THE YOUNG MARRIAGE

THE YOUNG MARRIAGE

A Handbook for Those Who Marry Young
and for the Early Years of Marriage

MARY ANNE GUITAR
and the
Editors of *Good Housekeeping*

1968
DOUBLEDAY & COMPANY, INC., GARDEN CITY, NEW YORK

Library of Congress Catalog Card Number 67–11196

CONTENTS

INTRODUCTION

This is a book on starting a marriage, putting it on such a firm footing that it will survive the inevitable crises of married life. But it is also a book on the art of sustaining and nourishing a marriage. Read it now if you are about to be married. Consult it during your first years together and don't hesitate to turn back to its pages whenever you need help.

Marriage demands a kind of loving vigilance if it is to work. When you can cope with the ever present problems at their germinating stage you stand a good chance of keeping them under control. What are the problem areas common to all marriages? Sex, money, in-laws, communication—these are the well-recognized ones. Married couples have always faced these crises. Additionally, each generation must confront special kinds of stress, seek guidance on problems other Americans have simply not experienced.

Your marriage will be very different from your parents' marriage and certainly from your grandparents'. The roles of husband and wife change with the generations and so do their expectations. This is why marriage is such a lively, durable institution.

Chances are that your expectations of what marriage can bring are based on a more realistic appraisal of the opposite sex than what your parents' generation could have had. Early dating, going steady and the constant companionship of potential marriage partners—social customs new with your generation—have given you firsthand knowledge of a close relationship. When you marry you can build on this early experience to create a lasting and deep kind of rapport.

The equality of opportunity which both men and women can now experience should help, not hinder, your marriage. Who wants to go back to the old days when an authoritarian head of the house dictated family plans? Both wives and husbands can share a responsibility for making marriage work. You can decide the roles you wish to play, the division of chores, the ultimate goals. It is your marriage and you can pretty much shape it the way you like. You have more choices than any young marrieds in history.

Improved birth-control methods let you decide the spacing of your children, the size of your family. No longer must this important factor be left to chance. Your freedom in this area is matched by that in others.

You can decide to continue your education while married. Both men and women are taking advantage of this opportunity. The college-based marriage is no longer the exception; it has become a way of life for thousands.

The working wife has earned her chance to carve out a career alongside her husband. More married women are working than ever before. At the turn of the century the proportion of women in the labor force was one in six. Today, it is one in three.

Efficient, labor-saving household aids have liberated the young wife from the time-consuming chores. She can hold down a job while carrying her housekeeping responsibilities with relative ease. Many newly wedded women elect to do just that. Not only are they interested in using their minds and education, they are anxious to contribute to the family nest egg. After the babies begin coming the job will likely give way to full-time homemaking. But today's young women know that this period too will pass. By the time their last child is in high school they will be ready to go back to work.

We are living longer and this will affect your marriage. Your grandmother never worried about what she would do when her children grew up. She had more of them, had them later, and could not expect to live to be eighty. Her husband worked until the day he died. Retirement was no problem for them.

Right now, of course, retirement seems like a million light years away. Yet the prospect of increased leisure in the years ahead will have a powerful effect on your marriage. You and your husband will have some fifty years together—a good part of them alone after the children grow up. Right now, at the outset of married life, you can begin building the foundation for a rewarding, companionable relationship.

You believe, naturally enough, that you'll never fall out of love.

You know you agree on all the important things.

You are sure that nothing, or nobody, could ever drive you apart.

You trust each other, and always will.

You're never at a loss for words. How could this change?

It doesn't have to change, except for the better. But you owe it to yourself to get off on the right foot. When you marry you set a marvelous chain of events in motion. You need help in coping with them, in appreciating the changes that will take place in you through marriage.

For most young marrieds the sound of wedding bells heralds a whole new way of life. You move from financial dependence on parents to self-support. You leave home to start one of your own. You usually switch from learning to doing. Instead of taking in, you begin giving out. The biggest change is that from childhood to parenthood. Once you're married you are formally grown up, with all the pleasures, privileges, responsibilities that adulthood can bring.

This book is dedicated to helping you make the most of them.

Where the Action Is—in Marriage

Someone once described the state of feeling married this way. "For the first couple of months I felt as if I were slipping in and out of being married. Some days I knew I was a married man; other days I felt like my old self." This is your marriage. Whatever else happens to you, marriage will change your point of view, your behavior, your goals. You won't be the same after you have been married but the changes will be gradual, so imperceptible that you will not be wholly aware of them until you look back with astonishment at your unmarried state.

You will put on the robes and roles of "married" the day you say "I do." But they won't quite fit until you've worn them for a time. It's only natural to feel still single and at the same time know that you are part of a pair. Only when the husband remains the intransigent bachelor or the wife a "baby doll" forever does the situation warrant alarm. You will have to ease into marriage, not take a leap and expect to be completely different. You are going to yearn for some of the pleasures of single bliss, wonder if the good old days are gone forever.

Your generation has been described as "the action, go-go kids." What happens to the action when you marry? Must you resign yourself to a steady, slow pace? Or can you find the thrills, new sensations, accelerated living that you have become accustomed to?

The answer is yes and no. Your definition of what action is will surely be modified through marriage. Said one happily married young man, "I never thought that I would be contented with life as I live it now. It is slower and some of the passion has changed but it is so much better than I ever dreamed. We have a mellowness I never anticipated."

The action doesn't have to be frantic. When you hear an old married couple describe an evening together—"We had a couple of drinks out back, then dinner, listened to music and so to bed"— it sounds dull compared to evenings when they danced until dawn. They don't think so, and neither will you someday. "The drink you have together before the company comes may be the best drink of the evening," says one old hand.

Marriage provides the stage for a kind of emotional action you have not yet experienced. Getting to know another person really well; depending on him; discovering strength in yourself you weren't sure was there—that's the action.

Quite possibly the most gratifying part of marriage is its extraordinarily commonplace aspect. What is, after all, so earth-shaking about eating dinner with the same person night after night? Why would anyone go into ecstasies over meeting the commuter train on the dot of six? What man would flip over hauling the groceries home from the supermarket on Thursday night? Yet these very homely acts often are the ones that make a marriage worth its salt. Rapture, sure, but more important the notion that you can count on someone else for the steady kind of love that wears forever.

Companionship is one of those words that doesn't begin to suggest the dimension of the relationship it attempts to describe. It is the extra dimension of a real marriage, when two people know each other completely and accept each other with all faults understood, where the feeling is mutual, where fidelity is taken for granted, not because of those vows but out of respect and love for the other—then you have a going marriage.

Your Expectations

Marriage cannot solve all problems, cure all social ills. It can be enormously fulfilling if you do not expect to live happily ever after without any effort on your part.

You can expect to be happier while married, more secure and comforted. People who are married live longer, enjoy better health. Men who marry early go farther faster than those who wait or remain bachelors. Marriage should give you confidence, provide the most favorable climate for personal growth. When you have a partner you can count on you will venture farther, accomplish more. You have every right to expect that marriage will possess its own unique personal excitement, generated by the discoveries you two will make. You will possess the physical intimacy married people take for granted, the sharing that this partnership insures.

It has become fashionable to accuse young marrieds of unreasonable romanticism if they expect excitement, sustained pleasure, fun and games to last much longer than the honeymoon. Why *shouldn't* marriage be a romantic adventure? If you recognize the problems confronted by all newlyweds, if you determine to solve them, you can keep your marriage fresh and vital forever. The secret is to keep your feet on the ground while you have stars in your eyes.

The first year or two are the hardest as any young married will testify. Said one young husband, "It's a big adventure. If you survive it brings you closer together. You work for the same things. That first year is critical. You feel cut off from your old friends and your family. Then there comes a time when you feel you belong. You make other friends. You take your place. Each baby, each stick of furniture, all the things you're adding on, are very exciting."

If you are in your teens you face a weight of evidence which indicates that an early marriage has less chance of succeeding than one contracted when partners are in their twenties. Let's be frank about it—the prognosis for success in marriage is not too favorable when both partners are in their teens. According to statistics quoted by the Institute of Life Insurance, the younger the bride is the less chance her marriage has of succeeding. The odds are even more discouraging when both bride and groom are in their teens. Marriages between teen-agers have twice the breakup rate of those where the woman is at least twenty-one and the man over twenty-four.

Marriage counselors say that immaturity is the prime reason why these marriages don't work. What do they mean by immaturity? Neither partner is willing to adjust to the other, to recognize that marriage means putting yourself out for someone else.

A young wife wonders if her marriage can hold up under the demands of a husband who wants the household to revolve around his casual way of life. "He hates to be pinned down," she explains. "I ask him when he wants dinner and, believe me, I'm prepared to eat at midnight if that's what he wants but I have to know *when* so I can get the food ready. He tells me, 'Don't be a drag. I'll eat when I'm hungry.' I can't imagine what we'll do when we have children."

This particular young woman has resigned herself to living with a rebel, feeling that there are other compensations. But one wonders why her husband isn't more considerate. Does he really love her? What will happen when they have children and he has to conform to a family schedule? Isn't he being selfish and isn't that a sign of immaturity?

When marriages break up partners are apt to hurl charges at one another—"selfish," "childish," "spoiled." They complain that the other wanted to be treated like a baby. "He [or she] wouldn't grow up," is a common accusation. What they seem to be saying is that true maturity involves a deep awareness of someone else, a willingness to extend oneself, a profound caring. You don't have to lose your own identity in the process. Indeed, if you are not sure of yourself, confident of your own powers, you will have a difficult time with sharing and caring.

The best yardstick for measuring maturity is to apply this definition of love to a relationship. It was written by psychiatrist Harry Stack Sullivan, and happily married people would agree that this is, indeed, what love amounts to. Mature love, that is.

"When the satisfaction or the security of another person becomes as significant to one as is one's own satisfaction or security, then the state of love exists."

Note he does not insist that you put the other person ahead of yourself. No masochistic self-denial is called for, but you should be able to respect and care for your partner as much as you do for yourself. Otherwise, it isn't love.

Social psychologist Nelson Foote has elaborated this concept of love as it can be expressed in marriage. "Love is that relationship between one person and another which is most conducive to the optimal development of both—love is to be known by its works. One commits himself to another not on the basis of romantic forced illusions but of real possibilities which can emerge with proper cultivation."

Love does not mean exclusivity. You will be wrapped up in each other, quite properly so, for some years to come. But you should be in touch with the world so your love can flourish. Remember Saint-Exupéry's remark, "Love does not consist in gazing at each other, but in looking outward in the same direction."

What Makes a Marriage Work?

Maturity cannot be equated with age even though we tend to think that the longer you live the more seasoned and sensible you become. However, some people are extraordinarily mature at sixteen; others never achieve maturity no matter how long they live. Even marriage counselors concede that "age *per se* is not an adequate criterion for predicting the degree of marital competence of couples." Says one, "Numerous factors related to readiness for marriage are correlated with age but . . . for some categories of youth marriage may not entail any greater risk than for the population as a whole."

"If both parties are emotionally educated for marriage almost any pair can make a go of it," says another counselor. And a minister adds, "Growing up in marriage is knowing how to handle feelings of love and hostility. So, you could be chronologically late in your twenties and still not know what to do with these feelings while perhaps a couple in their teens would have such insights."

Thankfully, you do not have to bring to marriage all the maturity it needs for eventual success. You have a good chance of developing the capacities required as you respond to the challenge of marriage. Counselor Aaron L. Rutledge, of the Merrill-Palmer Institute, says, "Marriage can be the greatest single stimulus to continued growth and maturation of young people who are determined to make their relationship work."

Many believe that your youth can be an asset if you are wise enough to learn from experience and can develop the skills needed to be an effective husband or wife. You possess flexibility for one thing. You haven't lived long enough to harden into a rigid pattern of life. You have energy and bounce. You can respond spontaneously to problems and if they are unyielding for the moment move in on them from another angle. You have a greater potential for change than someone older who may have explored a great many possibilities but settled for a static life.

In assessing the differences between three generations of the American families he has studied, one authority (Reuben Hill of the University of Minnesota) concluded that young marrieds today are more innovative than their parents and grandparents. They are "more oriented to the future and less fatalistic." Your generation is willing to take risks but your willingness to plan, to change if necessary, to work hard for what you want most certainly cuts the risks to manageable ones.

Significantly, researchers find that young marrieds have a greater ability to communicate with one another, to manage conflicts successfully than did their parents. They are not afraid of fighting, view family arguments as simply a way to locate a basis for agreement.

Today, counselors are guardedly optimistic about the prospects of success for brides and grooms who are still in their teens. One college president who has seen a lot of married students handle both marriage and a full course-load, sums up the new point of view.

"Marriage doesn't mean the end of anything. We must get rid of the idea that marriage means settling down. It is a part of life and can take care of a lot of the emotional problems. We're more concerned with what they do with what they've got than whether they are living their lives the way we did. They're not saved nor are they sinners. What they've got to do is figure out where they are and what they're going to do about it."

Social worker Norman W. Paget, who has done considerable

research into the problems of young marriage, estimates that "the single most important crisis faced by the very young couple would have some relationship to the discovery that they are alone with the responsibilities of marriage."

Of course you aren't wholly alone. Friends and relatives are pulling for you. They can provide support, both emotional and practical. Counseling is available if the going gets rough. But if the marriage is to work you will have to make it work. That won't just happen; it takes energy, drive, determination to create a happy marriage.

You stand a better chance of realizing your expectations if you don't expect miracles. There is no such thing as instant success in marriage, although a few cherished myths about marriage would lead us to believe otherwise.

Most couples firmly believe that "everything will be all right once we are married." Have we oversold the image of marriage as a cure-all, capable of resolving all problems connected with money, sex, parents? Marriage can't wipe out your past. Your husband (or wife) can't make up to you for everything you didn't have, provide you with all you want. Your partner is no magician. He can't be a parent as well as lover and friend. You can, however, find something infinitely better. Who wants a mummy or daddy when they can have a responsive husband or wife?

Some people believe, trustingly, that once married old relationships will be simplified. But it isn't that easy. Your mother is still your mother and she is going to keep on treating you like her child no matter how grown up and married you feel. One of the jobs before you is to slowly and tactfully put your other relationships on a new footing. It takes time. The fact that you are married won't automatically confer a new, adult status.

One of the favorite myths is the one about "love conquers all." We like to believe that we can cope simply because we want to. You can be deeply in love and still not be able to manage new responsibilities. Even a good sex life can elude you if you don't learn how to achieve it. Your respective roles as husband and wife must be defined to your satisfaction. You have to master any number of practical skills as well as the subtle interpersonal ones. It can be done but not by assuming that it is as good as accomplished once you've said "I do."

The younger you are the less you know about the workaday

aspects of living. A girl who has never learned to cook, a boy who has never held a job, are not particularly well equipped to set up housekeeping on their own. They can learn, however, to cope with this new and exciting life if they are willing to ask questions and take advice.

Much of what you know already will come into play during married life. But you must acquire insight into problems which are peculiar to marriage. You will have to develop as a homemaker, good shopper, Mr. Fixit, family chauffeur, decorator, cook, hostess, investor, parent, daughter- and son-in-law.

You can learn to earn and manage money; housekeeping skills can be acquired. You can even develop the ability to listen to your partner, communicate what you feel deeply. You aren't born with these talents. They may take years to perfect, but if you make a start now you'll build a firm foundation for the years to come.

Without true communication most marriages just don't stand a chance. With it, the young marriage can work. You may think you know all there is to know about the person you married, but the side you know best is the courting personality. Naturally, that's the most appealing side. The rest of the person you married is out of sight. It will emerge as marriage brings it into view.

If you are a woman you will have to recognize that you married a male who is sometimes inconsiderate, sometimes doesn't shave, wants to be waited on and even babied. If you are a male you will face the fact that you married a real, live human being and not a living doll. She's a female who can nag until she gets her own way. You're going to wake up some morning and wish fervently that the 180-pound male you married was big enough to get his own breakfast.

As you live together you will discover, accept and, hopefully, enjoy each other as real people. Your flexibility is your strength. You are not set in your ways, rigid and uncompromising. You are willing to be shown, to discover one another. Marriage will test your adaptability. You are products of completely different family upbringing. You have your own tastes, your own standards, your expectations of what marriage will bring.

Although marriage is a partnership it's very important that it permit both partners to express their individual and unique selves. You don't want to be submerged in marriage, you want it to help you be your best self. What exactly is this self? Who are you?

THE YOUNG MARRIAGE

I

WHO ARE YOU?

You're the best swimmer in your neighborhood . . . prettiest girl in class . . . oldest child . . . the one who got the fellowship to study abroad . . . the folksinger . . . the only boy to be elected president for four years . . . the child of divorce . . . the one member of your family who likes to be alone . . . the girl who put herself through nursing school . . . the best in math . . . the one who paints . . . Mrs. Baxter's little girl Alice. . . .

These are important facts because they contribute to the external image you project. But there are other, equally significant, aspects of you. What about your feelings, your fears, expectations, hopes, joys, needs? You can't know all about these signs of the Inner You because much of the unconscious remains buried. But since a lot of it will surface once you marry and are interrelated with another person (who, after all, possesses his own fears, hopes and needs) you owe it to yourself to understand some of the forces which motivate you.

There are clues. Most of us have strong feelings, likes and dislikes which we express rather freely. In a way we hope people will pick up the clues and get some idea of who we are. Admittedly these are subjective statements but they are most revealing. You've heard them, perhaps even voiced them.

"I would die if I didn't know exactly where I'm going to be next week."

"I have to have some kind of surprise; the deadly dull offends me."

"I can't bear to have anybody yell at me."

"People who don't say what they mean drive me crazy."

"I guess I'm a perfectionist."

"People tend to walk all over me."

"I'm old-fashioned, I guess, but I think a wife should do as her husband says."

"I'm a romantic."

There are ways in which you reveal yourself to others. If you listen attentively, noncritically—to what you are saying you will get some insight into that most elusive person—you. Developing self-awareness is a lifetime pursuit.

When you insist passionately, "I can't stand fighting," what does it mean? Being for peace is, of course, a Good Thing, but is peace at any price worth it? What does it say about you, that you are so threatened by a single argument that you would rather dodge the confrontation? Or suppose it's the opposite. What if you like to think of yourself as the challenger: "I just can't bear not knowing where I stand." Are you going around with a chip on your shoulder, daring someone to knock it off?

Are you possessive, have to feel that what's yours is yours for keeps? What if you have married a man who can't stand being fenced in? Are you going to be threatened by his independence, or can you change?

Let yourself grow into the person you will become. Don't try to force virtue upon yourself. Accept yourself, the good and the bad. You are bringing a unique set of characteristics, background, to the marriage. Inevitably they will be altered or solidified as you brush up against your spouse and *his* background, habits and different set of values.

Try to understand why you react so strongly to, say, criticism. Why does it bother you so much? Could it have anything to do with your family, the way they treated you as a child, the way you learned to deal with your mother and father?

Looking into Your Past

It is only natural to look back once we get into a brand-new situation. When you were away at camp or school, thoughts probably turned toward home. From that distance it looked awfully good.

Instead of concentrating on nostalgia, try looking backward with an eye to discovering the influences that made you what you are today. What kind of parents did you have? Strict, easygoing, penny-pinching, wildly extravagant, solid, fun, a little dull perhaps. Did you get along? What were your fights about?

Every child (the healthy ones anyway) goes through a period of adolescent rebellion when parents can do nothing that is right. Anyone over twenty is a drag. Some of this quarreling arises out of the perfectly natural desire of the young to question authority and prove that they, too, are grown up. You probably went through such a period when you were openly critical of the way your mother operated ("Why don't you wear more makeup?") or of your father's pocketbook ("Do we have to keep this old car another year?") or the way of life you lived ("This boring house, dumb room"). You outgrew it, moved onto a new plane where you could be sympathetic with your parents, see them as people and not as the family bosses.

But they left their imprint on you, probably influenced your choice of a mate. You have been conditioned by your experience with them.

Writing in *The Happy Family*, an excellent account of what psychological forces prevail in family life, Dr. John Levy and Ruth Munroe point out: "Parents do teach their children more than love in the abstract. They teach them love (and hate) for a particular kind of person—namely, themselves. Children never quite get over this bias, even those who develop most normally." Fortunately, as these authors demonstrate, the bias can lead to a happy marriage. In one study of married couples a researcher found that "when the marriage was successful the wife usually somewhat resembled the mother. This resemblance between mother and wife does not, of course, mean complete identification. The wife remains herself, but she is the same general kind of human being the boy learned early to love and revere.

"If the boy has remained too closely bound up with his mother he may be afraid of the woman who is like her . . . The boy who has disliked his mother will pick a wife as different from her as possible."

Inevitably, to some extent, you will be like your parents. Without realizing it you have picked up many of their values, their attitudes toward marriage, their expectations for success. Although it is common—and healthy—for young people to rebel against parental standards while they are adolescent, these standards will influence them later on.

If you grew up in a close, affectionate, large family you will probably want to re-create this atmosphere. If you were an only child, if your parents fought like tigers, you will have difficulty believing that marriage can be tranquil no matter how ardently you crave peace.

An only child may be quite accustomed to loneliness and, indeed, crave solitude. Even after he is married he may tend to draw away from his wife and children to seek that state in which he feels comfortable. He says he needs "peace and quiet" but what he really wants is a kind of equilibrium which is incomprehensible to those who like being with other people most of the time. One only child, now happily married, confesses that he still feels a bit uneasy sitting with his active family in his own living room. Another automatically gravitates to his bedroom after dinner. "That's what we did in my family. Each one went off to his own private retreat." Mothers of small children probably suffer most from togetherness if they spent their own childhood alone. "I had to learn to play by myself," one woman recalls. "I can't understand why my own children want me around all the time. After all, I still need some time to myself." Some people are going to crave more privacy ("the freedom to withdraw") than others simply because they were used to it as children. They may welcome the warmth and confusion of big-family living but not be able to tolerate it twenty-four hours a day.

As counselor Aaron L. Rutledge points out: "By the time people reach the age of marriage it is amazing how much of their daily living consists of fairly fixed patterns and habits, most of which are quite healthy. Indeed, without the economy of habits there would not be enough energy to get through the day, what with all the decisions to be made about tying shoes, chewing food, combing hair and perhaps even about kissing mother or wife good-bye on the way out to school or to work.

"On the other hand, there are many areas of habituated expression which can get in the way of intimate man-woman living in marriage. Part of the responsibility of the young couple is to undo these unhealthy conditions and replace them with newly learned forms of behavior that are less destructive, and more promising of satisfactions within marriage. . . . Parental and social expectations may have succeeded all too well in convincing the woman from girlhood that she does not have sexual feelings, or if so she does not express them, or that it is the husband's responsibility to see that she is satisfied or a fault of his technique if she is not."

Family custom can shape the externals of love. A man who grew up with parents who never touched one another in public, who frowned on casual kissing and hugging, may simply think it's not proper to show much affection. If his wife needs to be petted and patted she will assume (mistakenly) that he doesn't love her. She couldn't be more wrong. He simply feels self-conscious about being demonstrative.

Accepting Yourself

Parental influence doesn't shut out all other experience. A favorite teacher may have imbued you with a sense of outrage against injustice; your best friend has given you a competitive drive; your first employer inspired you with an urge to work hard for success. We are the product of dozens of inherited prejudices and attitudes, or we have reacted against them to create our own equally rigid standards. Often we are very positive without having examined either conscience or conviction. But you should make an attempt to examine some of your standing opinions.

When you say something like, "I know it's unreasonable but I just can't bear stuffy people," and then, with hard-won insight, acknowledge, "I think they're looking down on me, I guess," you've taken an important step toward learning something about yourself and accepting it. The greatest thing you can do for yourself is learn to accept who you are with a certain tolerance, even pleasure. You may detest your nose or mouth or tendency to gain weight. You know, in your secret heart, that you are not the "sweet guy" you appear to be. There are times, in fact, when you feel quite capable of punching someone in the nose. You hate keeping up appearances, of being the eternally good listener. "When is someone going to care about *me?*" Suppose you suspect that you are a fraud, that the good marks you got so easily, the popularity contests you won, in no way reflect the real you. "If they only knew," you think.

If you don't think well of yourself then you will have a hard time giving other people approval. You must like yourself before you can like someone else. Liking yourself doesn't mean that you like everything. Of course you will be conscious of failure, embarrassed because of the way you acted once, mindful of how far you have to go before you become the person you'd like to be. But if you really do feel unworthy, unhappy as a human being, then you're in trouble.

Too often people marry, hoping to find in another the qualities they lack themselves. Nothing could be more disastrous. You will discover complementary traits (he's venturesome while you are security-minded; she's got taste but you've got drive), but don't expect your mate to be you. That, you have to do for yourself.

That age-old question, "What does she see in him?" might better be rephrased, "What did she see in herself that made her marry him?"

A Marriage in Which the Partners Are Similar

Although many people marry to complement themselves, even more marry someone who is a lot like them. Marriage counselors think this is a pretty good idea. If you are conservative, they reason, you won't be happy married to a radical. If you want to change the world, then certainly you will be restrained by a solid citizen type.

Similar backgrounds, religious belief, race, color and conviction can help build a compatible marriage. If you see eye to eye on the important things you will, according to the prediction, be more likely to make a go of marriage. This sounds rather like a marriage between twins, totally sexless and devoid of challenge and excitement. It can be just that, but remember there are other discoveries to be made besides finding out how you feel about politics and religion. Consider this pair. They always knew they were meant for each other.

Paul and Annalee grew up in a small (population twelve hundred) Ohio town. Both were active in the Methodist Church and high school band. Both did well in school; Annalee was valedictorian of her class.

They began to date each other when she was thirteen and he was fifteen and, admittedly, "never really cared or bothered to date anyone else." They became engaged when Annalee entered a small state college. Paul was already there, by this time a junior. A year later they were married.

Annalee explains that college life itself motivated them to marry. "Most of the social life here includes a lot of drinking, wild parties, things we're not interested in. This is one of the reasons I wanted to get married. I was unhappy in dormitory life. The girls smuggled in beer and liquor and just lived so differently from the way I wanted to live. Of course, there are rules against this, but they could get away with an awful lot—and did."

Paul, too, believes that the casual social life on campus could have threatened his values. ("I'm against fraternities because so many people get hurt by them.") But because they have each other they are able to cope. "We see eye to eye on religion, and we feel the same way about all the other important things. So there aren't many disputes," Paul says quietly.

Both Paul and Annalee look extraordinarily young and cherubic to have assumed such firm charge of their own lives. However, their common past is undoubtedly the rock on which this very firm marriage stands.

Paul was a go-getter at the age of eleven, taking on odd jobs, carpentering, painting, mowing lawns. He never had a motorcycle or hot rod. He was reliable, hard-working and uncomplaining. Annalee, too, was a diligent worker, both in and out of the classroom. She divided her summers between teaching Bible School and helping her father in his engineering office.

Neither Paul nor Annalee objected to parental restrictions placed on them during the dating days. Paul recalls this period with evident pride. "Even in my freshman year in college I wasn't allowed to hold Annalee's hand or put my arm around her in public. Parking was against the rules. Another guy would have just given up, I bet."

Annalee approved of the discipline they developed during courtship. "My parents just put us on our honor. We were even heavily restricted in the use of the telephone. We could talk ten minutes at the most because the phone was also used for Daddy's business."

"We were closely supervised, all along the way," Paul explains, "but we're thankful for it now."

Annalee echoes his gratitude. "I think you have to be absolutely sure you're doing the right thing before you marry and that takes a lot of careful thought and prayer. A long waiting period would also be advisable."

When asked what he thought made young marriage work, Paul answered unhesitatingly, "Prayer. We have found that the spiritual side of life is the important one. It's what holds young marriage together. There are so many temptations, otherwise, to create trouble. Without something in the way of a spiritual life, I don't think young marriage can work. If you don't have more than physical love to hold you together, it's not going to work."

Paul and Annalee have religion as their bond but, more than that even, they have the security of knowing that they are as alike as two peas in a pod. They even look alike, sturdy and blond with candid blue eyes.

This unusual couple sounds like the answer to a marriage counselor's prayer. Most young marrieds, however, have to make more effort to adjust to their mates. They have to learn to recognize and accept the personal forces which make them unique and also give the other person equal time and consideration. They have to discover the person they married and it may take a lifetime.

A Marriage in Which the Partners Are Different, but Complementary

Most couples are not going to be perfectly matched; most will find that marriage amounts to balancing off personality traits and background. However, couples who do seem happily adjusted to one another seem to share common goals, values, convictions, aspirations. The surface differences are incidental when the deeper bonds are strong. Consider this couple—Rick and Martha—whose marriage satisfies basic drives common to both. On the surface they do not look compatible but their needs are complementary and so the marriage works extraordinarily well.

A terrific automobile salesman, Rick is energetic and immensely good with people. He admits cheerfully that he is "a real party boy." An eager joiner, he has been president of his fraternity, the junior chamber of commerce, the tennis club. His own house is, in fact, a neighborhood gathering spot. Before he married Martha, Rick had gone steady with a dozen girls. Nevertheless he settled into married life with no regrets at losing his freedom. "Nobody enjoys his home more than my husband," Martha says with pride, "but it takes a lot of housekeeping to keep ahead of the mobs he brings in."

Housekeeping is not Martha's forte, as she readily admits. A tall, slow-moving but beautifully coordinated girl, she devotes herself to tennis and golf. In her family, sports came first. Both Martha and her brother brought home the cups and prizes while their mother ran the household. Domesticity came as something of a shock to Martha, but her energy, competence and resourcefulness have helped. She takes all the shortcuts she can and concentrates on what she does best, namely casual entertaining, generally in the open air. Although Martha is more reserved than her husband and would relish an occasional quiet evening, she is willing to have open house when he brings people home. Rick has learned to accept her indifference to flawless housekeeping.

Martha has considerable insight into what attracted her to Rick. "He gave me confidence and encouraged me to do my best. It means a lot for him to see me win at tennis or golf. He always calls me 'Champ' and brags about the score. He'll feel the same way about our children, I'm sure of that. What it amounts to, I guess, is that he feels he's winning too when I come out on top. I know I'm pleased when he beats his old sales record. It's a joint effort for us; we want to win as a team."

Martha and Rick are agreed on their family goals. A big family is high on the list but Martha does not think motherhood will interfere with her outside activities. She'll be a good mother but not a possessive one. The children won't be able to brag about Mother's famous pound cake and their socks may have holes in them, but Mother herself won't feel guilty about being nondomestic.

"I admit I was worried about how good a wife I would make," Martha confesses. "Keeping house is just not my thing. I was lucky (or unlucky) enough to have a mother who really loved taking care of us. She didn't teach me anything about keeping house and

I never wanted to learn. My idea of nothing is to spend hours polishing silver and cleaning windows. Luckily Rick doesn't mind if the place isn't spotless."

Rick really doesn't mind and for reasons he readily admits. "My mother always talked about the sacrifices she was making. I wanted my wife to have her own interests and not be a martyr to me or our children. As long as the place is reasonably clean and we can have fun in it I'll be happy."

By now you ought to know what is important to you, what you are prepared to defend. Trivial habits, tastes can be modified through marriage but the really vital values are so much a part of you that they will never vanish. In point of fact you may not realize how important they are to you until your partner challenges one of your cherished convictions. Hopefully, you will be agreed on the big things; but you won't see eye to eye on everything. You don't have to.

Marriage is full of surprises and one of the biggest is discovering yourself. When you come up against another person, intimately, day by day you have to look at yourself. You may be pleased by the way you respond or frightened by fears you didn't know you had. Something he, or she, says will set off alarms. Or make you happy that a deep rapport does exist. The old you will expand to include the new, married you but not overshadow it. How could you ignore, if you wanted to, the forces that shaped you, your parents, friends, education, background?

Marriage will change you and you it. You won't recognize the person you are today after twenty years of marriage. But some of your values will persist, your way of looking at things, your special self, despite the influence of your partner. If you can grant yourself the freedom to keep on being you you'll be able to respect the identity of the one you married.

II

DISCOVERING YOUR PARTNER

Opposites may not always attract but often enough they do and eventually they marry. What seemed like an entrancingly different personality during courtship may, after the wedding day, seem totally alien. It was cute when your fiancé put his feet on the coffee table (how appealingly masculine), boorish and unbecoming in your husband.

You knew he liked music but you didn't know you'd be eating dinner every night to folk-rock.

To your surprise he is quite unwilling to discuss a problem once, according to his lights, "we've settled it."

You may be a morning personality while he likes to watch the late show and sleep until noon.

Let it be said that your husband will come in for his share of surprises once he starts living with you on a twenty-four-hour basis.

He liked your immaculate look but how could he know you would wash his socks as soon as they hit the floor, insist that every ashtray be scrubbed before the guests were out the door?

How could he know you would be so cautious with money? Instead of his bachelor's rule of easy-come, easy-go, he must now account for every penny.

Personal habits, even in the one you love (or, perhaps, more especially in him because you crave perfection) can be intensely irritating at first.

There are going to be times when your husband gets in the way. You want to finish dinner so you can have a bath and relax.

He wants to talk all night about the fascinating lunch he had with his boss.

Your wife will feel like a drag on occasion. You would so like to have a beer with the guy next door and watch the ball game. But should you leave her on a Saturday afternoon?

You wish he would stop rustling around in the garage and settle down for the evening.

You'd like to tell her to knock it off and hang up the phone. She can talk with her sister tomorrow.

Part of the problem lies in unfamiliarity. You have to live together long enough to get in step, or tolerate being out of step. Equally important, however, is the realization that you really are two different people in spite of mutual attraction. You can't lose your identity through marriage; you have to learn to live with it and respect your partner's urge to be himself.

Young marrieds confess that to their astonishment they don't want to be in each other's arms all the time. Once married they have the accessibility and privacy they lacked during courtship and yet, after the first few months, their sexual activity slows down considerably. "We go to bed two or three times a week and that seems to satisfy us both," said one young wife. "Of course, being together so much we do express affection more constantly and casually. I'll admit, though, there are plenty of times when I just want to get off by myself."

As a couple settles down, a lot of energy is moderated, or channeled into such mundane efforts as washing dishes, taking the car to the garage, watching television after dinner. Young marrieds confess that during the beginning of marriage they have a surplus of psychic energy. "We were bubbling over with it," one woman explains. "We could stay up all night talking, reveling in one another, explaining in detail how we got the way we are, reliving the time we met. But pretty soon the energy dwindled. I don't know whether it was because other things (fixing up the house, getting ahead in business) took precedence or whether we had simply talked ourselves out."

Quite possibly they aren't talked out; they are simply experiencing the kind of standoff which overtakes young marrieds after they feel they know all about one another. The emotional demands of being so close can be exhausting. You tend to draw back a bit, take a long, hard look at the person you married. You make judgments and appraisals. "How could I have known he [she] would behave this way?" You liked your partner because he was different but somehow believed that he would become your alter ego once you were living together. Now you are unwilling to settle for the differences, let alone enjoy them. Now you ask, "Why can't he [she] be more like me?" Why? Because you are you and he is he.

Emotional Differences Between the Sexes

Not only are you two unique individuals who have spent some twenty years apart; you belong to, and possess the characteristics of, different sexes. This, of course, is the powerful attraction that drew you together. But it can drive you apart unless you recognize and accept the differences between men and women. Differences in biological function, physical strength, psychological attitudes plus the training we receive in how to play the roles accorded our respective sex still influence the way men and women behave.

The most commonly discussed difference and the one likely to cause you the most trouble is the "passive-aggressive" distinction between women and men. Because women have traditionally looked to men for protection and support they have earned special considerations accorded members of "the weaker sex." Most women like the small courtesies. They like being helped on with their coats; like having doors opened; enjoy having a man escort them protectively along a crowded street. But most women would reject the obligation to play a totally passive role all through married life.

The girl who has never had the slightest conflict about expressing herself in class finds it demeaning when someone suggests that she let her husband do the talking. The girl who is competent and enjoys her strength can't be happy if she must pretend to be a clinging vine. True, many women admittedly *are* happier behind the throne, playing a supporting role, eager to look up to a stronger mate; but other women chafe under the presumed obligation to consult their husbands at every turn and resent the implication that they are "aggressive" when they are simply acting according to their deepest need.

On balance it seems absurd to label woman the "weaker sex."

As many researchers have pointed out she possesses certain physical advantages over man. She lives a longer and healthier life than most males because of certain built-in physiological assets. Her reputation for instability, moodiness and a certain inability to last the course probably comes from the special stress the reproductive system puts on her.

Women, thanks to their physical endowment, are susceptible to a different physical rhythm than men. They menstruate every month; they conceive, carry and bear children. Naturally the massive physical changes created by their reproductive system are going to have an effect on female temperament.

It may come as a shock to the bridegroom to realize that his wife is not herself on certain days of the month. If he stops to figure things out he will realize that her temper tantrums, tears and depressions seem to follow a predictable cycle. The best thing to do, say husbands, is to keep your distance until she is herself again. Don't feel guilty because you can't make everything all right. Her hormonal system is to blame, not her husband.

Little wonder that women have a reputation for moodiness. It seems rather unfair to assume, however, that all women are vulnerable to the blues all the time because of the brief period each month when depression strikes. Besides, many a man can feel down for reasons that have nothing to do with his hormonal balance. Having your ups and downs is quite healthy, provided the ups aren't manic and the downs aren't precipitous.

If women are more emotional than men, it is presumably because they respond readily to grief, anger, joy. Such spontaneity can, of course, be an asset. If you are free enough to express your feelings you should be emotionally healthy.

Men are supposed to be strong and silent. Is this always a good thing? Is the label even justified? Aren't some men exceedingly verbal and admittedly dependent on occasion? Why must they strive to live up to a characterization that had its points during the caveman era but surely is not appropriate today? Why can't a man blow up, sound off, even cry if he feels like it?

Women are considered more intuitive, quicker to assess situations, and this is either an asset or a liability depending on what you want to believe. Men are supposed to be rational, logical, fact-minded. Most of them are. But not every man could live up to this obligation all of the time. Men are just as warm and impulsive as women but they have been taught from childhood that it is somehow unmanly to express feelings, to act on purely subjective evidence.

For every female who rejects the passive role there is a male who resents being cast into the part of aggressive doer. Men do have a lot of drive but not all of them are blessed with limitless energies. On occasion even the most assertive male would like to relax and be taken care of.

Unfortunately, dependency is a drive we have learned to despise. This is a pity since we all (even men) indulge in it at some time or another. The fiercely independent male can be fighting the urge to lean. Men, more than women, fear the dependent role. They are afraid of being thought weak, effeminate, passive— all Bad Things in this society. What bothers them more than the actual struggle to be wholly self-reliant (surely an unattainable goal) is the fear that someone will find out that they like being taken care of. Men are supposed to stand on their own feet, never show that they are hurt, anxious or afraid. Isn't this too much to ask of any human being?

Men and women are, as one psychiatrist put it, "more human than otherwise." Each is capable of loving and laughing, crying and fighting—all the emotions we recognize as human. It would not be accurate to say that women are more compassionate than men; that men are tougher; women more nurturing. Every trait you can label "typically female" you can pin on a male. And *vice versa*.

You would do well to avoid the stereotypes of male-female behavior. If you like the way your partner operates don't worry if he (or she) is living up to the conventional picture of the opposite sex. What matters is your own contentment.

If you are dissatisfied don't accuse your partner of being an inadequate member of his sex. It can be quite devastating to have someone you love slash away with, "No real man would do that," or say accusingly, "If you're a woman why don't you act like one?" Instead of attacking on this level try to understand why you are reacting so angrily to his behavior. Are you mad about something else? Feeling deprived? Or are you confused about your expectations? You may feel that because your mother or father behaved a certain way that all women, all men must follow suit. Your partner, however, grew up with different models. His idea of role-playing can be quite different.

There are differences between men and women but they are not the cliché ones. Most important for your understanding of the opposite sex is an understanding of what shaped your partner's attitudes and behavior. If you don't try to understand him as an individual instead of as Everyman (or Everywoman) much of what your partner does will be mystifying, even frustrating. The differences do not represent an unbridgeable wall. You have more drawing you together than dividing you. As one young husband put it, "Be glad you're different but don't glory in the differences."

Personality Differences

More important than the well-known sex differences are personality differences. You may have married your husband because you respected his go-ahead personality. You, let us say, are more deliberate, more inclined to wait and see before you move. You thought he would stimulate you to action, turn you on. Now that you're married to him, however, you feel he's pushing you. You are obliged to accelerate your tempo to keep in step with him. Sometimes it's exhausting.

How about the man you married? He's impatient with your deliberation. He wishes you would spark to an idea as soon as he utters it. You are lacking in imagination, faith, adventurousness, says he. He admits, however, that he rather liked your slow but steady ways before marriage. "I thought I needed someone solid," he says.

If you can acknowledge the complementary forces of your personalities, habits, backgrounds, you will have a rich marriage. Learn to live and let live and enjoy the differences. Don't fight them.

Consider, for example, the marriage of two distinct opposites. Louis and Bea are in their early twenties, but that is just about the only thing they have in common. She is from a small town; he is a big-city boy. Bea's family are thoroughly middle class; Louis' widowed mother runs a café. Louis never finished college because he was much more interested in working with his hands than in abstract discussion. He supports himself as a woodworker but is about to reenter the academic world, go to museum school for a degree in sculpture. He has designed and made all the furniture in their apartment.

Bea has just gotten her master's degree in education from an elite Eastern college. She is besieged by job offers, a good thing since she must support the household while Louis gets his degree. Bea comes from a Mormon background which she has rejected. Louis is completely disinterested in religion and professes none. Bea's strict, religious background still influences her life although she protests that she is liberated from it. She is afraid to introduce her parents to her new husband, and has managed to put off the encounter.

According to the marital-success indicators this couple has several strikes against them. They come from widely different backgrounds—geographic, class, religious. She is better educated than he. (When there is a difference the marriage counselors like the man to be superior in education.) She is going to support them (reversing their marital roles and putting a strain on the marriage). They have no contact with in-laws. They aren't even interested in the same things.

Neither of them claims that adjustment has been easy. (Probably this directness in confronting mutual problems is their greatest asset.) Bea believes that both of them had developed set personalities before marriage. They were on their own early in life and developed personal and effective ways of coping. In particular, Bea feels that she is quite used to being self-sufficient and finds it hard adjusting to another person. They have eased this problem in their characteristic no-nonsense way. Each does what he feels like doing but they do it together. Does that sound contradictory? Here's how it works.

They rarely go out, preferring their own home. They eat at home consistently but dinners are very simple—a hefty soup and salad most often. Louis has set up a workshop in the basement of their apartment and spends a lot of time in it. He takes orders for furniture, both to keep his hand in and also to add to the family income. He also has an art studio in the apartment. While he works Bea reads, corrects papers for her classes, prepares assignments. Neither is lonely and neither wants for company. Each is doing what he likes best. Conformity is at a minimum. They don't own a television set. When company comes, and because the atmosphere is warm and welcoming people do drop in, they are treated to a big bowl of onion soup or coffee and cake. Outsiders are struck by the successful meshing of two strong personalities. Said one friend, "They rarely argue openly. Louis listens to Bea. He is more playful than she but she responds to his humor. All in all, they are never dull."

Louis and Bea have a marriage that works because they truly accept one another. A marriage of distinct opposites can work but not if either partner tries to make over the other. Or if a wife tries to submerge her real personality so there will be less friction. (Sometimes the husband allows himself to be swallowed up in the name of harmony.)

Neither Louis nor Bea is worried about role-playing. They don't think about who is supposed to be aggressive or passive. Sometimes Louis is totally dependent upon his wife and at other times she plainly leans on him. At this point in their married life Bea is the breadwinner but both expect that Louis will hit his stride professionally and eventually bring in the major income. Even when he does assume the financial responsibility Bea will keep on working. Her career means a lot to her and this pleasure in working is not diminished because at this point she is using the job to keep her marriage solvent. Neither Bea nor Louis could be happy married to someone who might expect more conventional behavior. They don't want to play a set piece in which the roles of man and wife are clearly formulated. Instead, they are evolving their own roles within marriage.

This couple represents a "mixed marriage" which works exceedingly well. Not all such marriages go smoothly. Even couples who try to anticipate the problems their different religions and race will create are not prepared for the complications marriage brings.

The Mixed Marriage

It has been pointed out that every marriage is really a mixed marriage because we are obliged to marry outside family bloodlines. Through marriage we get to know other kinds of people who have attitudes, habits, values and backgrounds different from the family we belong to. Of course, when there are sharp differences in class, color, race, religion, additional problems of resolving them arise. Trouble lies ahead. This prediction will be difficult for the principals in a mixed marriage to accept. Most likely they will deny that they have any problems. They are determined to make their marriage work despite certain foreseen odds. This is a commendable attitude but pure and simple loyalty, plus determination, doesn't always solve the problems implicit in a mixed marriage.

Unless both partners discover how much (or how little) the other one cares about his religion, say, he is going to be surprised after the wedding takes place. One bride was astounded, and hurt, when her Catholic husband left her the first Sunday they were married to go to Mass. "I guess I never thought his religion would come first. I supposed he would skip church for a while."

Family quarrels can erupt over any kind of commitment to religion. If one partner wants to give money regularly to his church the other one may resent it. If he keeps on serving his church as a volunteer the partner may be jealous of the claim.

In a kind of counterattack the partner who feels left out may question the beliefs and conventions of the church. Although this kind of probing may begin as a sincere effort to understand it can degenerate into ugliness. The outsider ends up questioning with a chip on the shoulder. His hostile approach only succeeds in driving his partner into a defensive corner.

If one partner tries to convert the other he may succeed in achieving a homogeneous religious climate in the family. Many tepid churchgoers are quite willing to switch religions just to keep peace in the family. Others have always been anxious to belong to a different religion, and marriage gives them a good excuse to change their allegiance.

The problems of a mixed marriage nearly always surface when children are born. How are they going to be raised? Some religions are more insistent than others on this point. The partner who belongs to the more vocal church group will probably prevail when it comes to deciding religious affiliation for their young.

There are problems connected with in-laws in a mixed marriage. They may tolerate the loss of a daughter or son but are intensely concerned with their grandchildren. They will press to make sure the church of their choice gets the offspring.

How are the partners in a mixed marriage going to solve these and other problems? The best way is by confronting them, not apologetically but openly. If you have not discussed the issues before marriage you should certainly do so before these differences become divisive. You may not be a regular churchgoer but your religious upbringing will, nevertheless, affect your marriage.

Returning to Louis and Bea, let us look at the way they have handled their religious differences. Even though Bea has left the church of her childhood it left its mark on her. She recognized that some of her puritanical attitudes came from this background. She feels quite strongly that work is ennobling, besides being necessary. Louis is much more inclined to the good life and is not inhibited by religious scruples. This could be a point of friction between them if they were not so determined to understand their differences.

Tolerance is an acquired quality and you may have to work hard to develop it. You can't take for granted that your way of life is the only way. If you come from a religion or race or class where the rules are firm and clearly understood, you will have a hard time accepting the fact that not everybody subscribes to them. Give your partner a chance to express his own background. Learn from it. Accept some (if not all) of his traditions and observances. You will have more success in maintaining your own precious commitments if you give him latitude in preserving his.

A mixed marriage can remain mixed and be very successful. Jews married to Catholics, Catholics married to Protestants, Negroes to whites—this kind of mix is becoming more customary in our pluralistic world. Neither has to take on the beliefs of the other. They can remain separate but equal, developing a rich marriage in which the strains of other cultures mingle to form a wholly new one. You don't have to convert the other person to make a mixed marriage work.

Can You Change the One You Married?

It is tempting to consider the many ways in which you might bring your partner around to your way of thinking, your behavior, taste, interests, convictions. Do you really want to achieve a kind of look-alike style? Consideration for the other person is fine but chameleon living highly dangerous.

More women than would be willing to admit it secretly feel

that they will be able to change their husbands once they are married. If he is sloppy they will make him neat, if he takes a bit too much to drink they will gradually break him of the habit. They are overly optimistic and treading on dangerous ground. The question is—can you change him? *not* will you change him? The answer is—probably not. Change may come about spontaneously, of course. In an effort to please, in response to marital happiness many men do mend their ways and conform to their wife's view of good husbandly habits. Certainly they will never reform if they feel put upon and put down.

In the interests of reform women tend to nag. Without quite realizing it they behave more like a mother than like a wife. A parent may be forgiven a constant picking at the young, trying to bring them up to snuff. A wife, however, is supposed to be on her husband's side. After all, she did marry him for better or worse.

Since the wife is inclined to most of the criticizing, here is some advice from women who have tried to change their husbands but only succeeded in alienating them.

Never snipe at your partner in public. "Just look at that shirt and he's had it on only an hour." You only reduce him to the level of a five-year-old. Next time, out of revenge, he's likely to wear his oldest, dirtiest clothes.

Never point out that he gets his unattractive traits from his family. "You're exactly like your Uncle Harry and I never could stand him." Nobody likes to be told that they are simply another descendant in a long line of failures.

Don't repeat what you've heard about your partner from others. "Your mother always said you were lazy."

Don't feel free to bring up a confession made in a moment of confidence. "But you did say that you always felt uneasy with your father."

There is nothing more disturbing than the knowledge that your partner shares the critical opinion others may have expressed. When a wife says in a moment of anger, "My mother was right. You *do* want everything handed to you on a silver platter," she immediately puts herself against her partner.

Try to focus on the favorable aspects of whatever transference has taken place. If your husband is proud of the way his father has managed the family finances and if, indeed, he seems to have acquired the same prudent characteristic it will do no harm to praise him for it. You can say, with all honesty, "You certainly do have a real money sense like your father."

Suppose, however, your husband abhors saving and budgeting. You suspect this is a reaction to penny-pinching back home. Don't, for Heaven's sake, make a virtue of the in-laws' thrift. Do ease up on the budgeting and encourage your free-wheeling husband to go out and make more to satisfy his spending desires. You probably won't be able to have it both ways. The big spender is generally the big earner. And, although it might be nice to combine your husband's generosity and his earning capacity with thrift, the chances are you can't have it all in the same package.

Instead of dwelling on what's missing why not pay attention to what's right.

Setting Up the Safety Valves

Fortunately the human animal is a remarkably adaptive creature. He can learn to live with anything—and anybody. He may not like it but pretty soon he gets used to it. If, that is, other rewards are there.

In marriage you are going to have to get used to habits quite different from yours. You can do it if you're having enough fun, getting enough pleasure from being married. By the time twenty years have gone by you'll have a hard time remembering how exercised you got because your husband refused to wear a tie for supper.

The trivial differences can become all-important if you let them. Don't become obsessed by the minor variations between you and your husband. Concentrate on what really bothers you and try to resolve the important differences.

Give each other growing room. You don't have to travel in tandem. You can develop separate interests without jeopardizing your marriage. Wives, in particular, need to seek ways to be themselves, not just Joe's bride. Men already seem to appreciate the value of activities outside the home.

Most observers note that men can have a second and satisfying life outside marriage, but that women must feel wholly involved and fulfilled by marriage. Of course this isn't true of all women, most particularly those who have held a job. Now that women are all too aware of the need to prepare for a second interest before their children have grown we can expect them to develop that interest parallel with motherhood.

A second interest doesn't have to be a job. You can keep up with anything that once fascinated you. Was it music? Why don't you subscribe to a concert series, collect records, join the choral society? If you loved painting, there's no reason why you have to put away your brushes and oils just because you are married. You can paint in your free time, go to museums, even acquire a modest collection of reproductions or sensibly priced originals. Whatever intrigues you—community politics, theater, volunteer work, alumnae activity—deserves your support.

Your husband doesn't have to share this special interest of yours. Nor do you have to adopt something he likes. Some women learn to play golf so they can be with their husbands on weekends but never enjoy the game. Others claim to like nothing better than a day on the lake when, truth to tell, they are bored to death by fishing. You don't have to share his interests. Nor is he obliged to find pleasure in yours. You can be the most dedicated gardener in the world, the most involved member of your conservation group, a passionate collector of antiques without expecting him to join in. Don't apologize if you get enormous pleasure from this side interest. For some reason women tend to feel guilty if they enjoy something outside home and family.

For as long as people have been getting married the husband has cheerfully conceded that he has interests outside his home. To be sure, he is encouraged to do just that—to be wholly absorbed in his job so that wife and family can benefit. If he likes to play golf he is excused on the basis that it's good for his waistline and business contacts. Any poker playing or bowling is written off as his need for relaxation. And if he wants to hide behind the latest magazine or newspaper, he is forgiven because he must, after all, unwind and keep up with the world.

When his wife acquires or sustains other interests she rather expects to feel guilty about staying late at her bridge game, committing herself to committee meetings, taking the day off at the beach. If she holds down a job she worries that she's getting too absorbed in it.

Said one young wife who works several days a week for the local newspaper and who has become fascinated with local politics and power, "Really and truly I worry that I'm not being a wife." She explained, "I get too much fun out of my job, minor though it is."

Allow yourself some freedom from each other. You'll have much more to talk about if you make some friends on your own.

Privacy within marriage is hard to come by. Some people insist upon knowing everything about the person they are living with. You can shut the door now and then without shutting your partner out. You can't possibly know all about the other person even if you and he are determined to share word, thought and deed. Besides, there ought to be a little mystery in every marriage. Don't check up on one another, demand an accounting whenever you are away from his side. The Freedom to Withdraw, as one woman called it, should be written into every marriage contract.

Respect the other person's privacy. Don't ask, "Who's calling?" when he or she gets a phone call. Don't wonder out loud, "Why are you so late tonight?" Or "Where did you go just now?" It can be irritating and demeaning, this constant checking up. More irritating, it's true, for some people than for others. If your spouse bristles when you ask such a question, take note and try to mend your ways.

Courtship After Marriage

For courtship read consideration. You know when your wife is tired and you don't press her—to talk, to go to bed, to give you a special dinner. She used to be your best girl; who says, now that she's your wife, that she must be treated like a squaw? Try to cherish her openly even though you feel in your secret heart that by now she must surely know how much you love her. Do it in the little ways. They may seem unnecessary much of the time but they add up to the kind of gentleness, respect for her as a woman, that will enhance your marriage.

"Sure, who the Hell wants to walk around the car and open the door for her," said one young husband, "but I always do it." He doesn't do it out of duty but out of love.

Women, too, can continue the attentions that they showered on their mate before marriage. Much has been written about not appearing in cold cream and curlers. An occasional moment of truth isn't going to ruin your marriage. But a constant disregard for the aesthetics of the toilette will certainly make your husband feel he's not a man, just a piece of the furniture.

You can put yourself out in little ways and assure him that you still care about him as fervently as you did when you were courting. One woman, now a grandmother, unfailingly walks her husband to the subway each morning just as she did when they were newlyweds. Not only does she like getting his breakfast (even though she's one of the ones who would rather sleep until noon) she wants his company. Don't think he doesn't brag about it, even about her parting shot, "Make a lot of money for us, dear," she calls as she kisses him good-bye. Interestingly enough, he has.

III

FORMING A DURABLE PARTNERSHIP

Before a marriage can become a durable partnershp three conditions must be met. The couple must be able to confide in one another, trust one another and have empathy for one another. On the surface, then, marriage does not look so very different from any other partnership.

The partners are going to be asked to make joint decisions, set goals, handle money, make accountings to one another. However, marriage can never be a partnership run by business rules. You don't issue directives, write memos, toss your weight around in a marital partnership. Instead you depend on communication, empathy, arguing constructively to establish guidelines for the partnership.

Because you love each other you are able to express yourselves freely. Don't ever lose that power of communication. It is your greatest insurance against marital bankruptcy. If you lose it work to restore it. If it's gone it is not necessarily gone forever. There are silent periods in good marriages, a time when one or both cannot say what's on their mind.

You've seen old married couples dining out, without a word to say to one another. They seem to have lost the ability to communicate. You shudder—and rightly—at the thought of ever being so tied up emotionally that you couldn't share your hopes and fears, amusements and joys, with your partner.

This kind of frigid silence bears no resemblance to the companionable quiet which can envelop the happily married. Each knows what the other is thinking; there is no need for words.

They are communicating all right. It's called empathy, the art of knowing how the other person feels.

Empathy is not putting yourself in the other person's shoes because then all you comprehend is how you would feel if you were they. True empathy means being able to grasp how the other one feels because she is she.

For a good example of true empathy, consider this insight offered by a young husband. He counts as a turning point in his marriage the day he was "feeling pretty sorry for myself. I think this is inevitable. On Saturday when you have had to work until noon, take the car to the garage, set up the barbecue, you are going to feel that all the work goes to you. I thought so that weekend, I admit. But then suddenly I realized, 'Ah ha, she's probably feeling the same way. After all she's spent the morning cleaning house and the afternoon cooking for the party. I must say she hasn't complained at all.' I suppose she could feel some of my resentment and she was just lying low. Anyway, once I caught on that I wasn't the only one in the family with a gripe I felt better."

Empathy and marriage should go hand in hand and they do up to a point. You are tuned in to one another but not always. More significantly, when you don't want to pick up a signal you'll probably miss it.

Suppose your wife accuses you of not inviting her parents to come for dinner next Sunday.

"Couldn't you see I wanted you to?" she may ask just a little plaintively.

"Couldn't you see I needed a Sunday off?" you might like to answer. Instead you play dumb. "I didn't get your message. Sorry."

It's amazing, the way some brides (and grooms) expect their new mates to be mind readers. "But I thought you knew how I felt about that!" is one of the common pleas heard. Or, "Didn't you feel me freeze?"

You can't have empathy unless you are open to it. Certainly you can't communicate unless you are willing to say what is on your mind. The celebrated silence of the Husband Who Refuses to Talk can, often enough, be explained by anger. Often he feels all talked out. More often he is afraid to open his mouth for fear he will say something he will regret. He doesn't want to fight.

If you want to keep the lines of communication open you will have to risk an argument or two. What's so terrible about that?

The argument itself isn't the crucial thing. Your methods of handling it are far more important. Will you resort to fight or flight when conflicts arise?

Arguments

Most people react in one of two ways when threatened. Either they gird themselves for battle or they run away. If you are the kind of person who "can't stand scenes," then you'll probably flee the battleground. One young wife makes a point of clearing out whenever the going gets rough. When tempers are at white heat she announces, "I've got to get away before I do something I'll regret." One wonders if this is her only motivation. Perhaps she hopes her partner will run after her, making concessions just to get her back. Or is she simply trying to win the argument by default? He is the guilty party because he has driven her away. She'll come back when she can win.

One counselor points out, "Before you're married you won't be your real mean self. You don't want to scare the other person away. But after you've lived together you know that if you don't win this battle now, this year, then you're going to fight from a losing position next year. The year after you're going to be worse off."

Clearing out can be immensely frustrating (is that why this technique is so effective?) to the partner who stands his ground. After all, you can't fight it out without an adversary. Neither, and more importantly, are you going to be able to resolve conflicts if you don't confront them. Men are as likely as women to simply skip out when the arguments become threatening. They are abdicating a certain responsibility when they do so. As one young wife complained, "When you are married you ought to be able to talk out your difficulties. It's no help to have a husband who just runs away when a problem comes up, who just jumps in the car and drives away fast to some place where he can have a drink."

Flight takes many forms, including simply ignoring the partner who tries to get a discussion going. Turning a deaf ear is the solution of those who seem to believe the issues will disappear if they try to remain oblivious of them. Others seek a different refuge. You probably have developed your own escapist pattern.

Most of us have. You may decide to hide in the bedroom or lock yourself in the bathroom or retreat to the basement. You could withdraw into hurt silence, refuse meals, ignore all overtures to kiss and make up. These are flight patterns in the great traditions but aren't they self-defeating in the end? You never can resolve an issue if you refuse to face it. But, does "facing it" always mean a rousing fight?

The fighting can be done just as effectively with words as with actions; witness the protagonists in *Who's Afraid of Virginia Woolf?* Verbal taunts can certainly draw blood—"Stupid!" "Sloppy." "What did I ever see in you?"—but aren't they a dangerous weapon? Some marriages survive when one partner has said "the unforgivable thing" because, of course, if there are other compensations you learn to forgive and forget. However, when the attack is constant and the blows hit you where you live, the marriage is bound to suffer. Each of us cherishes an imagined self whose motives are pure, conscience clean, spirit generous. When this self is questioned by someone who is supposedly trustworthy it really hurts. It is tempting to lash out with a personal attack when the discussion of issues goes against you. Resist the impulse. Don't say anything in anger that you will regret later. No excuses that "you weren't yourself" will soften the blow. Bite your tongue if you hear yourself about to say, "Can I just tell you something for your own good?" Words can hurt. Never forget it.

What about using physical violence then? Is that preferable? Of course not. But the possibility of physical attack is always present in a marriage. Some married couples are more controlled, civilized, even inhibited than others. They would never dream of hitting, slapping, scratching, biting, kicking each other. But even the most disciplined, sophisticated men and women can give in to violence on this level. As a matter of fact physical violence is rather relished by some masochistic souls.

You may draw back in horror from any suggestion that your marriage could deteriorate to the level of brutality. It isn't a pretty picture but, unhappily, it is valid for any number of marriages. How do they survive?

If you like being beaten up regularly, you will adjust to this kind of life. If you feel frightened by your partner's potential for violence, then you'll probably try to get out of the marriage. If you have a capacity for righteous indignation and a low boiling point you'll hit him back. Some women are quite adept at throwing china, scratching and kicking. In fact, some women do violence to their husbands without provocation. There are occasions when physical expression of anger is a natural reaction. One might hope that it could be controlled short of mayhem. These infrequent occasions can be borne by the partner who is victimized, but if the violence becomes a regular thing you are going to need help. What prompts so much violence? What do the blows really mean? What is being concealed? A counselor, analyst, social service worker can help you gain insight. One thing is obvious. This kind of warfare solves few problems. There are better, more grown-up ways of coping.

Solving Problems Through Sex

If fighting isn't the solution can heavy doses of love bring about a consensus? Many young couples think they can resolve their conflicts by going to bed whenever they can't agree. This can be a dangerous way of solving problems. Not only do you put an unreasonable strain on your sexual relationship but you fail to become more practiced in other forms of communication.

When couples come to counselor Aaron Rutledge with a sexual problem he finds that they have, often enough, counted on physical intimacy too heavily. "They did have a very good relationship sexually," says Rutledge, "but—in the absence of other kinds of nearness and other kinds of sharedness—all of life's messages got canalized into this one form of expression. Any line of communication, similar to a telephone system, can take just so many messages at a time before everything goes a-jumble. Typical in these marriages is the expression through sex of love, fear, shame, loathing, bitterness and hostility; the relief of all sorts of physical and emotional tensions; the need to share at any and every level—intellectual, social, emotional. They try to express all of this almost exclusively through the sex drive. Then one day this line of communication like an overloaded telephone circuit breaks down. Their sex life is a mess, either non-existent or conflicting and they come for help. By this time they usually have a great deal of pent-up bitterness, and are making accusations that 'he must not love me any more, must have a girl friend.' 'She must never have loved me, or we're incompatible.' Then they say, 'What have we left? There is nothing.'"

The message is clear. Don't try to do all your communicating through sex even though that may be your most effective way of demonstrating tenderness and understanding. You may lose this vital strength if you expect too much of it.

Airing Your Problems

You can discuss problems without necessarily resolving them. Just getting feelings and attitudes out in the open where they can be recognized as valid (for you if not for your partner) is a great way to let off steam. If you go through married life convinced that you have no right to have your say you will inevitably feel martyred. Quite possibly your partner will never agree with you on anything important, never concede your point. You can live with this kind of standoff, if you are granted the satisfaction of having your say. Some couples never see eye to eye on major issues but they manage to get along quite harmoniously. There's really no point in hammering out a consensus through constant bickering and argument. What is important is the respect you accord one another, the listening ear, the compassion. Don't go through life ignoring the other person's attitudes and values. You should recognize his point of view, his stand on matters of importance. "I didn't know you felt that way," is an admission that you simply haven't cared enough to find out.

Hopefully, you will find a confidant and listening post in the person you married. But you can't depend upon your partner to absorb all your anxieties, hopes and fears. You may well turn to a friend or relative, letting yourself exchange confidences with them. You're not going to share deeply private secrets, let strangers in on the intimate details of married life. But there are going to be moments in marriage when you wish you had an outside shoulder to lean on. You want to explore your questions and problems with a neutral third party.

In a five-year study conducted by the Community Service Society of New York, researchers concluded that marriages were helped when wives could air their problems to a trusted friend. Many of the women studied confessed that they actively sought advice from other women. They learned from them, compared notes and found relief in talking out their problems. It always makes you feel better to know someone else is in the same boat. You don't have to copy another solution but you can certainly pick up ideas on making your own marriage work more easily when you hear about other people and their ways of coping.

When you can recognize what is bothering you, you are going to have a real grasp of what counselors call "insight." This is hard to come by without a lot of self-analysis and talking out of the problem. It is self-defeating to bottle up your feelings and then blow up over an inconsequential issue. Speak up when you are disturbed. Get the discussion centered on the real issues. Listen to the other person's views. Only by examining the questions which disturb you can you ultimately arrive at workable answers.

Take your time. You don't have to find instant solutions. Some marital problems take a lifetime to resolve. You will come to accept much more than you ever thought possible, but the acceptance will come as you look at yourself and your partner, share your reactions to ideas and events.

Sharing the Good and Bad

In a durable partnership sharing is all-important. In marriage bed and board are shared and usually a good many other things, most importantly, the self. If you hoard yourself, refuse to participate in joint planning and decision-making your marriage will have little chance of succeeding. You have to give as well as get. Hopefully, you will want to give out of love.

The couple which has no trouble communicating is the couple with things in common. They can talk freely because each believes the other one cares. They are willing to give attention, participate in each other's life. Man and wife must be separated during the working day but when they rejoin each other they can share individual experiences.

Problems arise when either the man or the woman begins to feel "What's the point of bringing it up? Who cares?" Women are most prone to this kind of hopelessness. "What's interesting about *my* day—cooking, cleaning, doing chores?" You don't have to tell everything that happened during the day ("Let's see, it must have been around ten because the laundryman always comes at eleven"), but you can give your impressions of the life around you. Some of it is inconsequential but your husband will be interested if you are. Did you read a book, walk in the woods, listen to music? Only when you are bored will the audience begin to drowse.

The young businessman may tell his bride all about the office cast of characters, assume she is as fascinated as he by the politicking and in-stories. Perhaps she is because she, too, has worked and knows the scene. If she isn't, she would do well to pay attention and become absorbed. When her husband stops telling what happened downtown she's in trouble.

The man who has been put down by his boss, snubbed by a hoped-for client, beaten by the competition, can at least find a refuge at home. If his wife is sensitive she will pick up the storm warnings when he comes in the front door. Let him be tense and irritable. Let him take it out on you (up to a point). Try to deflect the anger, absorb his resentment. The show of temper will not last long once he expresses it and feels secure in his castle.

If you snap back, "I know you've got your troubles; well, I've got mine," you only compound the miseries.

Sometimes, both of you need a pat on the back the same day, the same hour. Try to give it even when you are desperately longing to have someone listen to your troubles. In any partnership there has to be a certain amount of imbalance. Learn to bear with it, anticipating the change which will certainly come. Inevitably one partner will pull ahead of the other—in achievement, stability, contentment, ease of living. But, if things are working well, this is only a transient spurt. Pretty soon the other catches up, forges ahead.

Men do bring their business problems home. And their triumphs as well. As a wife you wouldn't want it otherwise. You have a stake in his other life. He should be able to turn to a trusted wife and confide in her. It means a lot. One man who was in the middle of an office upheaval said, "I don't know what I'd do if I couldn't come home at night and spill it out to Patsy. The other fellow in my department doesn't dare tell his wife what's up. He has to bear the burden all alone."

Building Up Your Partner

You did a lot of handholding during your dating days but you'll do even more after marriage. Not necessarily the physical kind although that's still fun, but the supportive, emotional brand. Some people, both men and women, need a lot of it and you may be married to this type. Give them all they crave—a pat on the back, a lot of reassurance, and "never mind, everything will be all right" pep talks.

You must want to build your partner up, not tear him down. Some people feel that once married they are privileged to tell him/her off. A partner has to "take it" because you're now members of the same family. If you grew up in a family where everybody spoke up and nobody was spared "the truth," you probably feel this right is yours. Is it really? Your partnership will be as durable as your mutual esteem. Cherish it now. You can never undo the damage done by a barbed remark, a taunt or sneer. People don't forget when they have been hurt and are especially wounded when the blow comes from someone they love.

There is no reason why the consideration, approval, affection you lavished on each other before marriage should cease on your wedding day. You have even more reason than before to let your partner know how much you care, how much you respect each other.

If ever two people needed to create a mutual admiration society it is you two. Your security and happiness depend on it. Your individual successes will be directly related to the support you get from your mate.

The wife who tells her husband how bright he is, how handsome he looks, how persuasively he speaks, is surely giving him the confidence he needs to make out in the working world. If she sends him off in the morning with a kiss and an optimistic pat on the back, he is better equipped to do battle in the competitive world. Assure your husband that you're behind him all the way, that you have complete confidence in his ability to win out. Don't tear him down.

The wife who complains, "I don't see why you let the boss treat you that way," who subtly undermines with, "My father would never have put up with that," who sows seeds of doubt, "I wonder why he asked Harry to write the memo," who puts her husband down, "Of course he didn't have time to see you. He's a busy man," is only defeating herself.

Women need just as much assurance as men do that they are lovable, attractive, functioning at the peak of their form. The wife who lets herself go to pieces after marriage may be taking her husband for granted. More likely, she isn't getting the compliments she used to and is simply responding with defeat. "Why bother, he won't notice anyway." Quite sensibly you can tell her to bother so he will notice. Otherwise she is simply creating a self-defeating vicious cycle. But it behooves the husband to put himself out a bit, never take his wife for granted. It costs so little to pick up a small bunch of flowers, pay a compliment ("You look just great tonight"), to acknowledge that the new hairdo is meant to impress him.

Men tend to assume that their wives know they love them. They can't be bothered to repeat it constantly. In point of fact, the demanding wife who is constantly seeking reassurance will only defeat herself. Men hate to be begged for a compliment.

It's hard for a husband, even a new husband, to realize that dinner didn't simply appear on the table, that somebody had to make the bed and empty the ashtrays, that the flowers on the table didn't just grow there. Of course, it's his wife's job to keep the house looking trim and attractive but she deserves a pat on the back for it. He likes to be told what a good provider he is. No reason for the home-based partner not to get her share of approval.

If you give it, you get it back—approval that is.

What Loyalty Is and Isn't

Loyalty is . . . sticking up for your spouse in front of other people. When he (she) is being picked on, badgered, harassed, you ought to turn the hostility off. Don't jump on the bandwagon and agree with his detractors. If your spouse is wrong tell him so at home. That ancient cry, "Don't criticize me in front of other people," really means, "But I thought you were on my side."

Every husband and every wife has a right to expect an ally. When an in-law or a boss, brother or sister, neighbor or friend starts to work on you, you ought to be able to feel that there is one person in whose eyes you can do no wrong (in public anyway). Does this mean that your partner (or you) must forever keep silent when you don't agree? Are you going to have to subscribe to your partner's politics, attitudes, convictions? Become a shadowy image of his beliefs? (For some reason nobody expects a husband to adopt his wife's convictions.)

Inevitably, you will come to view the world with a double vision. You have, after all, common goals and will slowly develop a partnership point of view. Meantime, there is no reason for either of you to lose identity. Any number of happily married couples disagree on politics. She votes her ticket, he votes his. You hear men and women express their personal opinions of public figures, government activity, local news. This is what makes for stimulating conversation. In fact, if you have nothing more to contribute than a weak, "That's right, my dear," your spouse will lose interest in talking to you at all.

Loyalty is not tactfully ignoring the slip that shows, the broken nail, the unpressed suit. You don't have to carp but surely your spouse wants to have someone looking after his best interest. Love implies protectiveness but not to the exclusion of honest criticism.

Accepting every habit uncritically. If you hate cleaning up a messy room, tell your husband you wish he would put away his clothes. If you think he drives too fast, ask him to slow down. You don't have to grin and bear it.

Handing out compliments indiscriminately. There is no reason to tell your wife she looks smashing if she doesn't.

Saying patronizingly, "I'm only telling you this for your own good."

Always letting your husband win, always conceding that he's right. His male ego doesn't need false support. "My best friend and critic" is the highest compliment any partner can pay the other.

Who's in Charge?

There are countless jokes about marriage which culminate in a single punch line, "Now you know who wears the pants."

The man obviously wears the pants but he can't be in charge all the time—nor would he want to be—nor would his wife let him be. The best guidelines are the simplest.

Let the person whose job it is be in charge. If your husband is driving the car let him drive it. Don't be the back-seat voice. If your wife is cooking dinner don't tell her how much onion to put on the hamburger.

Arrange to share the reins of power. One couple actually worked out a system whereby they decided who was going to be in charge that day. There was no need to take office every day, of course, since their routine was fairly well established. But on weekends they felt they wanted one or the other to assume responsibility for planning the activities, marketing, hosting the party, preparing the feast. It may seem artificial but for them it really works.

There is a lot of advice written on male and female "roles." Some of it is well taken; a good bit of it is unnecessarily rigid. When you marry you will assume the roles we customarily think of as belonging to husband and wife. But aside from that you will keep on doing what comes naturally.

If you are a man who likes to cook there's no reason why you can't keep on with it after you acquire a wife. She may or may not appreciate your help in the kitchen but you can work out ways to express your own skill at the stove. Sunday breakfasts, cookouts, Saturday night steaks, may turn out to be your specialties. Enjoy preparing them without any guilty thoughts that perhaps this is a woman's role.

Suppose you're a woman who really likes to drive a car. Must you give up the wheel when you're in the car with your husband? Not necessarily. If he likes being chauffeured you're in luck. If he doesn't perhaps you can work out a share-the-car system. One couple does it this way. The wife drives her husband whenever he's on his way to work, thereby allowing him to rest and relax. He takes the wheel when they're driving home from the office. On

pleasure trips he does the driving. Anyone who has ever met a
commuter train knows the common pattern of husband-wife
chauffeuring. He is driven to the station but at night his wife slips
over and gives him the wheel for the ride home. Trivial perhaps
but all-important to any couple interested in playing the correct
role.

According to sociologists role-playing in marriage has lost some
of its intensity. Men and women are not so rigidly obliged to
conform to the role set up by previous generations. Some critics
claim that as a result we are creating a neuter society where men
perform as women and vice versa. They are particularly concerned
that children will no longer have models to observe, on which to
base their own sex development. There is some truth in the charge
but our society does allow plenty of opportunity for role-playing.

When you're both working it becomes all too easy to slip into a
palship-partnership. Beware the Roommate Relationship. You
can neuterize each other if the roles are too interchangeable.
What difference does it make who defrosts the hamburger? Who
cares if George does the vacuuming on Saturday while Sally gets
her hair done? This even-Steven arrangement has its advantages;
husband and wife can play either role. It also has its hazards.
Here is a breakdown of the roles usually attributed to men and
women. You don't have to live up to them explicitly. They are
not laws but, rather, a means of sharing the work and responsibilities of marriage. Adapt them to your own situation but do
make an effort to divide the work. Neither of you should feel
overworked.

The Woman's Job

She's the family's purchasing agent. Her husband may join her
in the market and help load the car with provisions but she is
the one who keeps tab on the family larder. She makes sure that
they buy sensibly, get the most for their dollar, keep a well-stocked
house.

She cooks the meals. If she finds this a bore she may devise
all sorts of ways to vary her chef's role. But she should get up to
fix her husband's breakfast, make sure they have a well-balanced
meal at night.

She sees to the clothing. Washes and irons it (or sends it out); keeps it mended. Likely as not she picks her husband's suits and ties. She's the one who puts the winter things in mothballs, airs the blankets, makes sure the socks are matched and in good shape.

She keeps the house looking bright and inviting. Except for heavy work such as refinishing a floor or painting the ceiling, she manages the cleaning. Thanks to new, lightweight, fast-moving equipment this isn't the job it used to be. (There are shortcuts.) She pays the bills, keeps household books. Women usually handle the bookkeeping, at least on the family expenditures.

She arranges their social life. The woman always issues the invitations and accepts them. When a man is invited to a party he quite properly replies, "Call Helen, she keeps our date book." Naturally, she consults her husband before she makes engagements.

Women, whether they like it or not, are the human-being experts in the home. They are responsible for its tranquillity, its atmosphere, its warmth. Often as not they are asked by their husbands to "take care of it for me, dear." By that is meant, "deal with him, or her, or the baby."

Much is made of the not so astounding information that women must be all things to all men. They are supposed to know how to run the car, operate the washing machine, fix the appliances. True, their mechanical horizons have been broadened. But the real chore, the actual cause of the housewife's frustration has to do with her obligation to be interpersonal. She could probably tolerate having the washing machine break down but she has to talk to the man who comes to fix it. She has to beg him to come, assure him he can do it, listen to his troubles while he works, fix him a cup of coffee, congratulate him when he solves the difficulty, and thank him for coming. She has ongoing relations with dozens of people all day long—the butcher, baker, shoe man, cleaner, newspaper boy. She is the one who will confer with the teachers in and out of school—music, dancing, art, camp counselors. She is obliged to be the peacemaker with the in-laws.

Her husband sees his working-life associates and, if he can manage it, has a secretary who will shield him from them. His role-playing is much more circumscribed than his wife's, his responsibilities more clearly defined.

The Man's Job

Men generally bring home the bacon. They are charged with the responsibility for earning family income. Their wives may work, indeed a good many of them do, but this income is usually earmarked for extras. The man pays for shelter, food, protection, the basics of living.

Men, because of their strength and stamina, handle the big jobs around the house. They carry out the garbage, haul heavy stuff in the garden, maintain the furnace, move furniture. He does the heavy repair work around the house.

Men usually buy liquor and cigarettes for the household.

Men buy the insurance, negotiate charge accounts, establish credit at the bank.

The car is the man's responsibility. He keeps it in tune, makes sure repairs are done properly, buys gas and oil.

The man usually makes the family investments, the biggest one being the house.

Changing Roles

Don't think about your role as rigidly defined. You can take on another if it is agreeable to you and the other person. Do try to figure out if you are hidebound about roles, insist that they be played the way Mother and Dad played them. The traditional parts for husband and wife may have to be modified for today's partnership.

All too often husbands and wives refuse help because they think "he/she shouldn't be doing this." If they want to do it, relax and enjoy the assist.

When he offers to load the dishwasher let him. If he insists upon emptying the ashtrays after a party, thank him for it. But if he firmly insists or implies that this is "woman's work," just grin and bear it. There is plenty of man's work around for him to do.

You want the help to be freely given, not grudgingly paid. If you insist upon doing everything in the beginning, you will frustrate his desire to help around the house. He'll give up offering just about the time you feel overwhelmed by all there is to do. This can only lead to great feelings of self-pity on your part and self-righteousness on his. Isn't it better straight off to line up the jobs according to who can do them best, who likes to do what and, possibly, who should take on what roles?

If you love to cook but hate to sew, then don't force yourself to do the mending. Save money on the food bill with your inspired casseroles and with the profits hire someone to mend for you.

A good many new wives are astounded that their husbands are not as handy around the house as they had hoped. There seems to be a persistent notion that all men are born able and willing to use a hammer, fix a fusebox, repair a leaky gutter. Not only are some males admittedly disinterested in such activities, they simply aren't trained to do it. The solution: pay someone to do it. Don't carp, "I thought any man alive could go up a ladder and nail down a shingle." Just accept the fact that your particular man isn't interested in the chore.

The old jokes about the bride's biscuits fall into the same category. If your wife can't cook, don't badger her about it. Encourage her to develop a basic repertory, even if it means hamburger every night. (Nobody ever starved subsisting on hamburger.) Don't kid her about her lack of culinary talent.

According to one researcher (Dorothy Beck of the Family Service Association) a marriage can work even though, to the naked eye, it does not look perfect. Says she, "The level of giving and receiving need not be equal provided the ratio of gratification to frustration is acceptable to both. Mutuality in emotional support and affection are central components but not the only ones. Even here the fit need not be perfect. The needs met may be either 'neurotic' or healthy."

In other words, a young husband can shoulder much more of the family burden than a "referee" might consider "fair," but be quite satisfied to do it. A wife can "hold up" the family by being on twenty-four-hour call, always ready to help and advise, even bring in a major part of the income but the marriage doesn't have to collapse. The point is, both husband and wife should feel satisfied, rather than frustrated. The ideal "fit" is something each couple works out in their personal life. They learn to accommodate to the other through trial and error, rather than according to "rules" handed down by marital oracles. What works for one couple would be disastrous for another.

During the early years of marriage the balance may be quite precarious, but, say the experts, any unfavorable shifts are often reversible. "Most partners have the capacity to grow and change. Breakdowns occur not because of difficulties but because of the inability to handle those differences together."

Making Decisions

Only recently you learned to make decisions independently of your parents. You decided whether to pledge a fraternity, to major in history, to get a summer job out of town. It was all-important to stand on your own feet, let the adults know that you could cope. Having successfully learned how, you made your biggest decision of all, finding a mate.

Now then how must this independent decision-making skill change with married life?

Certainly role-playing has an effect on your decisions. In one survey researchers discovered the husbands and wives were inclined to give each other specific responsibility for making decisions in their areas of competence. For example, decisions about food were made by the wife, which car to buy by the husband. The choice of life insurance protection was also made by the husband. The most frequent areas of joint decisions concerned housing and vacations.

If you have confidence in your partner's ability to make good decisions you will encourage him to do so. However, there is some danger involved in turning all decision-making over to one partner. As one observer pointed out, "People do not think of all alternatives, nor think of themselves as making choices between two things, usually. They decide whether or not to do one thing (a choice of one thing against all its alternatives, perhaps without even the next-best competitor being specified)." If the other partner is silent or simply given the chance to vote yes or no, the options are severely reduced. The more you study the alternatives in decision-making, the better the decision is likely to be. Let there be two voices, more options in every family council. At least where the decision is an important one. Naturally you don't have to consult endlessly over whether to buy pork chops or hamburger.

Right now your problem may be one of learning to share the pleasurable decisions—buying a car, picking out fabric for the living room curtains, choosing a vacation hideaway. You may be surprised to discover that your partner feels quite capable of making decisions you thought you were entitled to make alone. The man who couldn't care less what kind of suit he puts on may have violent feelings about the rug you bought for the living room.

Nothing creates as much resentment as being left out of a major decision, unless it is being obliged to make the decision without the help and support of a partner. Don't assume that your partner wants to make the decisions or that she doesn't. You will find out the real state of affairs as your marriage progresses.

One area where there can be considerable conflict is the work situation. Should a man change jobs without telling his wife, or quit in a huff? Shouldn't she have a right to help him make the decision since she is dependent on the paycheck? Most wives think their husbands have the right to make this major decision but point out that by talking things over at home the husband may gain insight and make a better decision. Here's how it worked for one couple. The husband was a recent college graduate, miserable in his first job.

"I came home one night, and I announced, 'I'm going to quit. I can't stand it.' My wife just said, 'I knew you were going to do it and I wondered when you were going to tell me.' We talked it over and although I had wanted to go in the next day and tell the boss off I listened to my wife. In the end I stayed there three months while I looked for another job. Now I think it was the thing to do."

Some young marrieds mistakenly feel that they must simply announce to their spouse a decision which might have been made jointly.

"I hope you like the hat. I really needed it."

"I had a chance to get a good buy on this car so I took it."

"I told the Masons we'd be there for dinner Saturday."

What is the ethic?

If you feel you must always "ask" before you decide on what you want, you are likely to feel childish, tethered to somebody's apron strings. On the other hand, if you plunge ahead the way you were used to doing before marriage aren't you assuming too much? Won't you feel guilty? Hurt your partner's feelings? Create a situation that can only be handled by a show of independence on the part of the other?

In a misguided effort to be protective some men do try to shield their wives from the brutal side of business. "I don't see any point in letting her know how near the edge we are until I have to," said one.

If a man has had the experience of seeing his mother react strongly to crisis he may feel that some women are too emotional to take it. Or he feels so strongly about the issues in question that he can't bear to think about them at home. He wants to wipe the office out of his life the minute he comes in the door.

There are others, however, who are inclined to dump all their problems in their wife's lap. Not that they really expect her to solve them but they do think she ought to know what they are up against.

"I've learned," says one wife who is accustomed to hearing her husband's office woes in detail, "that he doesn't really want me to suggest anything. He would be offended if I did. It's up to him to find the solutions. What he wants from me is concern and sympathy. I made the mistake early of pointing out that maybe his boss acted this way or that because of something he was doing. I'll never make that mistake again. Even though I can see how he could improve his tactics I only hint at that part. My job is to build him up, make him know I'm on his side."

Her husband agrees. "I don't want an answer when I ask for advice. I just want her to say, 'whatever you think is right.'" Any number of men would quarrel with this approach. "Fat-headed!" said one. "I trust my wife's judgment and I need to consult her. Together, we make better decisions than either of us could make alone." It is not considered nice if you are a woman to be aggressive or competitive. You can, however, reach your goals by working in partnership with your husband. There's nothing wrong with having ambition, just don't let it dominate your life.

Don't worry about the Joneses. Your ambition should reflect you, not them. If you aim to outwit them, outdo them, show them up, then your ambition is sadly warped. Set your own goals, but be sure you can realize them.

Don't be disappointed if you don't succeed at first. You can't achieve all you want overnight. It may be years before you'll be living in the style to which you became accustomed as a youngster.

Don't live through your husband. A little bit of the power behind the throne goes a long way. He needs to feel you're behind him, but don't shove.

Don't feel guilty if at first you don't succeed. Measure up to yourself—not to your parents' expectations.

Taking Your Place

As a married couple you will be asked to assume social and community responsibilities. You owe something to your country as well as to the town in which you live. Your privileges as adult members of society are matched by certain obligations, but there is great satisfaction in discharging most of them.

You will be invited to serve on committees and boards, participate as a volunteer in church, political, club activities. Your time, energies, pocketbook will be tapped for any number of causes and good works. As a functioning member of society you will be expected to support your country with taxes and defend her when asked.

You owe your community, as well as your country, some measure of time and support. Now that you are a partnership you have twice the resources to contribute. Do it generously and openly and you will get back in full measure that welcome feeling that you belong not only to each other but to the human race.

Military Service

Every able-bodied American male between the ages of eighteen and twenty-six must be available for military service for six years. This obligation can be discharged in any number of ways. You may never be asked to serve, or your service time may be limited by various personal factors. Parenthood will affect your eligibility. So will educational commitments and certain types of employment. It is wise to assume that you could be asked to serve for six years. If you have not already done so, you should surely examine all the options open to you. Will you wait to be drafted, claim a deferment, join the Reserves? Now that you are married you will certainly want to include your wife in making this important decision. You owe it to her, as well as to yourself, to make the most of the many opportunities offered by the Armed Services.

Marriage *per se* does not change your service eligibility but your Draft Board should certainly know as soon as you do marry. When you marry, move to a new address, change schools, finish your education, quit a job or get one, acquire any physical disability, become a parent—the Draft Board is entitled by law to hear about it. Even if you go away for a trip you should notify the Draft Board. This is for your own protection. You have ten days to appeal any decision by your Draft Board. If they do not know you are away and mail you a notice of classification, you will lose your chance to appeal.

You must register in person with your Draft Board within five days after your eighteenth birthday. If you do not register within that time you are liable for imprisonment up to five years, a fine up to $10,000 or both.

The Draft Board then classifies you as ready for active service, deferred or exempt. These are the classifications.

I-A: Available for military service.

I-A-O: Conscientious objector available for noncombatant military service only.

I-C: Member of the Armed Forces of the United States, the Coast and Geodetic Survey, or the Public Health Service.

I-D: Member of a Reserve component or student taking military training.

I-O: Conscientious objector available for civilian work contributing to the maintenance of the national health, safety or interest.

I-S: Student deferred by statute.

I-W: Conscientious objector performing civilian work contributing to the maintenance of the national health, safety or interest.

I-Y: Registrant qualified for military service only in time of war or national emergency.

II-A: Registrant deferred because of civilian occupation (except agriculture and activity in study).

II-C: Registrant deferred because of agricultural occupation.

II-S: Registrant deferred because of activity in study.

III-A: Registrant with child or children living with him in a bona fide family relationship or registrant deferred by reason of extreme hardship to dependents.

IV-A: Registrant who has completed service; or sole surviving son.

IV-B: Officials deferred by law.

IV-C: Certain deferred aliens.

IV-D: Minister of religion or divinity student.

IV-F: Registrant not qualified for any military service.

V-A: Registrant over the age of liability for military service.

When your Draft Board receives a call for men this is the order in which they are chosen.

1. Men who have reached the age of nineteen and who have been declared delinquent for failure to comply with the Selective Service law. They are called in order of their dates of birth, with the *oldest* being selected first.

2. Volunteers for induction who have not yet reached the age of twenty-six, in the order in which they have volunteered for induction.

3. The nonvolunteer who is nineteen or older—but not yet twenty-six—and who does *not* have a wife with whom he maintains a bona fide family relationship in his home; and the non-volunteer in the same age bracket who was married after midnight August 26, 1965, and who is childless. Men in this category are called in the order of their dates of birth, with the *oldest* being selected first.

4. The nonvolunteer who is nineteen or older—but not yet twenty-six—and who *does* have a wife whom he married before midnight, August 26, 1965, and with whom he maintains a bona fide family relationship in his home. Men in this category are called in the order of their dates of birth, with the *oldest* being selected first.

5. Nonvolunteers, twenty-six to thirty-five years old, in the order of their dates of birth, with the *youngest* being selected first.

6. Nonvolunteers, eighteen and a half years old or older—but not yet nineteen—in the order of their dates of birth, with the *oldest* being selected first.

If you are drafted you will receive your order to report for induction not less than ten days before the day on which you must report. After a physical examination you will be inducted into the Services for what is generally a two-year stint.

You are liable to be called for the draft at any time between
the ages of eighteen and twenty-six. If you are not called by the
time you are twenty-six the chances are that you will not have to
serve, barring a national emergency. If you are deferred for any
reason your liability extends to age thirty-five. However, you may
well never have to do military duty because your country does not
need you.

According to Lieutenant General Lewis B. Hershey, national
director of the Selective Service system, "a man who is deferred
isn't getting out of any obligation to serve if and when he is
needed. At the same time, men who have served tend to believe
that their obligation is met after a term of service. But this depends on whether the nation remains at peace or enters a war of
some kind.

"The registrant who is deferred past 26 at the present time has
liability until he is 35, but he carries it lightly because at present
he is in low priority. But that situation could change quickly and
completely."

If you think that you qualify for deferment as a conscientious
objector you would be well advised to seek help in establishing
this status. Your priest, minister or rabbi may be able to answer
your questions. Or you can write the National Service Board for
Religious Objectors, Washington Building, 15th and New York
Avenue, N.W., Washington, D.C. 20005. The Central Committee
for Conscientous Objectors, 2006 Walnut Street, Philadelphia,
Pennsylvania 19103, is another source of information.

You are entitled to a student deferment if you are still in high
school. This is the I-S deferment, good until age twenty. The II-S
deferment applies to college students and those in graduate
school. You must carry at least thirty credits and rank in the upper
half of your class if you are a freshman, upper two thirds if a sophomore, upper three quarters if a junior or senior to qualify. Or,
you can qualify for exemption by passing the nation-wide achievement test given each year by the Selective Service administration.

Once you are married you are entitled to a new classification
but you are not necessarily deferred. You have to prove that your
family would suffer hardship if you went into the service.

If you have children you will be entitled to a deferment.

If you work in an occupation which is critical to the public
good you may be entitled to a deferment. Agricultural workers can

qualify. Employees of companies which produce war material and have government contracts are usually deferred.

If you are a member in good standing of a Reserve or National Guard unit you are deferred.

You can fulfill your six-year military obligation by serving in the Reserves. Here are the choices open to you.

You can serve on active duty for a minimum of two years and then serve in the active Reserves for three years. After a total of five years' service you can request transfer to the standby Reserves.

You can enlist in the Ready Reserves, take a minimum of four months' active duty for training and serve in the Reserves for the balance of a six years' enlistment.

You can enlist in the Reserves and serve two years' active duty. When you return from two years' active duty you must complete the time necessary in order to total five years of active duty and active participation with reserve units. At that time you can request transfer to the Standby Reserves.

Ready Reserves are required to drill regularly and to complete forty-eight meetings per year. Most units drill about once a week for four hours; others carry on their drill over weekends so that the men can fulfill their month's obligation in one session. An enlisted man in the Reserves is paid a full day's pay for each drill session. This ranges from $3.13 a day to $11.57, depending upon rank and length of service. A private first class can receive about $200 a year from his training time. Officers are paid more, according to their grade and time in service.

Some members of the Ready Reserves are not obliged to drill because they have been placed in the "reinforcement pool" or "control group." They may, however, be asked to attend the summer training camp. And, if they are needed in an emergency, they are liable to be called up in short order.

If you think you are in a critical occupation or if your family situation is such that recall to active duty would work a hardship then you may apply for the Standby Reserves. Your Reserve headquarters will send you a questionnaire each year to establish your qualifications for Standby or Ready duty. However you should talk to your unit commander as soon as any extenuating circumstance arises. You are always considered ready for recall to active duty unless you have applied for a change in status.

Until October 11, 1966, the President could not call the Reserves to active duty unless he declared a state of national emergency. Congress has now given him the power to call the Reserves without such a declaration. Joining the Reserves in no way assures you of protection against active military service.

IV

THE BUSINESS SIDE OF MARRIAGE

Every partnership must be solvent. You can't enjoy each other, sexual relations, and marital security until you get your financial affairs on an even keel. Admittedly, this is a highly unromantic concept of marriage. It may even sound cold-blooded to some. A couple madly in love is convinced that they will be "able to manage," that it's dreary to budget. This is a couple headed for trouble. You simply must know not only how to earn money but how to manage and keep track of it. Your marriage will go bankrupt in more ways than one if you do not think of it as an economic partnership.

This chapter is going to concern itself with the capitalization of your marriage. We are going to talk about the many ways you can build equity (the value of what you own is called equity), how you can multiply your assets so they will be substantial enough to invest, borrow on and live off of in retirement. Now that you are married your "discretionary income," the money earmarked for extras instead of necessities will shrink. You have new obligations to meet, a partner to support. You should become more cautious with your spending, building capital for a house purchase, a business of your own, education for your children, comfortable retirement. Most newlyweds start married life with a nest egg of wedding presents and cash. Don't blow it on a sports car, trip to the Islands, ski equipment. Let it grow in value.

Some of this money will have to be spent for furniture but try to keep from outfitting yourself completely. Don't imagine that you will be relieved of major purchases forever. On the contrary, the more you acquire the more you will want to own.

The bills you had as individuals won't stop with marriage—the dentist and doctor, for example. You still need clothing. You are both consumers—of food, cigarettes, entertainment. You can share a common roof, bed and casserole but just about everything else will have a double price tag.

Try thinking of your marriage for a moment as a small, productive, thrifty, well-managed corporation. What are the goals? You certainly want intake to equal outgo, if not outstrip it. Your credit must be good, not so you can exhaust it with installment buying but so you can count on a cushion in the emergencies, take advantage of good buys when they come up. You would hope to build a capital reserve both to produce income and provide the resources for a flier now and then. You want to be able to seize opportunity when it knocks, be able to buy stocks, invest in your own business, get the dream house. Hopefully, you will never face bankruptcy, but you should be aware that a majority of bankrupt families are in their twenties.

How can you achieve these goals? By scrimping and penny-pinching? Not necessarily. A good buy can be an excellent investment. You will be spending more than you did while you were single but you will have to be better spenders, more careful with each dollar. This takes training and a certain amount of self-discipline. Now that you are married you are obliged to make some accounting to your partner and this in itself is a good thing. Somebody else can put the brakes on if the spending gets out of control.

You owe it to yourself and your mate, not to mention your children, to manage your earnings and investments so that you will have something to show for the work you do. During your working life you will earn close to half a million dollars. It doesn't have to go down the drain unless you let it. You can make some of this money bring in more money, use it for protection and peace of mind, beat the high cost of living and inflation through judicious spending. First, of course, you have to get your hands on it.

Making the Money

The median wage for the American family is $5,490 a year. This is the median, mind you. When you are in your twenties you will bring in less than that. Consider these statistics on the earning power of men twenty to twenty-four.

99.8%	make	less	than	$10,000
97.5%	"	"	"	7,000
93.7%	"	"	"	6,000
86.3%	"	"	"	5,000
75.3%	"	"	"	4,000
57.6%	"	"	"	3,000
39.8%	"	"	"	2,000
20.2%	"	"	"	1,000

Because work has become more complex, requiring extensive equipment and group effort, there are fewer of the self-employed. More Americans are working for somebody else. However, there are still those who want to go it alone and do so despite the odds. Something for a newly married couple to consider is that an understanding and supportive wife can be a great help if a young man is considering going into business for himself.

An argument could be made pro and con going out on your own in your twenties. Some people claim that you have less to lose, so can gamble more and perhaps win a higher pot. Your responsibilities are minimal and while you're trying to establish yourself you don't have to worry about keeping up with the Joneses. There comes a time when it is too late to start over, what with children in school, a mortgage to pay, expensive family tastes.

Others insist that you need a seasoning period, time to discover your abilities, learn a business, make contacts and gain exposure. One engineer in his forties who abruptly uprooted his family from their comfortable suburban home to start his own electronics business is of this persuasion. "When I was working for G & D, I got to know the field, the competition, and they got to know me. I'm sure I couldn't have raised the capital I needed to start my business ten years ago. Those guys would have thought I was just a fresh kid. They respect me because I did move up in the company before I went out on my own. I have a kind of backing I just had to earn by putting in the time in a big company." Apparently it's never too late to start over but this man had an unusually sympathetic wife willing to go to work herself so he could have his chance.

Some fields will always attract lone-wolf types who want to be in business for themselves. Artists, writers, designers, musicians tend to work alone and they can earn a rather precarious living, at first anyway. Their wives seem quite able to adapt to an uncertain present, count the companionship and stimulation of a creative husband more important than regular bank deposits. The artists themselves are not unmindful of the sacrifice they must make.

Said one illustrator who resigned a regular studio job to try free-lancing, "It's tough if you married at eighteen as I did. However, if two people are right for each other the marriage will work regardless of age. I have found that it is much easier for the young husband to accept and adjust to an early marriage than it is for the young wife. The husband has to work and be self-sufficient anyway, in order to be socially acceptable. It's part of our way of life. The girl who marries at the age of seventeen or eighteen and has children right away has to wait a good eight, ten or even twelve years before her husband has his feet firmly on the ground and can afford to give his family the things that she has dreamed of in marriage."

Often enough the self-employed outstrip the organization men in money earned as well as independence but it does take time to get the training, build up a clientele and establish a reputation. This, of course, is especially true of doctors, lawyers, and architects, who tend to work alone.

Which of the self-employed workers makes the most money? Doctors do, with a median income of $14,689. Household service employees make the least, $1,770.

Which is the best business or profession as far as income potential is concerned? According to *This U.S.A.*, "The three wealthiest groups, in 1963, by industry classification, were 'finance, insurance and real estate' ($8,222), 'professional and related services' ($7,635) and, surprisingly, 'public administration' ($7,709). Also remarkable; the 'government worker' (greatly underpaid we are often told) earns more on the average than do 'non-government wage and salary workers' or than 'self-employed workers.'"

American incomes have risen in *real* dollars by 50% since 1947, according to *This U.S.A.*, "A typical 1963 family lived on $120 per week; their 1947 counterpart lived on $80 per week in *constant* 1963 dollars."

General good times account for the rise in family income but other forces are at work, namely, the wife. Consider figures from *This U.S.A.* on the $10,000-plus, or "ample" family. "In 1949, 19% of the ample families had the wife in the labor force. Eleven years later, in 1960, just twice as many—38%—had wives in the labor force.

"The amount that a working wife contributes to household earnings can be quite substantial.

Median family income when family has one earner $5,614
Median family income when family has two earners $7,202

"Thus, a working wife adds close to 30% of the family income; in the case of a family making $10,000 a year this would work out to about $7,700 per year for the head and about $2,300 for the second earner."

No wonder the authors of *This U.S.A.* advise any young man who wants to be well off to encourage his wife to work. Many young wives don't need the encouragement; they do need help in dovetailing their job into marriage.

The Working Wife

One out of every three married women work. Some are doing it out of necessity but a sizable number work to increase the family's spending power and double their pleasure in living.

The young wife who wants to start her family right away may wonder if she should get a job. "As soon as I became useful, I'd probably get pregnant and have to leave." Fair enough. But there are hundreds of part-time jobs, community projects, short-term employment opportunities available to the bright young woman who wants to be active outside the home.

Sometimes an early job experience can lead to a continuing home-centered assignment. Young mothers who complain that their days are built around diaper-changing and formula-making are grateful for a working link with the outside world.

Ann C. is one. She used her college English major to good advantage, got a job as a researcher for a small publishing firm when she graduated. After she got married she "retired" from the job because her husband wanted her to. But she stayed in touch and asked to be put on the company's part-time list. Even now, when she must take care of her baby, she keeps up with her part-time job.

She can do the work at home, using the telephone to check facts and get interview material. When she goes to the office to get an assignment, attend a meeting or pick up research material she hires a sitter to stay with the baby. This expense she thinks is well worth it.

"I'd go wild if I was tied down at home all the time. But if I left the baby just to have lunch with the girls or go to a museum or library I'd feel guilty. This way I'm bringing in some money we can use to buy a house or car. I'm in touch with the working world and stimulated. It's not the kind of job I'll ever outgrow either. I should be able to do it the rest of my life, devoting more time or less as our family comes along."

Ann is lucky because she can work at home, thereby having the best of two worlds. Most young women have to show up at an office if they want to work. How does this kind of schedule jibe with the needs of home, husband and family?

When there are just the two of you the problem of scheduling an outside job isn't too difficult. But you should try to work out a schedule. You can't expect household chores to do themselves while you are away. You will have to become something of an efficiency expert if you are to juggle the working wife responsibilities.

Here are some guidelines.

Your husband comes first, his well-being, happiness, sense of being cared for, has priority. If you have a boss who likes to work late, who begins to dictate around four in the afternoon, then you'd better change jobs. Your husband deserves to come home to a good dinner and a wife who is there. If the job bugs you, puts you under too much pressure, then you'd be better off in another one. Any sympathetic husband will, within reason, listen to your troubles but he doesn't want to hear ad infinitum about the ogre in billing or the supervisor who doesn't understand you.

Try to figure out a pattern of living that suits you both. If your husband is willing to do the dishes, by all means let him. If he thinks such chores are "woman's work," accept this gracefully and ask him to take on some jobs that he doesn't mind—i.e., taking out the garbage, washing the windows, paying bills, tending the yard. Clearly, if you both work you will both have to make some contribution to the home.

Be very clear about what your job nets you both. It costs money to hold a job.

According to studies by several government and private organizations concerned with the family's well-being, taxes and job-related expenses eat up a third to a half of the average working mother's earnings.

Here are some specific expenses that should be taken into account:

Taxes. Social Security taxes take 3⅝ percent of the first $4,800 of annual earnings. Then not only are the wife's earnings subject to income taxes, but the family may well be pushed into a higher tax bracket, so that the husband's income gets taxed more than before.

Wife's job expenses. These might include dues to union or professional organizations, uniforms, lunches, transportation, etc.

Indirect expenses. Working wives tend to spend more on clothing and personal grooming (according to the U.S. Department of Agriculture, their clothing bills on the average are double those of nonworking wives, as are expenses for laundry and household help.) The family food bills, too, are likely to be larger, with more meals eaten outside the home and greater use of "convenience foods."

Child care. This will generally be the largest single item of expense, and the most variable, depending on the age of the children, the availability of baby-sitting help from friends and relatives, and other factors. In some cities, there are day-care centers whose fees are scaled to the family's ability to pay, usually with a maximum of about $15 a week. Private nurseries generally charge somewhat more.

The Budget Standard Service of the Community Council of Greater New York estimates that job-related expenses for the average working mother add up to $15 a week, before allowing for child care and income taxes:

Expenditure	Weekly Cost
Lunch	$ 4.75
Transportation to work	3.00
Union dues	.80
Additional clothing	2.55
Additional personal care	.40
Additional laundry	1.15
Social Security tax (on a salary of $65 a week)	2.35
	$15.00

For a working mother with school age or preschool children, child care and/or additional household help might bring total expenses to $30 a week. Federal and state income taxes will add another $5 to $10 a week (depending on the family's income tax bracket), leaving $25 to $30 as the net increase in the family's weekly earnings.

You will have to weigh the intangible satisfactions of working in with the net income you bring home before you can really decide if the job is worth it. If you need the stimulation of life outside the home then even a modest profit makes working worthwhile. But if you aren't driven toward a career, relax and enjoy domesticity. You can "make money" by being a creative homemaker.

If you sew, cook well, have some decorating and do-it-yourself talents, your contribution to the family budget may well be greater if you stay home than if you work. One young bride who thought she was making a substantial contribution to the family nest egg discovered that her household expenses ran 30 percent higher because she worked.

"It had nothing to do with buying clothes for the job or eating lunch out or carfare. I found that I depended on short-order cooking because I was just too tired to try a stew or fricasse. I bought desserts instead of making them. We had to have a cleaning woman because it was too hard for me to do the housework and incidental laundry."

Even if a wife is no great shakes at do-it-yourself creative cooking and sewing she still earns her salt by handling the regular chores around the house. One college home economics department estimates that she "earns" $150 a week if you rate her services on the pay scale of housekeeping professionals. She would get $2 an hour for cooking, table-setting, serving. Dishwashers charge $1.25 an hour and so do laundresses and cleaning women. On an annual basis the housewife can figure she adds almost $8,000 in services to her family's pocketbook. It would cost that to replace her.

Job Opportunities for Women

Every year more women get jobs, on either a full- or part-time basis. In addition to the many thousands of women who enter the job market, many others start thinking about that possibility, particularly mothers who feel that in a few years they will be able to spare the time from their primary roles as homemakers. For such women, it is vital to know *today* where government and private employment authorities believe the most job opportunities will be in the next five to ten years. This will enable a woman to start getting the training, if any is needed, for the job she really hopes to get. Job opportunity areas singled out by experts include:

Typists and stenographers. The current demand for well-trained secretaries will continue with business growth. Those who can take shorthand as well as type have the best chance of quick employment. A secretary with only typing ability can get a job if her employer uses a dictating machine and she can transcribe from a recording. College-trained women frequently find that many career opportunities require typing and that starting as a secretary may offer an opening in the field of her choice. Secretarial school courses are six to twelve months.

Service and sales. Jobs such as a beauty operator or a hotel assistant manager may take from three to twelve months of special training. The need for waitresses, hostesses and maids will continue in restaurants, hotels, resorts and hospitals. Little training is needed. Sales jobs, whether in stores or door-to-door, are increasing. A suburban housewife may find full- or part-time work as a salesclerk in shopping centers in her area. Real estate and insurance are also widening career fields for women. Some insurance companies require a college degree for agents, but others accept high school graduates and provide on-the-job training. Real estate selling can be learned on-the-job. Courses for real estate and insurance agent license exams are offered.

Business offices. Clerical employees without special skills are being displaced in many places by automated office machines. However, persons with training in computer-card punching, billing machine and calculators will be needed. Use of business machines is taught in some high schools. Other training programs of from a few weeks to six months, depending on the type of machine, are available in colleges, private data-processing schools and from equipment manufacturers. High school graduates with mathematical training will find opportunities for clerks in bank and insurance offices.

Medical and dental. Opportunities in these fields are for both high school and college graduates. Some high schools have courses in practical nursing. Hospital aides also are needed and the training period is only a few weeks. Dental technicians and hygienists and X-ray technicians require about two years of special training beyond high school. College-trained women or those who go to specialized schools will be needed as dietitians and home economists, medical technologists and laboratory assistants, nurses, chemists and physical therapists.

Counselors and youth advisers. Neighborhood recreation and expanding social agencies will use more helpers who have been college trained, but do not have the advanced degrees required for social and welfare workers. College graduates without teaching certificates also are being used in schools as teacher-helpers.

Professional careers. The expanding fields of science and technology will require trained women with advanced college degrees for market analysis, electronics, statistics, biology and psychology. More teachers and librarians are needed.

What Every Job Hunter Should Know

Job-hunting is something of an art. Before you begin, it pays to evaluate your experience and skills realistically. When you are ready to look for a job, plan your approach carefully.

First, collect personal records required for the job application, resumé and interview. You can fail to land a job because of incorrect or incomplete facts. To most employers this indicates a haphazard, unbusinesslike approach. You should have your Social Security number, names and addresses of business and personal references, dates and addresses pertaining to your schooling and work experience. If you attended college, obtain a transcript of your academic record. (Some colleges will send a transcript only to the prospective employer.) Include in your personal folder any letters of commendation you may have received and details of achievements and awards.

A resumé or summary of your personal background and work experience is important. It should be brief (usually one page) and neatly typewritten or duplicated on white paper. At the top of the page list your name, address, telephone number, marital status, height, weight, and, if you desire, date of birth. In subsequent paragraphs list your educational background, including names and addresses of schools and colleges you attended, dates of attendance, major fields of study, degrees if any, scholarships and awards. Next list work experience. Give names and addresses of companies you worked for, dates of employment and a brief description of what you did. If you have skills, such as typing or stenography, mention them. Include the words-per-minute you type or take shorthand. Finally, list several references, people other than relatives or former employers who know you well.

The next step is to search for job leads. Inquire among friends, relatives and acquaintances who may be in a position to help you, including former employers or business contacts you may have made in earlier jobs. Learn how to scan the "Help Wanted" advertisements in newspapers, because jobs are sometimes listed in several different ways. Additionally, you may want to register with a commercial agency, the local office of your state employment service or a college placement bureau.

When you have a promising job lead, ask by letter or telephone for an interview. A letter of application should be brief and neatly typed. Try to address it to the personnel director or appropriate supervisor by name rather than to the company. Remember, too, that *any* written material you submit to a prospective employer —a resumé, application form or letter—is a reflection of your work habits and personality. Read such material carefully before you send it out. Be sure that spelling is correct and the document is neat.

The impression you make in an interview depends on many things—your grooming and appearance, your personal manner, your alertness, interest and preparation. An interviewer expects you to be a bit nervous and knows you will become more relaxed during the interview. Adele Lewis, an executive of Career Blazers, Inc., a New York employment agency, says, "A surprising number of people fail to show up for interviews or arrive late. Be prompt." If you cannot keep an appointment, call and tell the interviewer. These suggestions help to make a good impression:

Dress simply and conservatively in good taste. A cocktail dress is as inappropriate as slacks. Wear lipstick, but do not use heavy eye makeup or lace stockings. If you do not have a comfortable, appropriate business suit or dress, it pays to invest in one.

Let the interviewer conduct the interview. Show interest in the company, but avoid an aggressive approach or a barrage of questions about such things as fringe benefits, coffee breaks and vacations. The interviewer usually mentions these.

Wait for the interviewer to introduce the subject of salary. Be realistic and reasonably flexible about salary. Some jobs may prove to be better than others which pay a little more but offer less opportunity.

Legal Rights of Working Wives

Do a wife's earnings belong to her husband? Does a woman have a legal right to work even though her husband disapproves? Can she go into business for herself and control her own finances? If so, is her husband legally responsible for her debts? In general, what *are* the legal rights of working wives in relation to their primary roles as wives and mothers?

In recent years, federal and state legislation has been enacted to help insure equality of women's rights. Among other objectives, this legislation is intended to provide equal job opportunity, equal pay and promotion policies and to prevent discrimination based on sex. Nevertheless, certain laws in many states still discriminate against women. For instance, in many states there are legal restrictions on the personal and property rights of married women.

Laws may vary considerably from state to state, but a number of laws commonly prevail in most states. Key rights of working wives under these laws include:

A married woman has the right to choose whether to work or not to work. Often, of course, a wife's decision to work is based on financial need. In other cases both husband and wife welcome additional income even though the husband alone can support the family. Harriet F. Pilpel, a New York attorney who served on the committee on civil and political rights of President Kennedy's Commission on the Status of Women, says, "Actually, although a wife is free to work even though her husband disapproves, most marriage partners find that a problem such as this requires full and frank discussion before a decision is made. If the couple has children, their welfare should be the primary consideration." Many other factors may be involved. For example, suppose a woman works on an assembly line in an electronics factory. Her husband's firm transfers him to a branch office in a small city that has no electronics factories. If she wishes to continue working, she will probably have to find a different kind of job. Since a husband is legally responsible for family support, *he has the right to decide where the family lives.* (However, if a husband is sick or disabled and cannot support his family, his wife must provide support to whatever extent she can. And, in some states, both husband and wife are legally obligated to pay family expenses.)

Money you earn by working is your separate property, to use in any way you wish, in most states. You may keep it in your own bank account, invest it or buy things with it. However, in eight states and in Puerto Rico, property, including earnings, acquired by either husband or wife after marriage is known as *community property* and belongs jointly and equally to them. Generally, though, in community-property states the husband has greater power than the wife to control and manage funds and property. The eight community-property states are Arizona, California, Idaho, Louisiana, Nevada, New Mexico, Texas and Washington.

In all states, whether she is employed or not, a woman may maintain a bank account in her own name. A married woman does not need her husband's consent to do this.

A working wife also has the right to make contracts. Among other things, this generally means that you may establish a business, form a partnership or corporation or be self-employed. In a few states, though, you must have court approval to establish a business, and in some states you need your husband's consent. If you establish your own business, *you,* not your husband, are responsible for the debts of the business. In a few states the right to make contracts is limited to certain kinds of contracts. For example, in several states a wife cannot act as *surety,* that is, cannot guarantee payment of another person's debts. In most states, too, you can make a contract with your husband, although in some states you and your husband can do so only through a third person who acts as trustee. Suppose you work in a business owned by your husband. Is he legally obligated to pay you? In most states, he is not. In some states, though, you may make a contract with your husband which obligates him to pay you for working.

A major family purchase, such as a car or furniture, usually is considered the property of the husband unless it qualifies as community property or there is evidence of the wife's part-ownership or of the husband's intention to make a gift to the wife. Thus, if the bill of sale or title is in both names, it helps to protect the woman's interest in the property if her husband dies or the marriage ends in separation or divorce.

Further information regarding legal rights of women in your state is available from the Women's Bureau, U.S. Department of Labor, Washington, D.C. 20210. If you have a specific legal problem, consult a lawyer or the nearest Legal Aid Society.

Community Property

When a man and woman marry, who owns the property they acquire after marriage? For instance, when a husband speaks of "my wife's car," is it really hers? Or does he own the car, or do they own it together? Ordinarily, this depends on whether the car's ownership is in the name of the husband, or wife, or both, and on whose money was used to buy the car. However, it *may* depend on where they live and when or how they acquired the property. This question of who owns what becomes important when a husband or wife dies. It is important, too, if a marriage fails and property must be divided.

In this country, most states recognize two kinds of marital property: the wife's and the husband's. However, since the major earnings are usually by the husband, he is likely to accumulate and control much more property than his wife.

A third class of property exists, though, in eight western and southwestern states and in Puerto Rico. This is *community property*, owned jointly and *equally* by the husband and wife. If the husband buys a house, his wife legally owns half even though the house is in his name. Since several of these states have had great population increases in recent years, more people are becoming affected by community-property laws daily. What happens when a married couple moves to a community-property state from another state? Their separate property usually remains separate. However, what they earn or acquire in the new state becomes community property. Generally, people in community-property states have little or no tax advantage over those in other states. (In the 1940's several states—Hawaii, Michigan, Nebraska, Oklahoma, Oregon and Pennsylvania—adopted community-property systems for tax purposes but later abandoned them. In some of these states a person may still have rights which were acquired under the community-property system.)

The details of community-property laws vary among the states that use this sytem. However, such systems share certain common features. The concept of "partnership," or equal sharing, is basic. With a few exceptions, community property includes all property acquired *after* marriage, as well as any gains or profits from the property. "Property" includes such things as wages and earnings, real estate, savings, stocks and bonds. The exceptions—property which is owned separately by husband or wife—include:

Property received by gift or under a will or inheritance.

Property bought with separate funds and specifically bought as the separate property of husband or wife.

Property owned by a husband or wife *before* marriage is separate. It remains so unless it is expressly made community property. Likewise, it is possible to transfer community property to the status of separate property by agreement between husband and wife.

The community-property system recognizes the married couple

as *equal* partners. The husband and wife each owns one-half of all community property. When one spouse dies, the survivor automatically holds half the community property in most states. The other half is subject to provisions of the will of the spouse who died. If he left no will, his share may be divided among relatives according to law, or pass by law to the surviving spouse, and is subject to any claims against it. The survivor may also receive the *separate* estate of the dead spouse.

In states that do *not* have community-property systems, a wife is entitled to a minimum share of about one-third of the estate when her husband dies. If there are children, she may receive as little as one-fifth. Thus, community-property laws usually protect the wife by assuring her an equal share of the marital property. In some situations, though, a community-property system may not be advantageous to the wife. This is particularly true when the value of the husband's *separate* property is large and his community property relatively small.

If a married couple in a community-property state are divorced, the half-ownership rule applies in *theory*. Generally, divorce property settlements tend to be more advantageous for women in community-property states than in other states. However, most states have made special provisions that give courts considerable freedom in dividing community property.

In most situations, the husband in a community-property state has greater power than the wife to control and manage property. He is general manager and agent for the community property. He has full power to manage and dispose of "general" community property, subject to certain restrictions. However, he usually cannot transfer or mortgage community real estate without his wife's consent and in most cases her signature.

Community-property laws are complex. Too, they may vary considerably in detail from one community-property state to the next. Thus, consult an attorney if you have questions regarding the way these laws may affect your situation.

A Second Income

For the first time in history more than half the families in America now have a second income. For a substantial number that extra income is represented by the wife's paycheck, but for many it comes from nonwork sources. These sources include savings and investments, rental profits, pensions, veteran's payments, workmen's compensation, alimony or support payments. It would seem that the American dream now has a new dimension—to "have a piece of something, to have something going for you." Whether you buy into your brother-in-law's hamburger-stand franchise, invest in growth stocks, sock your money into a vacation house which will pay its way as a rental property, you could be moving toward the security of a second income. There is just one catch. Before you can make money earn money for you, you have to have money to invest.

When a famed economist bade farewell to a Yale graduating class he said, "Gentlemen, I have but one piece of advice to give you. Gentlemen, acquire capital." We could all profit (quite literally) by his wisdom.

There may be other ways—like winning on the races, moonlighting another job, borrowing from your family—to get a chunk of money to invest. The surest way is to start saving it. Start right now. Save off the top of your income, instead of promising to put whatever is left at the end of the month into the bank. Earmark a certain amount for saving and put it in your account before you sit down with the bills. It can be as small as ten dollars a month and still add up over the years to a tidy sum. Think of this ten or twenty-five or fifty dollars a month the way you do any other obligation—the light bill, or car payment, or club dues. It's a necessity. It has priority. If you train yourself to save regularly, you will not only have the peace of mind which comes when you know you can fall back on a nest egg, but that the nest egg will grow.

Always deposit money you don't intend to touch in a savings bank which compounds interest. Your interest becomes principal every time it is compounded. Your money earns more than it does in a bank paying "simple interest." For example, $5,000 invested at 4½ percent compounded quarterly would grow to $7,821.85 in ten years, compared with $7,250 at 4½ percent simple interest.

If you were to save fifty dollars a month beginning at age twenty-five in a bank paying 4½ percent a year from day of deposit, compounded quarterly, here is how your savings would grow. At age sixty-five your account would be worth $67,014 even though you only deposited $24,000 in those forty years.

You can set money aside on a regular monthly or quarterly basis, and watch it grow, by investing in government bonds. A payroll deduction plan is a good means of keeping your investment program on target. Or, you could participate in the Stock Exchange Monthly Investment Plan. Or you might consider a monthly payment into a mutual fund.

The important thing is to earmark some of your income for savings and investment now. Form the sensible habit of putting money aside with regularity. If you need help in disciplining yourself to save, then sign up for a payroll deduction plan so you won't see the money and won't, therefore, be tempted.

Being young, you have one great asset the older investor lacks. You can afford to take some investment risks because you have more time to recoup your losses. You might take a flier on speculative growth stocks, knowing that even if you didn't make the profits anticipated you could save enough from future earnings to compensate for the loss. The older investor, thinking of retirement, is looking for the safer stocks that will pay dividends but not always grow in value.

You do, however, lack the experience a seasoned investor possesses. It may be wise for you to study the stock market before investing even in mutual funds or any group investment plan. Put your money in the bank while you bone up on the possibilities of increasing it.

Read books on investment. Follow magazine and newspaper articles. Get the habit of reading the financial page. The New York Stock Exchange will send you free booklets which clarify the role of the stockbroker. Most community colleges offer night courses in investments; your state university can probably provide an extension course in rudimentary economics. Investment clubs offer the novice a useful way to learn about the market and at the same time practice investing on a modest scale. The National Association of Investment Clubs, 1300 Washington Boulevard, Detroit, Michigan, can give you information on joining or starting such a club. If you join a club you are encouraged to form regular investment habits. Members of the club are asked to become "experts" on certain kinds of stocks and report to members on their findings. Together you can pool your information and cash and buy more sensibly and extensively than you could as individuals.

Mutual Funds and Government Bonds

Mutual funds attract individuals who want to get into the market but are not confident that they can manage their own investments. They also would rather not put all their eggs in one basket, buy only one stock with the modest sum available to them. The mutual fund is a professionally organized and managed investment institution. When you buy into a fund you are buying a fraction of all the investments it is currently making. Your personal stake is, therefore, spread out. If one stock in the portfolio goes down another may be going up. You also get the advantages of professional management, but you have to pay for this. The mutual fund investor must usually pay a commission running to 8½ or 9 percent plus management fees of nearly 1 percent. Usually the commission is taken out of your initial purchases. You must, therefore, be prepared to stay with a fund over a period of years to earn back the commission and also take advantage of what investors call "dollar averaging." Simply put, this means that because you are investing at regular intervals your fixed payments buy more shares when prices are low, fewer when they are high. The net result is a price average in your favor.

No matter how worthwhile saving for investment may be, you should always keep money in the bank (half a year's salary) for emergencies. You never know when accidents or illness may hit, when you will have to travel on short notice, when a parent may need help, when your job may fold. It is far better to meet these emergencies with savings than have to borrow to do it. Incidentally, you may want to borrow against your savings rather than draw them out. A "passbook loan" secures your account against the loan but since your savings will still be earning interest the cost of the loan is only a percentage or so. Also, you are more inclined to pay back the loan and release your savings. If you simply drew them out it might be a long time before they were once more built up.

U.S. government savings bonds, for millions of families, have proved to be a safe, practical way to set up a retirement fund or to pay for a child's college education. More than 40 million persons, many using payroll deduction plans at their place of employment, now hold more than 500 million savings bonds worth almost $50 billion. Although it is currently possible to get higher rates of interest on savings funds, many people prefer to invest in savings bonds for both sound financial and patriotic reasons. The savings bond interest rate recently was raised to 4.15 percent from 3.75. Last June's sale of U.S. Series E savings bonds was the highest June sale since 1945.

Unlike other types of U.S. government securities (including bills, notes, certificates and other bonds), savings bonds are not subject to market fluctuation. They are never redeemed for less than the amount invested. Too, these other types of securities, despite their risk factor, are limited to a 4.25 percent interest return on a five-year maturity or longer. Franklin R. Saul, Assistant to the Secretary of the Treasury (Debt Management), says marketable Treasury securities not redeemed by the government before maturity are subject to price fluctuations. An investor may take a loss in principal if there is a need to sell before maturity.

In considering the purchase of savings bonds, it is important to understand the differences between Series E and Series H bonds. Series E are sold at discount in denominations with maturity values of $25, $50, $75, $100, $200, $500, $1,000 and $10,000. E bonds increase in value; they do not pay interest directly to the holder. For example, you pay $18.75 for a $25 bond. In seven years the bond is worth $25. Series E bonds can be redeemed at any time two months after purchase. However, the accrued interest is less than full rate if the bond is cashed in during the early years. Here is an example of yearly return on a $25 bond:

VALUE AT END OF

One year	$18.96
Two years	$19.70
Three years	$20.52
Four years	$21.42
Five years	$22.37
Six years	$23.36
Maturity	$25.00

Owners of E bonds may retain the bonds after the original seven-year period for another ten years to earn interest at the full current rate.

The Series H is a ten-year bond sold in denominations of $500, $1,000, $5,000 and $10,000. Interest is paid semiannually by check. At the current rate, a $1,000 bond would earn $417.40 during the ten-year period. The bond may be redeemed for face value on the first day of any month at least six months from the issue date by giving one month's written notice. An individual can buy no more than $20,000 of E and $30,000 of H bonds (face value) each year.

Federal taxes on Series E bond earnings can be paid annually or when they are redeemed. Series E taxes can be further deferred if E bonds are exchanged for Series H. The tax on the accrued interest of the E bonds is delayed until the H bonds are redeemed. Federal taxes are paid annually on H bond interest. Savings bonds are exempt from state and local taxes.

If you are saving for a child's college education, you can buy the E bond and register it in his name as sole owner. The bond becomes a gift from the parent to the child. The child files his own tax return at the end of the first year, listing the increase in bond value as income. If the child has earned less than $600 he will not have to pay any tax on the bonds. The first tax return establishes the intent and no further returns need be filed if annual income remains less than $600. For a retirement program, tax on interest may be reduced or eliminated because of increased exemptions and/or lowered income after age sixty-five.

No fees or commissions are charged for savings bonds. Series E bonds can be bought at banks or by mail from any Federal Reserve Bank, its branches or the Office of the Treasurer of the United States, Washington, D.C. 20220. Only the Federal Reserve Banks, their branches and the Treasury Department are authorized to issue Series H bonds. However, commercial banks and trust companies will forward applications for their purchase.

Interest rates on bonds of certain Federal agencies recently have risen to more than 5 percent. For instance, the Federal Home Loan Bank has issued one-year and eighteen-month notes paying 5.75 percent interest. The smallest denomination of such bonds is usually $5,000. While not specifically guaranteed by the

U.S. Treasury, these bonds carry an implied backing of the federal government and are considered very safe by investment authorities.

The Most Common Investing Mistakes

More people than ever before are investing in stocks. The New York Stock Exchange reports that the number of stockholders (more than 20 million) in the U.S. has tripled in the last ten years. Wise investing, though, requires knowledge and intelligent planning. A haphazard approach to investing can be costly. George J. Leness, president of Merrill Lynch, Pierce, Fenner & Smith, Inc., the world's largest stockbrokerage firm, answers these questions about investing.

Who should invest in stocks? Any person *who can afford it.* By this we mean that a person should be able to cover living expenses, have adequate insurance and enough cash for emergencies. With this protection, he can safely invest *extra* money in stocks. Actually, most people who buy stocks are relatively small investors.

Can you "make a killing" in stocks? Almost invariably, this attitude causes lost dollars and disappointment. A beginner should think of investing in stocks as a way of using his money to provide a reasonable return, not as a way of getting rich quick. You may have a fortunate friend who bought a stock that showed a dramatic profit in a short time. Such cases are rare.

Should a beginning investor buy low-priced stocks? Many beginners would rather own one hundred shares of a two-dollar stock than ten shares of a twenty-dollar stock. Usually the higher-priced stock is a wiser purchase than the so-called "penny stock," which, in essence, is highly speculative. Beginners tend to assume the two-dollar stock is better because they will make that much more money when the stock goes up, say, to twenty dollars. This does not happen often.

Should an investor act on a "tip"? This practice is more likely than any other to cause heavy losses, particularly among amateur investors. *Never* buy stocks from a stranger who approaches you by phone, mail or in person. A reputable broker never solicits business this way. It is risky, too, to act on advice or so-called tips from well-meaning friends who know little about the stock market. On the other hand, a respected businessman may have good information and be well informed about a stock.

What kinds of stocks should beginning investors buy? This is determined by their particular goals. Certain kinds of stocks and bonds have general characteristics. Some, for example, are considered particularly *safe* investments, while others provide more liberal *dividend income* and still others offer an opportunity for *growth* of the investment. A few stocks may combine two of these features, but *none has all three.* Thus it is important for a beginning investor to know his goals and the characteristics of the stocks he is considering. Of course, some risk is involved in buying any stock. Although the general trend of the stock market has been upward over the last thirty years, not *all* stocks have shared in this growth. Sharp drops in the market have occurred. Thus, your stock can go down as well as up.

How do you decide when to sell a stock? Many investors make a mistake when they sell stocks that are making a profit. Frequently it is wiser to sell stocks that are going down in value, and to take a loss, if necessary, than to sell stocks that are rising in value. Since this is not an ironclad rule, consider the circumstances carefully and consult your broker or other adviser.

Where can investors get good advice? Seek help from a *reputable* person experienced in investing, such as a stockbroker, banker, lawyer or investment counselor. As in many other businesses, sharp operators exist. If you have any doubt about a broker's reputation, check with your banker or local Better Business Bureau. Beware of anyone who urges you to buy a stock fast "before the market goes up" or who uses high-pressure tactics to persuade you to buy a particular stock. A reputable broker usually recommends several stocks suited to your goals. Responsibility for the decision is *yours*.

How can beginners learn more about investing? Free, informative material about investing is abundantly available. Many of the larger brokerage houses and stock exchanges offer readable booklets that explain the basic principles of investing—how to buy stocks, how to read a financial report, and so on. In addition, some firms give free investing courses for beginners (in some cases a small fee is charged). Occasionally these courses are conducted at places most convenient to women shoppers—for example, in large department stores.

From these sources, too, a person can learn how to find out about a particular stock. This is not as mysterious as it may seem. A woman shopping for a new refrigerator may know little, technically, about refrigerators, but she knows how to shop wisely. She looks at several models in different stores. She compares prices, considers quality and brand names, and finally buys a refrigerator with most of the features she wants at a price she can afford. She should shop this way for stocks, too, learning about the different kinds available and the companies behind them. Up-to-date reference books available in libraries and brokers' offices list information about these companies.

Budgets

"Budget" is probably the dreariest word in the English language. And yet, unless you have some idea of the expenses you face you won't be able to meet them on payday. Some married couples go through life always wondering, "Where does the money go?" They could find out and stop the drain on their pocketbooks and themselves. Why don't you get off on the right foot financially by determining not to know where every penny goes but certainly where every ten dollars goes.

There was a time when a wife did not know how much her husband earned. She was given "household" money to spend—for food, clothing, help, utility bills. He paid for the car, rent or mortgage, insurance. If they had anything left over he invested it or saved it or they splurged on a trip, a new carpet, remodeling.

It's different today. The wife is more likely to be a full partner in the business of buying, selling, saving, investing. Very probably she brings in some share of the family income. If she doesn't work she figures that she could. By staying home to take care of the baby and the house she is earning her keep. Therefore, she is entitled to have a say in the family spending.

Most husbands agree with this, in principle anyway. A good many men would, in fact, be just as happy if their wives spent the paycheck on the necessities and banked the rest. Said one young husband, "I don't mind having an allowance for lunch,

haircuts, a drink with the boys. If I ran our finances I wouldn't
get half as much mileage out of them as my wife does."

There are as many ways to set up a financial partnership within
marriage as there are outside it. Here are some of the options open
to you. They've been tested by couples who find they work—for
them anyway. Depending upon your personality, your income,
and your training in money, you may find one or two worth experimenting with.

Plan A. Husband and wife figure their expenses together, estimate their income, map out a plan. Naturally the plan has to have
built-in flexibility. You never know when you'll face a small emergency (the car needs a new clutch, you break your glasses). But
you can make a rough estimate of what your expenses are going
to be. Here's how such a system works for Joe and Kitty.

Kitty says, "As soon as a paycheck walks in that house we know
where it's going, which bills are important, which can wait. We
were each living on $250 a month when we were in college. That
hasn't changed even though now I'm working and Joe has his
graduate school grant. Our combined income is around $500 a
month. At first it seemed like lots more than we were used to
even though it adds up to the same amount. Then we began to
realize that we would have expenses we hadn't counted on.

"Medical bills, for one thing. When I had to have glasses or
my teeth fixed, my parents paid for it. They didn't take it out of
my monthly expense check. Joe didn't have to buy life insurance
before he was married. Neither of us had a car then; now we feel
we need one because we live so far away from our jobs."

How do they budget their expenses?

"I allow about $30 a month for medical bills and medicine. Food
takes about $100, rent $115. We spend $30 for cigarettes, and
$25 for the telephone. We could cut down on these two items
I suppose but I like to talk to my family and now that I'm married
I don't feel that I can reverse the charges. Besides, Joe uses the
phone for business. We both buy a lot of books. I spent less on
food and more on books before I was married."

Food is the big item in their budget but Kitty works hard to
keep the cost trimmed down. One strategy is to shop alone. "I
shop better by myself. I'm not distracted by wondering if he
would like this or that. He is tempted to buy the usual cheeses and
olives that men like. If we are ahead for the week because we've

been asked out or because the leftovers worked out I ask him to come along. But if we're working on a tight budget I wouldn't dream of it."

Even though insurance comes to a couple of hundred a year and car maintenance (and payments) run around $100 a month, Joe and Kitty manage to save some money. They started marriage with a $1,000 nest-egg present and intend to build on that at the rate of $50 a month.

Plan B. Wife gets an allowance for all household expenses with the understanding that anything left over belongs to her for clothes, lunches with the girls, books, investment, presents, travel. Husband gets an allowance too for his personal necessities. He also pays for the big items. They agree that what is left over goes into the savings account. Four times a year they assess their savings and decide on a modest investment in bonds, stocks. They keep a cushion in the bank against emergencies, feel they are protected against disaster with life and medical insurance.

This is how their income-outgo breaks down. Husband makes $600 a month. He gives his wife $200 to pay all household bills—food, laundry, cleaning woman, oil, electricity, garbage man, telephone. He allows himself $100 a month for transportation, clothes, recreation, lunch. The rent is $125 and he pays that. Car maintenance, insurance bills, taxes, medical expenses run around $100 a month. They always save at least 10 percent of their gross income but when household bills are light manage to put aside more than that.

Plan C. In this situation the wife earns $400 a month as a legal secretary. She buys the food for the couple, pays household expenses and takes care of her own clothes, transportation and job-related costs. She manages to save $100 each month and puts that into a kitty to be spent eventually for a house or trip, something they can both enjoy.

The husband earns $500 a month and must spend $150 of this on the apartment rent, insurance, taxes. He takes another $100 for the car payments and upkeep, plus $50 for his personal expenses. Their medical expenses and entertainment allotment run around $100 a month, leaving $100 for the husband to put in their joint savings account.

Plan D. The wife is an advertising copywriter earning $600 a month. She wants to quit work and start a family as soon as they have saved enough money to buy a house. They want to make a big down payment and avoid a lengthy mortgage. Her husband makes $800 a month which is quite adequate for their needs. Her entire salary is put in the bank with the understanding that it will pay for a house someday. They live on his income entirely.

Things to consider. If the husband feels that his manhood is threatened when his wife has an outside source of income, then they had better put her money aside for a joint project. He likes to feel he is supporting her. If the husband rather likes the idea that his wife is also a breadwinner, then they had better split the expenses. If the wife likes to work but has always believed that what she earns is "mine," then she will do better paying her share of bills with her money. This may seem like a roommate arrangement but it works for many couples.

Depending upon which one has the best head for figures, the actual budgeting and accounting need not be a joint enterprise. The husband pays all the bills, even his wife's personal ones, balances his and her checkbooks. She earns more than he does at this point but he is the family money manager. Nobody's pride is hurt.

Usually the wife does the paper work but some women feel overwhelmed by it as family responsibilities grow. One husband admits: "When we were first married I used to bring my check home on payday and put it on the table. My wife paid all the bills. I never asked where it went or how much we owed or if we were saving anything. A few years later when we owned a house, were starting our family, had life insurance and investments, it became obvious that the arrangement wasn't fair. My wife felt, quite rightly, that she carried the total burden for the finances. She really was oppressed by it. So now we sit down twice a month for our bookkeeping evenings. She reads off the bills; I write the checks. We decide what we'll pay and what can wait. We both hate it but it's better this way."

Another husband describes his seemingly casual handling of the family finances. "I put both our paychecks in a joint account. I pay all the bills and give her cash when she wants it. Every time the checking account gets too big I put some of it in a savings account.

"We are able to do all the things we want but, of course, we don't yet have any children. We carry on a running conversation

about decisions. We always know how the other feels and so far
we haven't had any fights about money. The reason our system
works is that we conceive of every expenditure as being for *us*.
Sometimes that gets pretty ludicrous I'll admit. I come home with
books and records I want and announce, 'Look what I bought
us.' "

This young husband did hit upon the most important single
explanation for the very varied ways couples arrive at a mutually
satisfactory plan for spending and saving. "The way people handle
money," he observed, "reflects the way they consider each other."
Your plan will be as unique as your marriage. Don't struggle
against this fact of life.

You will do well, however, to decide what you value most and
then adjust your budget so you can satisfy both the necessities
and the "luxuries." One man's luxuries (books, records, travel)
may easily be another's necessities. If you are constantly struggling
to satisfy your soul on a modest income and at the same time
conform to your parents' notion of appropriate housing, something is going to have to give, hopefully not your soul. Some necessities are indeed just that—food, shelter, clothing, protection,
but you don't have to live beyond your means. The key to workable financial planning lies in determining priorities and then
figuring out how you can meet them. You have more options now,
in your early married years, than you will ever have again. You can
elect to live a rather Spartan domestic life, subsisting on hamburgers, just so you can have a month's vacation abroad. With
no children to care for as yet, you can do a certain amount of job-
hopping. There is no reason why you have to accumulate possessions at this point in your life. You might prefer to travel light
until you have decided just how settled down you want to be.

How to Plan a Budget

Most families *need* a budget to manage their dollars most effectively. But keeping a budget is not simply a restricting, dreary
game for penny pinchers. A budget is a realistic *plan* for determining what to do with a family's available dollars. The basic purpose
of most budgets is to keep the family's spending within the limits
of its income. But a good budget has other desirable features. It

usually is the best way to decide how and where to save money. And, rather than restrict your spending, a budget sometimes can show you ways to *afford* spending on things that matter most to your family—a new car, a vacation, needed kitchen improvements. Finally, preparing a budget is one of the most effective ways to pinpoint the areas in which you may unwittingly be spending too much money. These basic steps in drawing up a budget can be used by any family:

Decide your family's goals. A budget can be used to achieve any of several goals, or a combination of them. For instance, you may want to plan for long-term goals over ten or twenty years, such as education of children and saving for retirement. Or you can plan a budget to help attain goals for the near future—say, the next three to five years. These goals might include saving for a down payment on a new home, buying a car or making home improvements. Again, you can budget for even more immediate goals in the coming months or year. For example, you may want to reduce debts, buy a home appliance, or start a reserve fund for emergencies or vacations. Most budget experts and family-welfare authorities agree that if children are old enough, it is a good idea to let them take part in, or at least listen to, these discussions of family budget goals. And, these experts add, each family member should have a personal allowance, no matter how small, to spend as he likes.

Estimate your income. To plan a budget, you must know how much money will be available during the planning period. (A budget can cover any convenient period. Many families plan a budget for one year, but you may want to establish a three- or six-month trial period, particularly for a first budget.) Thus, this next step in planning is to estimate your family's net income—the amount you have available for spending after taxes have been deducted. This should include your husband's take-home pay (and yours, if you work), and any other income you expect to receive. You may have income from part-time jobs, pension payments, sale of property or rental income. Other possible income sources are stock dividends, cash gifts and interest on savings accounts and bonds.

Know your spending habits. Before you decide how future income will be spent, it helps to know how you *have* been spending. Checkbook stubs, bills and receipts may help you to recall previous expenses. However, unless you can account quite accurately for most of your recent spending, you may find it valuable to keep a record of current spending for two or three months. It is not necessary to keep track of literally every penny you spend, but your record should indicate where most of your money goes. Careful study of this record may reveal poor buying habits, overuse of credit and other areas in which you may be overspending regularly without realizing it.

Estimate budget expenses. When you know how much money you have available for spending and what you actually have been spending, you are in a position to establish a budget. Write down all expenses you can anticipate during the budget period. You probably can estimate quite accurately the regular (or *fixed*) expenses your family has each month. These may include rent or mortgage payments, utility bills (gas, electricity, telephone, water), installment payments, transportation costs. Next, list expenses that usually vary from week to week or month to month. These may include such items as food and beverage allowances, savings, recreation and personal expenses, contributions, medical care, home repairs and certain items of household operation and equipment. Too, remember to allow for expenses that occur seasonally and may be substantial, such as taxes on real estate, personal property and income; fuel; schoolbooks and supplies; insurance on life, household and car; holiday gifts; winter clothing; vacation costs and heavier summer use of a car; and organizational membership fees. If the total amount of your estimated expenses during the budget period is the same as or very close to your estimated income for that period, your budget is balanced. And, if you have adequate savings for emergencies and planned savings for future goals, you may reasonably decide that the budget is satisfactory. If your income is greater than your estimated expenses, so much the better. You may decide to increase your savings for future needs or to satisfy more of your family's immediate wants. However, if expenses exceed your income, you need to look critically at your spending and consider ways to trim expenses.

How much should you spend? A budget must be geared to a family's own needs. Even though two families of the same size may have exactly the same income, their budgets may be markedly different because of differences in living standards and family goals. For example, your neighbors may spend two or three times as much as you on clothing or home improvements, while you may prefer to save toward retirement or a more costly vacation. It must be emphasized that there are no rigid formulas for determining the amount you "should" spend for rent, food, recreation or any other category of expense. However, to use for general comparisons, it is helpful to know roughly how your spending habits compare with those of others. The following figures, the most recently available, are based on a joint survey by the U.S. Departments of Labor and Agriculture in 1960–61 of more than 13,000 urban and rural families. Their average income before taxes was about $6,250; after taxes, about $5,600. They spent approximately these percentages of their income on the items listed:

HOUSING	26%
FOOD	22
TRANSPORTATION	14
CLOTHING	9
MEDICAL CARE	6
PERSONAL INSURANCE	5
GIFTS AND CONTRIBUTIONS	5
RECREATION	4
TOBACCO, ALCOHOLIC BEVERAGES	3
PERSONAL CARE	2
READING, EDUCATION	2
MISCELLANEOUS	2

Establishing Credit

You can afford to make mistakes because you will have many years to correct them. However, one mistake you should try to avoid is abusing your credit rating. If you begin thinking of credit not as an invitation to use charge accounts, buy cars on time, borrow against payday but as debt, pure and simple debt, you may become wary of getting in over your head.

Most people who have money in the bank and are employed can acquire credit. When you apply for a charge account you will be asked for your employer's name, your job category, your salary, your bank, a personal reference or two. If you own property or have another charge account the clearance for credit will be even easier. This information about you is transmitted to a central clearing house where your credit rating is established. If you are a "slow payer" this will be noted and held against you. If you pay promptly your credit rating will be A-1. If you should default on a payment to the point where bill collectors are assigned to your case, where your salary is attached, the purchases repossessed, your credit rating will show it. And you will have trouble reestablishing your good standing.

You should get a credit rating (a good one) as soon as possible. By the time your family is grown you will probably borrow over $60,000. This is the way it breaks down. A house will cost $20,000, two babies $1,000, new cars $15,000, home improvements and equipment $5,000, college for the kids $20,000. Happily you don't have to borrow all of it right now. At this point you should simply establish your right to borrow when you need to. Then, when you face an emergency (the washing machine goes on the blink, the roof leaks, the car breaks down), you can borrow on a moment's notice or charge the replacement.

How Much Debt Can You Afford?

Although the vast majority of those who buy on credit do not get into trouble, some families find themselves hard pressed to keep up loan payments. Authorities on family finances say people who get overextended on time purchases usually are those who buy on impulse. These authorities use a number of broad guidelines in discussing how much debt a family can afford:

Never go in debt more than one month's salary on a loan repayable in one year.

A family should have a reserve fund, preferably of one month's pay, before buying on the installment plan.

Such guidelines do not necessarily apply to an individual family situation. Differences in income, job tenure, skills, health and spending habits mean the needs and limitations of each family must be considered in particular. The first step in finding out what your family can afford to borrow is to know what money you have left each week or month after essential living costs are met. This requires some form of budget which lists expenditures and subtracts their total from your income. The difference is the money you have to save, to spend on luxuries or to use for payments on an installment loan or time purchase. This is called your *discretionary* income.

Discretionary income varies greatly among families, depending on total income, standard of living and spending habits. For example, one family might pay $150 a month in rent, while another pays $75 monthly on a house mortgage. If their incomes and standards of living are the same, the second family has $75 a month more discretionary income than the first. However, the homeowning family might need a car. Some of its discretionary income could be used for time payments on the car.

Aside from rent or mortgage payments, which are considered essential living costs, lending institutions do not like to make loans where debts amount to more than 15 to 20 percent of take-home pay. When installment purchases or charge buying reach this point, it may not be possible for a family to get an additional loan in an emergency. This means that if a family's take-home pay totals $6,000 a year, debts of $1,200 (20 percent) could be considered a top limit. A prudent person might only borrow $600 (10 percent) with the thought that he could probably borrow up to another $600 in case of an emergency. Also, you should consider future situations:

Is a husband's job steady and will your income remain at the same level or possibly increase? (Where a wife works, keep in mind that this income may end if she becomes pregnant.)

Do you expect any major expense in the near future? Young families should consider the possibility of a first child or another baby.

Will an item bought on time purchase still be usable for some time when all the payments are made?

A person's debt limit is not only what he can borrow, but what he is going to be able to pay back. Lenders consider the age, marital status, number of dependents, type of job, record of previous debts and purpose of a loan when applications are made by borrowers. If a lending institution or store refuses or limits credit, it is wise for that family to take notice. The safe debt limit may have been reached. Additional credit can possibly be obtained from sources which accept high risks (that is, of not being repaid). In general, the higher the risk the higher the interest rate. A person who keeps his debt within his ability to pay can usually shop around for the lowest interest rates.

In considering your credit limits, remember, you cannot borrow yourself out of debt. If you do become overextended and are unable to meet debt payments, go to your creditors and try to arrange terms which you can meet. Some communities offer free consumer credit counseling. Eight cities have such services, which can be found through local social or family agencies. Lending institutions often consolidate debts and set up longer reduced-payment terms. Don't consider your credit rating a license to borrow indiscriminately. The temptation to buy everything all at once on the installment plan is strong. Why wait for furniture, carpeting, appliances, color television and assorted creature comforts? Why? Because you will end up paying much more for these items when you buy them on the installment plan.

Credit: The Different Kinds and Their Costs

A key to buying on credit is to find out the true cost of the money borrowed. Sales and loan contracts should be read carefully and questions asked if there is any doubt about the terms or charges. The cost of a loan can be figured in *dollar costs*, the actual amount you spend for the loan, or in *true annual interest*. To get dollar costs, simply add the down payment, any trade-in allowance and monthly payments. The difference between this total and the selling price of the item is the amount paid in borrowing charges. True annual interest is the rate charged on money in your possession for a full year. If you borrow $100 at 6 percent true interest, after one year you would pay back $106. If you borrow $100 at 6 percent interest repayable in equal monthly installments, you would have kept an average of only one-half the amount for the full year. The true annual interest on such a loan would be nearly 12 percent, although the total six-dollar interest was the same. Among the sources of credit are:

Commercial banks. Loans from commercial banks are available for a variety of purposes, such as medical bills, taxes, appliance and car purchases and home improvements. A *personal* loan, one arranged on your signature alone if your credit rating is good, is frequently used to finance smaller purchases. Interest rates are usually quoted in *discount* terms, that is, the interest is deducted at the start of the loan. (The true annual interest rate on a 5 percent discount loan is nearly 10 percent.) Current nationwide rates for personal loans are between 10 and 16 percent true annual interest. Many personal loans carry life insurance on the borrower at a small added cost. New-car loans are slightly less costly (8 to 12 percent) because the car is security for the loan. Rates may be higher for used cars. Banks also will lend money on other collateral such as stocks, bonds or savings deposits at lower rates.

Credit unions. Members of credit unions, usually employees of a company or members of fraternal or social groups, can borrow at interest rates of up to 1 percent a month on the unpaid balance of a loan. True annual interest at 1 percent a month is 12 percent. Some charge less. Credit unions mostly handle small loans, but some will finance the purchase of a car.

Small-loan firms. These usually charge higher interest rates because they lend to borrowers who are greater risks. Loans are mainly small—usually under $1,000—and for a short period. Interest rates, regulated by state laws, can be as high as 36 percent true annual interest. Interest mostly is calculated as a percentage of the unpaid balance.

Installment buying. When buying on time, finance charges are included in monthly payments. The cost of an item increases with the time it takes to pay for it. Charges may be 1 to 1½ percent a month (12 to 18 percent true interest) on a store revolving charge account or 1½ to 3½ percent a month (18 to 42 percent true interest) on an installment contract. The buyer should know how much he will be required to pay in credit charges before signing any contract. It may be more advantageous to borrow money from another source and pay cash.

Insurance. A life insurance policy which builds cash value as premiums are paid can provide more than just protection for a family against the death of the wage earner. One can borrow money on such policies, including *whole* or *straight life* and *endowment.*

This money can be borrowed by the policyholder at a relatively low interest rate without a credit check or supplying references. In times of financial emergency, a major advantage of an insurance loan is that it does not have to be repaid in regular installments, as is the case with a bank personal loan. In fact, an insurance loan never has to be repaid by the insured and the policy will remain in effect as long as the premiums and the interest on the loan are paid. Repayment of the loan is the responsibility of the borrower. Insurance authorities suggest, though, that such loans be used only in emergencies that can be created by sickness, accidents or loss of a job.

The cash value of life insurance usually does not start accumulating until the second year a policy is in effect. The longer the policy is in effect the greater the amount that is added to the cash value each year. For example, one representative straight life $10,000 policy bought at age twenty-five would have $950 in cash value at age thirty-five and $2,500 at age forty-five. Up to 95 percent of this cash value could be borrowed at a *true* annual interest rate of 5 percent under most policies (and 6 percent in some written before 1940). On a $1,000 loan at 5 percent, $50 in interest would be due after one year. (The interest is deductible on income tax returns.)

To determine how much cash value has accumulated, all policies have a table showing the total in any year after the policy is issued. It is customarily given in amounts per thousand dollars.

Borrowing all or part of the cash value decreases the face value of the policy by the amount of the loan if it is not repaid before the policyholder dies. If $1,000 is borrowed on a $10,000 policy and is not repaid, the insured's beneficiary would receive $9,000 at his death, less any interest due on the loan. Consequently, insurance authorities caution against lowering needed coverage by borrowing on the cash value. Some suggest adding short-term life insurance to keep coverage at full value while the loan is being repaid. This, in effect, insures the policy loan in the same way that a bank personal loan is frequently insured. To cover a $1,000 loan, term insurance can be bought for from $8 to $10 a year at age thirty-five. This cost increases at older ages. Some policies have a built-in option which allows dividends to be used to buy insurance to cover the loan. Because no medical examination usually is required and little paper work is involved, this type of loan insurance costs less. For example, in one representative policy, $1,000 in such insurance costs $2.57 for one year at age thirty-five.

Interest rates on insurance loans are low compared to most other loans. Insurance companies generally charge 5 percent true annual interest and the U.S. Veterans Administration (on cash value policies held by veterans and armed forces members) charges 4 percent. Most unsecured personal loans from banks or savings institutions are *discounted,* that is, the interest is deducted from the loan at the time it is made. Inasmuch as the loan is repaid monthly, the borrower does not have use of the money for the full period of the loan and the true interest is about double the stated discount rate. For instance, the true annual interest on a 5 percent discount loan would be about 10 percent. Installment buying charges can be higher. If 1 percent is charged monthly on the unpaid balance, the true annual interest is 12 percent. Interest rates on loans from finance and personal loan companies are considerably higher.

Because cash values are available at such low interest rates, some people believe this money could be more profitably invested elsewhere. They reason that insurance cash values, unlike stocks, do not change in dollar value and are adversely affected by inflation. On the other hand, the stock market has been rising steadily for the past twenty years and values of most—but by no means all—stocks have climbed. In this sense, investing in good-quality stocks has proved to be a protection against inflation for many people. Nevertheless, investment and insurance counselors mostly do not recommend borrowing on policies to buy stocks. They say insurance cash values should be reserved for emergencies or for planned purposes, such as college costs.

Insurance advisers say there are exceptions when cash values might be used for investments. These include when a man's family situation changes, such as when children become of age or are on their own. He then may want to lower his insurance coverage and use the cash value for investing. Instead of borrowing the cash value, he may want to surrender the policy and take the cash value without paying interest.

Borrowing on life insurance usually takes only a few days to a week. Such arrangements can be made through an insurance agent, a branch office or by writing the home office of the company. VA insurance loans are handled by the Veterans Administration office which sends out the policyholder's premium notices.

Financing a Car

Your house and your car will be your biggest purchases and you will undoubtedly have to finance them. Consider the charges for financing a car and you will begin to have a healthy respect for the cost of borrowing.

Suppose you were to buy a car that cost $3,075. You make a down payment of $700 and get $375 on your trade-in. Your total down payment is then $1,075, leaving a balance of $2,000 to be financed. The automobile company adds $149 to that for insurance coverage and you agree to pay twenty-four monthly installments of $111 each. Multiply this and you get $2,664. Subtract the $149 for insurance and you discover that you are paying $515 in interest. That is more than a quarter of the amount you borrowed!

If you must borrow you owe it to yourself to get the very best bargain that you can. Don't be afraid to ask hard questions, probe for hidden charges, get everything in writing and read the installment contract carefully. Make sure it is filled in completely, and X out any blanks so that the seller will not be able to write in additional charges or conditions. Compare propositions before you sign anything. Once you sign you are committed to pay up and if you fail to do so your credit rating will be in danger.

Your credit rating is a precious possession. Don't jeopardize it. Pay your bills on time and if you are strapped for cash because of a family emergency be sure and advise the store. The credit manager will usually cooperate by letting you stretch your payments over a longer period of time. Families who get into trouble over installment buying are the ones who panic, then decide that since they can't clean up the entire amount they might as well ignore the bill. They stay away from creditors, refuse to answer telephone calls or letters and, as a result, bring disaster upon themselves.

Buying Protection

A young husband really knows he is married when the insurance agent comes to call. He probably already carries automobile insurance and probably a health policy. Now, however, he finds himself a choice candidate for life insurance, liability and disability policies, a homeowner's package. He wonders, quite understandably, how he can make the best choice of the dozens of complicated plans offered by persuasive salesmen. Should he buy all his insurance from one company or spread his policies? Can he depend upon a salesman to map out an insurance program suitable for his needs now and in the future?

There is merit in putting all your insurance problems in one basket. You can have one trusted representative to look after your interests, someone you can come to know and depend on to settle claims promptly. However, you don't have to decide on the first personable salesman who comes your way. (Don't feel you have to give your business to a brother-in-law or cousin either.) Shop around a bit, educate yourself on the merits of various insurance plans, become enough of an expert so you can ask knowledgeable questions.

An insurance agent can work out a long-term program of insurance protection and investment for your family so they will have the security you want for them. Don't think of life insurance as a necessary evil, something to buy and then forget. You should review your life insurance holdings at various crucial stages in married life—when the first baby is born, when children near college age, when retirement is only ten or fifteen years away. A good agent will keep you alert to the possibilities of converting policies, cashing in others, investing in still another type. Pay attention to his advice, weigh it carefully.

You may already know all you need to know about automobile insurance. Nearly everyone who owns a car carries such insurance; it is mandatory in many states. However, you may not know how much coverage is really necessary. When you marry you will probably decide to raise your coverage because the car will now be driven by two people, thereby increasing the hazards of accidents. It costs relatively little to increase insurance to maximum levels and you would be smart to carry as much liability insurance as you can afford. Judgments against car owners in accident cases have often enough exceeded $100,000. Collision insurance protects you if your car is demolished by an uninsured driver. If your machine is new you ought to carry collision insurance. If it is middle-aged to ancient, you might decide the extra premium isn't worth it.

Health insurance is certainly a must for you and your wife. Quite possibly you are covered by a group plan in your office. Make sure your personnel officer knows about your marriage, so that your wife is included in coverage. If she is working and covered on her own you might want to compare your respective policies and see if they provide enough benefits. You may be able to collect on both of them if your wife requires hospitalization. You will want to be fully covered by the time you start a family. Most policies call for a waiting period before they pay anything on pregnancy and delivery costs. Find out now what you must do to establish eligibility. Group policies may need to be supplemented with a private plan to which you and your wife subscribe. Ask your personnel director about major medical plans and disability insurance.

Disability insurance is protection against loss of income while you are out with a long-term illness. You may not think you need it if your wife is working. However, it is only sensible to find out just how much your employer would pay (also the state) if you were off the job for several months. Suppose your wife became pregnant or ill herself during this period?

Homeowner's Policy. This complete package of insurance protection against liability, fire and theft is a must for every homeowner. For about fifty dollars a year (or less, depending on the limit to which you want to be insured), you can adequately protect your newly acquired possessions. Once insured, you have simply to report to your insurance company what was stolen or damaged by fire and its cash value—usually this must be supported by some kind of proof, usually a police or fire department report—and the insurance company will reimburse you. The insurance company will only pay you up to the limit of your coverage, so you should be sure to correctly assess the value of your possessions and to review this figure at regular intervals. Included in the price of almost all homeowner's policies is a large liability limit, to protect you if, for example, someone is injured in your home and sues you for damages.

Some couples spend ten or fifteen dollars to buy a short-term policy to insure them against the theft or damage of their wedding gifts. This is a good idea since these possessions are particularly vulnerable while one is moving or setting up a new home and because most couples do not buy their homeowner's policy until they have become settled in their new home.

Insurance Plans That May Pay Drug Costs

Prescription drugs are one of the few major health expenses for which separate insurance policies are not sold. Such protection *is* available as part of other plans, such as major medical insurance, but most families do not have this coverage.

Now, various plans are being considered—and some tested— that might lead to nationwide availability of prescription drug insurance. For example, the national Blue Cross Association is studying the possibility of such a policy.

Interest in these plans has grown as drug costs have continued to take a large part of every family's medical expense dollar. According to the Health Insurance Institute, the industry information agency for a number of major health insurance companies, the average family of four spent about $53 last year for prescriptions. The chronically ill, such as diabetics and arthritics, and the aged have substantially higher drug expenses. Modern prescription drugs, of course, have frequently saved lives, eliminated or shortened expensive hospital stays and enabled many people to function effectively despite what previously may have been debilitating ailments.

To date, insurance for prescription drug costs, often called prepaid drug insurance, has been available in these ways:

Major medical insurance. About 40 million persons are protected by this coverage, the fastest growing type of health insurance. However, major medical insurance policies have a deductible clause, usually ranging from $200 to $500 for policies bought on an individual basis and $50 to $200 for those in a group plan. This means that benefits do not begin until this amount is exceeded in medical costs. Too, most major medical plans share costs with the policyholder after the deductible is reached, usually with the insurance company paying about 75 or 80 percent of expenses over the deductible.

Union and regional plans. A growing number of unions are starting prepaid prescription drug plans for members and their dependents. Most are financed by employers' contributions. One of the first plans started was by the Bricklayers Union in New York City. It covers about ten thousand members' families. The union member pays the first 50 cents for each prescription filled and the union pays the rest from a fund financed by a 5 percent payroll contribution by employers. Regional plans have also been started in a few areas.

Test plans. Blue Cross conducted a trial program among its own employees in Wisconsin for part of last year. Among the most comprehensive test plans is that of Wisconsin's Blue Shield. This program, started in 1963, has enrolled about three thousand persons. It costs $18 annually for a family and $7.80 for one person. An additional one-time enrollment fee is charged for anyone in a group smaller than twenty-five. This fee is $5 for a family and $3 for one person.

The policyholder pays the first $25 of prescription drug costs if he is under sixty-five or the first $50 if he is sixty-five or older. The plan pays all other drug costs. Over-the-counter (non-prescription) drugs are not covered. Any pharmacist can be used. The plan pays drug expenses on the basis of "reasonable charge" by the pharmacist. The insurer determines what is a reasonable charge. If this is less than the drug cost, the policyholder pays the difference.

A similar program begun in January, 1963, by Blue Cross for portions of Ontario, Canada, has been expanded on a group basis to cover the entire province. This plan costs a family $17.04 a year and a single person $6.72. It has a $25 deductible for a single person and a $50 deductible for a family.

Dr. William S. Apple, executive director of the American Pharmaceutical Association, believes drug insurance plans may become widely available in the next few years. He says these services will:

Reduce patient anxiety over costs.

Lessen delay in treating patients who postpone buying necessary medications because they are concerned over prescription costs.

Allow doctors and pharmacists to concentrate on services and not "on explaining the economics of the services."

Give the doctor greater choice of medication and not limit selection solely on the basis of cost.

Dr. E. M. Dessloch, chairman of the Wisconsin State Medical Society's Commission on Medical Care Costs, says the Wisconsin

Blue Shield experiment was begun because "insurance can no longer be ignored as a means to assist the patient in budgeting his drug costs." He adds, "It is apparent that prepayment of prescriptions would be of substantial aid to large segments of the public."

In general, private insurance companies do not consider separate drug insurance plans to be desirable. A committee representing the private insurance industry several years ago told the American Pharmaceutical Association that the answer to the problem of prepaid prescription plans lies in the promotion of major medical programs through "increased knowledge of that kind of coverage" by pharmacists. Private insurance companies, says J. F. Follmann, Jr., director of information and research of the Health Insurance Association of America, an organization of insurance companies in the health field, believe that insuring each type of medical care under separate arrangements with separate companies is not the most efficient use of the health insurance dollar.

Life Insurance

Life insurance premiums can represent a substantial annual expense for the man who is seriously concerned about providing his family with adequate financial protection in case of his death. However, some insurance authorities question whether the best possible protection plan is always obtained for the money spent. One remarkable aspect of life insurance is that it has amazing flexibility. Given the assistance of a knowledgeable insurance adviser, a family should be able to tailor a program to best suit its protection needs. These basic types of policies can be used singly or in combination to cover specific family requirements:

Term. Coverage under a term policy is for a specified time, often five or ten years. At younger ages, the cost is lower than for other types of policies, but the premiums increase at the end of each term. Term insurance rarely acquires cash values. Term policies can be purchased so as to be renewable or convertible to permanent insurance at the end of a term without a medical exam or other proof of insurability.

Whole life. Insurance which provides lifetime protection at a set annual premium is known as whole, straight or ordinary life. It usually starts building cash values after the policy has been in effect one or two years. This money is paid to the policyholder if he cancels the policy or he can borrow it at a relatively low interest rate, usually 5 percent.

Endowment. This policy provides the policyholder with a specified sum of money at a future date as well as death protection up to that time. Premium rates are higher than for term of whole life because cash values are built at a faster rate.

In planning an insurance program for a family, a wife should participate with her husband in determining current and future needs. They must consider their own ages, the ages of their children, the standard of living they want to maintain if the husband dies and whether children will go to college. In both long-range goals and short-term needs, the first requirements are financial protection in case of the death of the family's main wage earner, usually the husband. Certain needs are self-evident. These include funeral costs, taxes, possible debts and other expenses connected with settlement of an estate. There may be medical bills not covered by health insurance. An adequate regular income for the family must be considered. And special coverage may be needed for mortgage payments or education costs.

In weighing how much protection will be required, a family should take into account the group insurance or pension rights the husband has on his job, family savings or investments including equity in a home and potential Social Security benefits. (Social Security *now* can provide a widow under sixty-two, with two dependent children, from $66 to $339 a month. It is generally assumed these payments will increase in the future.) A family's need beyond what such resources provide can be covered by insurance.

Many people, especially young families, frequently find that estimated needs are staggering compared to their ability to buy insurance, particularly if only whole-life insurance is being considered. In such circumstances, term insurance can play an important role. For example: Housing can be assured by a term policy which declines in face value as the mortgage is paid off. Family income payments can be provided by a declining term rider—usually for twenty years—on a permanent policy. This provides regular monthly payments, in addition to the face value of the policy, and is excellent coverage for a period while children are young. A thirty-five-year-old husband who wants coverage at the lowest rate when other family expenses are high can have a term policy for $10,000, renewable at five-year intervals for the following premiums: first five years, $65; next five, $80; third five, $110; and last five, $155. A typical whole-life policy for $10,000 coverage would cost $190 a year at age thirty-five. However, after twenty years, the term policy would have no cash value. The whole-life policy would have a cash value of $3,500.

Cash values in whole-life or endowment policies can be used for planning on education expenses and for retirement purposes. A way to lower initial costs for cash-value insurance is to use a *modified* life policy. Premiums are lower than with a whole-life policy in the beginning and then become higher—usually after three to ten years—than whole life. Too, as family situations change, insurance terms can be changed. Authorities say it is less expensive to change an existing policy rather than to cancel it to buy another.

Coping with Paper Work

You may have traveled through life so far with only a driver's license and a draft card to worry about. Once married you will be deluged with official papers wrapped in red tape. Some of the paper work will be of your own making, a good part of it thrust upon you by officialdom. You can cope best by accepting the inevitable and trying to make order out of it.

Inability to produce a birth certificate when needed for passport, insurance or employment purposes can cause frustrating delays. Similarly, if U.S. savings bonds are lost, replacing them may take up to six months. To avoid such problems, many people keep these items in a safe-deposit box rented from a bank.

The American Bankers Association recommends use of a safe-deposit box for all personal papers that are difficult or expensive to replace. These include basic family records—birth, marriage and death certificates. Other items to consider keeping in a safe-deposit box are property deeds, stock certificates (if not left with a broker), passports, tax records and copies of wills (the original copy should be kept by an attorney or the person named executor). A household inventory should be in a safe-deposit box for insurance purposes in case of fire or theft. Too, life insurance policies may be kept in the box. However, some insurance authorities point out that safe-deposit boxes are usually sealed upon death of the renter and cannot be reopened until cleared by state tax authorities. Because insurance companies require presentation of the policy before they pay death benefits, this can cause a delay—the time varies from state to state—in payment. (If policies are kept at home, be sure to have a record of policy numbers and companies in the safe-deposit box.) Heirlooms, including valuable but seldom-worn jewelry, may also be kept in safe-deposit boxes.

Annual rental fees for safe-deposit boxes vary from about $6 to $100, depending on size.

If you don't have enough documents to justify a bank box, at least keep what you have in a safe place—together.

Be sure all your insurance policies, stocks, bonds, bank accounts, clubs, organizations, government agencies, charge accounts, have been apprised of your marital status. Beneficiary and title information must be updated to include husband and wife.

Make a will. You may think that your estate is not worth worrying about. True, it may not be large but it does amount to something and your surviving spouse will have a complicated and disheartening time trying to settle it without a will.

Facts About Checking Accounts

Do you write checks properly? Many people do not. Their carelessness in handling checks can cause them embarrassing and costly problems. Banking authorities suggest checks be written this way:

Fill out the stub first. Then, write the check *carefully*. Place the check amount, in numbers, next to the dollar sign and close together. Indicate cents in smaller figures, written as a fraction in one-hundreds (e.g., 30 cents would be written $^{30}/_{100}$). If the amount has no cents, write *xx* or *oo* over 100. Write the amount of the check in words as far to the left as possible and close together in the space provided. Fill out the space by drawing a line to its end. Care is necessary to avoid any possibility of someone changing the amount. If there is a discrepancy between the amount in words and in numbers, words usually govern. However, if there are differences, a bank can refuse to honor the check.

Sign your name as you wrote it when the account was opened. *Never* sign a blank check. Do not write a check payable to "cash" or "bearer" unless you will cash it at once. Such checks, if lost, can be cashed by anyone who finds them, although banks and businesses usually require an endorsement and identification. Checks should be written in ink. Pencil writing can be more easily altered. Do not cross out, erase or otherwise change any part of a check. A bank may refuse to honor it. Should you make an error in writing, bankers suggest that you destroy it and write another.

A check must be endorsed—that is, signed on the back—before it can be deposited or cashed. (Some banks accept unendorsed checks for deposit only in the accounts of those to whom they are written.) An endorsement can be *blank* or *restrictive*. A blank endorsement is simply the signature of the person to whom it is written. Once the blank endorsement is made, the check is negotiable and can be cashed by anyone who has it after he adds his signature under the first endorsement. (In practice, most banks and businesses will not cash such checks for strangers unless the bearer furnishes satisfactory identification.) For this reason, never write a blank endorsement until you actually cash the check. A restrictive endorsement is a specific instruction to your bank. For example, one type of restrictive endorsement would be to write "for deposit only" on a check and then your name. This means that the check can only be deposited to your account. Or you may want to sign a check issued to you over to someone else by endorsing it this way: "Pay to the order of John Jones," followed by your signature. The person who receives the check must then sign his name below the endorsement when he cashes or deposits it. Always endorse the check the way it is made out. If your name is spelled wrong, sign it that way first and then correctly.

You may want to stop payment on a check once you have issued it. This should always be done if a check is lost or stolen. Notify your bank to stop payment, by telephone if necessary. The bank will usually require a written order as well. If the bank then honors the check, it—and not you—is generally responsible for the amount, says the American Bankers Association. Most banks charge a fee, as much as $2, for stopping a check.

Writing a check that "bounces," that is, it is not cashed by your bank because you have insufficient funds, is usually caused by carelessness. Often this results when two people, in a joint account, write checks but do not keep the checkbook stub current. In addition, many people write checks before they make a covering deposit. This can lead to great embarrassment if the bank refuses to honor a check because it reaches the bank before the deposit. The use by most banks of electronic processing equipment often makes it possible for checks to be cleared within twenty-four hours after they are issued. Most banks charge a penalty, frequently about $2, if they have to return a check because insufficient funds are in an account. Such checks are usually marked "n.s.f." (non-sufficient funds).

Checks follow specific channels as they pass from the person receiving them back to your bank for payment. The numbers in the upper right corner and across the bottom left guide this process. Both sets are identification and routing instructions. The strange-looking numbers across the check bottom are a code written in magnetic ink. They allow faster electronic processing. This code includes your checking account number if your bank uses electronic processing. If your bank does not use electronic methods, the bottom code usually contains only routing instructions. This helps other banks that are using electronic equipment.

Two kinds of personal checking accounts, *regular* and *special*, generally are available. The regular accounts may require that a specified minimum or average balance be maintained. Charges depend on the number of checks written and deposits made with an allowance made for the average daily balance. A service charge is based on the daily average balance maintained. Special checking accounts require no minimum balance. Typical costs in one large Eastern city are 10 cents for each check written and a 50-cent monthly maintenance fee.

Income Taxes; Don't Overlook These Deductions

Keep your tax records in order. This is the year when you may decide to file a joint return. You will probably need help in making it out the first time. A good tax man is worth his price. He can save you headaches and dollars and get you on the right track.

Every year, a surprising number of families pay more in federal income taxes than they really owe. In 1966, for example, the Internal Revenue Service audited (that is, checked in detail) 3.1 million individual tax returns. It found that on 300,000 returns, taxes were overpaid, and taxpayers were entitled to about $279 million in refunds. People overpay taxes, says the IRS, because they are unaware of legitimate deductions. Among those most frequently overlooked:

Joint return. With few exceptions, married taxpayers save money by filing a joint return. Yet many still file separate returns instead and pay a premium price for doing so. If in doubt, figure your returns both ways.

Medical expenses. In most cases medical and dental expenses are deductible to the extent that they exceed three percent of gross income. You can claim drugs as a part of medical expenses to the extent that they exceed one percent of gross income. Transportation to a doctor's office, hospital or medical clinic generally is deductible. Costs of special equipment, such as a whirlpool bath, reclining chair or window air conditioner, may be deductible if recommended by a doctor and if used primarily as part of treatment for a specific illness. The cost of hospitalization insurance is deductible.

Contributions. Not only the cash you give to charitable groups but also the expenses you have (e.g., gas and oil, public transportation) in rendering services for the benefit of such groups can be deducted. However, you cannot include the cash value you place on the services themselves.

Taxes and interest. You can deduct real estate taxes if you are the legal owner of your home or other real estate. If you and your husband file separate returns and *you* are the legal owner, you can deduct real estate taxes only on *your* own return. Of course, they are also deductible on a joint return.

You can deduct the *interest* portion (but not the principal) of mortgage payments. If you have borrowed money for home repairs, improvements or additions, the interest is deductible. (Interest on all loans normally is deductible.)

Dividend exclusion. The first $100 of stock dividends (on a joint return, $200, if both have dividend income) from qualifying corporations is excluded from reportable income.

Business use of your home. If you use one or more rooms in your home for business, you can deduct expenses connected solely with business use. The same applies if you pay rent on all or part of your house or apartment. For example, if you use one room in your home as a business office (or if you pay rent on a room), you can deduct the cost of such things as maid service for that room, floor refinishing and depreciation on office furniture. You can also deduct a certain portion of your rent, light, heat and similar expenses. How much you can deduct depends on the number of rooms in your home, how much of the room you use and how often it's used for personal activities. Tax regulations are somewhat complicated on this point and it is best to discuss these matters with a qualified tax expert or at the IRS office in your community.

Your Financial Goals

Resolve to estimate your net worth on a balance sheet at the end of every year. Knowing your family's *net worth* can be an important guide to sound financial planning. Many people, though, have only a rough idea of their net worth. Calculated once a year, net worth can show whether you are increasing your financial security. If, with a rising family income, your net worth does not increase, it can mean you are not saving, adding to the value of your home or building reserves as you should.

Basically, net worth is the difference between what you *own* and what you *owe*. There is a relatively simple way to determine net worth. First, divide a sheet of paper into two columns. List what the family owns in the first column. These are your *assets*. The second column lists what you owe—your *liabilities*. Determining net worth—the difference between assets and liabilities—is done in the same way a Certified Public Accountant calculates a business balance sheet.

Family net worth should not be calculated on the basis of what was paid for an asset or on what it may be worth at a future time. It is the current market value—what an asset can be sold for—that gives a picture of a family's financial standing. With a realistic view and resisting the temptation to overestimate value, you can come fairly close to a dollars-and-cents evaluation of your current worth. Assets should include:

Home or other real estate. The current market value can be obtained by finding what similar properties have been sold for in the neighborhood. (For a fee, an appraiser will set a more exact market value.)

Automobile or boat. The current value of a car can be estimated from used-car advertising. This will give you the retail price and such a value may be realized if you sell to an individual. If sold to a dealer, you would receive the wholesale price, in many cases this is about one-fourth less.

Life insurance or retirement funds. Permanent life insurance (as contrasted with term) builds a cash value which increases each year. This can be determined from a table in each policy or by asking your agent or the company. To the cash value, add any dividends left on deposit. Some pension or profit-sharing funds have a current cash value.

Investments. Current market value of stocks, bonds, mortgages held or business ownership. The principal of a trust fund you eventually will receive can be listed.

Cash. The amount in savings or checking accounts and what you actually have on hand. Also, list cash due from loans, unpaid salary, dividends, rents, judgments, tax refunds and current payments from a trust fund or an annuity.

Home furnishings and appliances. Value of home furnishings drops rapidly after purchase and use, but value may be maintained on antiques or heirloom furniture if kept in good condition. Appliances, like cars, depreciate in value by about 25 percent the first year and continually drop until they generally have little resale value after five to ten years.

Personal property. Jewelry, paintings, coin and stamp collections, etc. are more likely to retain value than clothes, sports equipment or books.

In listing liabilities, include:

Homes and other real estate. Unpaid balance of a mortgage, rent due a landlord or amount owing on purchase price should be included. Also, property taxes or assessments owed.

Loans. The amount borrowed on an insurance policy, personal loans or balances due on installment purchases are listed.

Bills. Include current bills owed for services (e.g., to doctors or to stores). Also, wages owed employees, school tuition, club dues and income taxes, including capital gains taxes due if you sell certain assets.

How does your family compare with others in net worth? These figures from the Federal Reserve Board (in this case excluding household-personal items, cash on hand, salary due, insurance dividends on deposit) show net worth's relation to family income. The median figure is the point which separates half the group's families from the other half.

Income	Median net worth
$3–5,000	$3,320
$5–7,500	$7,450
$7,5–10,000	$13,450
$10–15,000	$20,500
$15–25,000	$42,750

Here is how net worth is related to age of family head.

Age	Median net worth
25–34	$2,080
35–44	$8,000
45–54	$11,950
55–64	$14,950
65 and over	$10,450

You don't have to account for every penny but you should be able to spot the soft areas in the budget. Suppose your goal is a house in the suburbs within five years. You want to make a healthy down payment and you are willing to forgo some luxuries now to achieve this goal. Certainly you can tell with each yearly accounting how close you are coming. Next year you can resolve to do better and know exactly where you might cut corners.

Estimate next year's income. Then make an educated guess at next year's expenses based on last year's bills. Where could you skimp? How could you improve your earning power? Are you willing to give up that thirty-cent coffee break each day to reach your goal that much sooner? Or would you rather live day to day as comfortably as possible? It is your decision to make. Once you have made it you will have to live with it. You can get some idea of the direction you are going. Instead of drifting you can understand where the money goes. Only by facing this fact of life will your small corporation remain productive and solvent. Only then will you reach your goals.

V

THE PLEASURES OF SEX IN MARRIAGE

"Sex is fun; it is also funny. And by this I mean to emphasize not only the humor which attaches to sex (although that is also there, as witness the penchant which most of us have for off-color stories) but rather to emphasize the playful element involved in sexual activity. Like the play of a child which is freely expressed and creative, sex is also playful. And this means that there are no laws attached to sex. I repeat: *absolutely no laws*. There is nothing which you ought to do, or ought not to do. There are no rules of the game, so to speak. And anyone who tells you there are may be guilty of mistaking social and cultural custom for divine sanction, or for what is sometimes popularly called natural law. . . .

"Sex is natural. This may seem self-evident to you, but what it means is that there is nothing special about sex. It is natural. It is not some special area of our lives divorced from all the rest. It is not for special people, at special times, or in special places, or even under special circumstances. It is natural. It is part of the created order of things. . . . We all ought to relax and stop feeling guilty about our sexual activities, thoughts and desires."

This is no hedonist speaking but rather a college chaplain, the Rev. Dr. Frederic C. Wood, Jr., addressing the students at Goucher College. He reflects a new approach to sex, advanced by forthright clergymen, psychiatrists, educators, family counselors and doctors. Dr. Mary Calderone sums up the new view: "Sex is not just something you do in marriage, in bed, in the dark, in one position."

This notion that sex is a pervasive life force which enhances our joy in living represents quite an advance over previous sex philosophies. It is a refreshing departure from the puritanical conviction that sex should be furtive.

Your Sexual Past

You were born with the capacity for sexual pleasure and from childhood have experienced an erotic drive, without quite knowing what was arousing your emotions. Freud was the first to identify the infant's sucking and clinging actions as intrinsically sexual. He observed that the parent-child relationship had its sexual overtones. Indeed, unless that relationship progresses to the point where the child detaches himself from the parent of the opposite sex his subsequent marriage will suffer. He cannot love his wife while still fixated on Mother. The wife, on the other hand, may feel that her husband is inadequate if she continues to idealize and romanticize Daddy.

During childhood you cautiously explored your body and discovered the pleasures of physical stimulation. Masturbation afforded relief from sexual tension but the relief was probably tinged with guilt. Even though masturbation is no longer considered a sin, a practice that might drive you mad or give you acne, we are only beginning to consider it a perfectly permissible sexual outlet. In the absence of other, more rewarding sexual activities, masturbation can serve an important function. A knowledge of one's own anatomy, erogenous zones, can only serve to improve the capacity for sexual pleasure.

As you grew into adolescence you developed crushes on members of the same sex. A favorite teacher, chum, scout leader—these were the recipients of platonic or homosexual love. Usually this homosexual period is a transient period in sexual development, a prelude to the heterosexual phase. However, the homosexual phase can be more lasting. If a man or woman, still fixated in this phase, should marry that marriage is headed for problems. With the help of psychiatry a person who prefers his own sex can eventually move comfortably into a heterosexual relationship. It is a long process and, needless to say, his partner must be wholly supporting and understanding throughout.

Most people emerge naturally from a homosexual period to heterosexual. However, all of us retain an affection for the members of our own sex and will end up spending at least half of our time with them during a lifetime. Sexual experiences are normally confined to members of the opposite sex and this erotic interest develops in adolescence.

When you began dating you became very aware of the body and emotions of the opposite sex. You kissed and fondled the other person, learning what makes him (her) respond. Not incidentally, you learned what aroused you, how you enjoyed this kind of sex.

If you went steady you were tempted to go beyond necking and petting to making out. You may have had intercourse, not once but several times. You wonder whether you should tell your wife (husband) about these experiences. (Don't if you think it will destroy his illusions; do if you want to be scrupulously honest in all things. Never make comparisons—favorable or otherwise.) If you come to marriage as a virgin you wonder about your capacity to respond. In other times your inexperience would have been a virtue. Today, we have a new sex morality which makes the female role demanding indeed.

Fortunately your generation has been spared the advice which used to be passed on from mother to daughter—to "submit" to your husband or else. Most mature men and women now accept the idea that the female of the species is quite capable of sexual pleasure and that she can actually seek fulfillment. However, the pendulum may have swung too far in the other direction. Women now have a tremendous responsibility to be liberated, even libertine.

In our emancipated age the woman who doesn't like sex the minute she gets in bed is considered sadly inhibited, cold and "not a real woman." Women may have been freed from the Victorian concept that they must submit to their husbands but they have been given another burden—to become Lady Chatterley. It is the rare woman who enjoys sex the first time she experiences it. She has to learn to use her body for pleasure. Although it sounds mechanical to say that practice makes perfect it is as true for sexual relations as for most other arts. She will discover what she likes best and how to arrive at it after much love-making. If she has had sexual experience before marriage (and come to enjoy it without guilt) her marriage may well profit.

The chances are that if she is not a virgin her premarital experimentation was carried on with the man she intended to marry. (And probably did.) Despite all the publicity about an increase in premarital sex experimentation some 75 percent of today's unmarried college girls are still virgins; about the same percentage were in their mother's generation. When a girl does have premarital relations today she does not feel she is being pushed into it or being exploited. She is looking for a close relationship and sexual love is simply another expression of fidelity. She will not allow herself to be used; for her, sex is freely chosen. She is going to insist on this choice after marriage as well and this can come as something of a surprise to her husband.

No healthy American male would think of marriage without expecting to have regular sex relations with his wife. He may be astounded to discover he cannot always have them when he feels like it. The stimuli which arouse him to heights of passion have little effect on his wife. He should not take it personally. Being female, her sex drive is quite different, as Kinsey noted in his celebrated *Sexual Behavior in the Human Female*. Kinsey concluded that the woman's sexual appetite is weaker than the man's and aroused less easily.

The male is immensely susceptible to an exposed leg or bosom; he whistles out loud when he sees a female who excites him. (It doesn't always have to be his wife.) Girlie magazines and shows can produce an unreasonable passion in him. One observer noted with justice that the world's pornographic literature has been produced by men and, not incidentally, consumed by them.

Women on the other hand can take sex or leave it alone. They are not wholly unsatisfied if they must go for long periods of time without intercourse. Women do not flip at the sight of a bare male chest, however tan and hairy. In point of fact, many probably appreciate a well-turned-out Brooks Brothers type more than an overtly physical beach boy.

Women develop a sexual appetite as they mature and with experience. Men are fully capable of intense activity at age fifteen. In fact, they are more capable of virility and potency then than they will ever be again. Naturally, this sex drive must find an outlet. The Kinsey Report on *Sexual Behavior in the Human Male* revealed an astonishing variety of male sex experiences. Ninety-three percent of all men masturbate at some time in their lives.

(A good many make a daily practice of it.) Eighty-five percent have had premarital sexual relations. Thirty-seven percent have had a homosexual experience at least once. Fifty percent are unfaithful to their wives.

The material in Kinsey on the frequency of sexual relations should be of particular interest to young brides. Half of the men under thirty who were interviewed desired sexual activity every other day. A considerable number had as many as ten to twenty sexual experiences a week.

When the average woman finds a sexual partner she can depend on and relax with, her sexual appetite begins to match his. Her capacity for orgasm is, actually, greater than the male's. When she reaches her thirties she may actually surpass her partner in sex drive. That is her peak and she retains such vigor into the fifties and sixties. Three-fourths of all men interviewed by Kinsey were still active at sixty-five and half were going strong at seventy. However, the intensity of desire may have slowed down.

A kind of sexual mismating where one or the other is always out of step has created considerable friction in modern marriages. The young husband may be full of drive and wish his wife could enjoy sex as much as he does. By the time they are in their thirties his wife will want more satisfaction. He, meantime, conditioned by her earlier denial of him is not inclined to gratify her now. Besides, his own sexual drive may be slowing down. This is one reason why both husband and wife should make a concerted effort to understand one another sexually at the beginning of marriage and establish a lasting and satisfying pattern of sexual activity. Read both Kinsey Reports for the valuable insights they offer.

The female is different biologically and this can perhaps account for her more moderate sex drive. Or, as some suggest, she has been conditioned to say "no" because nice girls don't allow themselves to be seduced. Even after marriage she cannot easily reverse herself and say "yes." The male is expected to be the pursuer and the aggressor and when the female regards him as such she may also hold back a bit for fear of being overwhelmed. When more adolescent boys and young men begin assuming responsibility for sexual restraint (instead of always expecting the girl to put on the brakes) a new generation of young women may feel freer to express sexual impulse. Meantime, the husband finds that once married he is no longer the one who pushes and pushes until he gets what he wants. Now he must woo his wife, win her trust. The classic marriage manual clichés are aimed at the husband ("A woman is like a fine violin; you will have to learn to play on her senses.") He has the responsibility for making his wife a sexually fulfilled person. She is supposed to be brimming with passion but he will have to find the key to unlock her emotions.

How Valid Is Marriage-Manual Advice?

If he follows the marriage manuals literally he may learn a good many exotic tricks but not necessarily succeed in pleasing his wife. Marriage counselor Dr. David Mace criticizes this approach as "the mechanization of sex." Says he, "The manuals teach a man to operate his wife like he operates his car, pulling that lever, pushing that switch. One patient complained to me that, in bed, she could tell by her husband's gestures when he was turning from page 15 of the manual to page 34."

When you consider how very basic intercourse is—the male inserts his erect penis into the woman's vagina, a series of rhythmic movements enables both man and woman to reach a climax or orgasm, the male sperm is ejaculated and both feel deeply satisfied and content—it seems surprising that so much could be written about the sex act. At least that is the way intercourse is supposed to take place, according to the marriage manuals. Rarely does it operate with such clocklike precision. There are thousands of variations on this basic pattern, common to all human beings (and the animal world). Different positions, preliminary love-making, readiness for intercourse all take their toll of or contribute to sexual pleasure. Volumes have been written describing the subtle variations in intercourse and how to achieve climax. Most of the sex manuals leave out one very important consideration, the partners' love and tenderness for one another.

Psychoanalyst Rollo May observes that "enlightenment has not solved the sexual problem in our culture. We talk a great deal about sex and a great deal about sexual activity, but complain of a lack of meaning and passion. The Victorian person sought to have love without falling into sex; the modern person seeks to have sex without falling into love. The problem has come full circle and we find a progression from an anesthetic attitude to an antiseptic one."

Dr. May illustrates our clinical approach to sex with this verse.

"The word has come down from the Dean
That with the aid of the teaching machine,
King Oedipus Rex could have learned about sex
Without even touching the Queen."

Certainly you should have a knowledge of male and female sex organs and how to use them for pleasure. Our sex education has been largely focused on reproduction, not pleasure and so you may come to marriage thinking that sex is only a means of having babies. It is much more than that. Not only does sex offer the most exciting physical pleasure man is capable of; it draws husbands and wives together in a rare closeness. Let yourself discover what pleases you and your mate. Don't worry if it doesn't measure up to the goals set by the sex experts. If you feel happy, satisfied and fulfilled you are doing all right.

Free yourself from what someone has called "The Tyranny of the Orgasm." Is it so important for a woman to reach climax every time she goes to bed? Must the earth move? Aren't there other pleasures open to her?

Kinsey discovered that one-quarter of the wives he interviewed did not reach orgasm during the first year of marriage. One woman in ten will never reach orgasm even though she may remain happily married and content with her sex life.

Dr. William H. Masters of Washington University is attempting a new kind of sex research which is far different from Kinsey's and which may have far-reaching effects on our sexual values. Masters believes that women do have a strong sex drive but it is different from the man's. It is more diffuse, for one thing. A woman is not so single-minded as the man when it comes to sex. When he is stimulated he thinks immediately of penetration and conquest. A woman may feel sexy when she hears a familiar romantic song or daydreams about love. She can find pleasure in touch, petting, cuddling without a wish to go beyond that. If her husband has orgasm she is pleased even if she has not achieved a climax. He can satisfy her in other ways. Her sexual needs must be recognized as powerful but they can be gratified by a willing husband in subtle attentions.

"The exploration of a woman is a lifetime work," says one happily married man. "As each of you changes love-making changes. Guys who say, 'I know what she is and what it's like and what it's going to be' simply miss the point. It's amazing what you can find out if you just stay with it."

Of course the husband must have some understanding of female sex organs before he can begin to comprehend the potential of his wife's sexual life.

Female Sex Organs

The nipples of the breast, the lips, inside of the thighs, small of the back are endowed with sensory apparatus which responds to the touch. Women like to be kissed, to be stroked on the back and thighs. Their breasts can be kissed or fondled to arouse great sexual excitement. Not all women have sensitive nipples nor do all of them appreciate this kind of sex play, but most do. The size of the breasts has nothing to do with the intensity of response. Some women worry that if their breasts are manipulated they will get cancer. They will not. When you consider the rough treatment breasts receive from a nursing baby you can begin to understand how indestructible they really are.

As a woman becomes sexually stimulated physical changes occur in other parts of her body. The nipples become erect and the breasts gradually increase in size. A lubricant appears in the sex organs and this will facilitate entry by the penis.

The external sexual parts which lie between the thighs of the woman are called the *vulva*. This part of the female anatomy consists of the two large lips of the vagina (the outer *labia*) and the two inner lips (the inner *labia*). The outer *labia* are covered with hair. The visible seat of sexual pleasure, the cushion protected with hair, is called the *mons veneris*.

When the outer *labia* are drawn apart an arched recess known as the *vestibule* can be seen. On each side of the archway the inner *labia* converge above and appear to be hanging skin folds. Depending upon the individual and upon sexual stimulation, the inner *labia* can change in size, shape and color, turning bright pink on occasion.

The inner *labia* form a cover for the *clitoris*, probably the most important key to sexual stimulation in the female. It is a vestigial penis with all the capability for erotic pleasure that the penis possesses. Its sensitive rounded end can produce intense sexual excitement when rubbed against the male penis or stroked by hand. The clitoris has a foreskin, is about the size of a pea and may enlarge and harden during sexual excitement. The location of the clitoris varies somewhat in individuals. In some women the clitoris is more highly placed than in others. But it is always located just above the area where the two *labia minor* can be found. The bladder opening, *urethra*, is placed between the clitoris and the vaginal opening.

The authors of *Human Sexual Response* (William H. Masters, M.D., and Virginia E. Johnson) have given us an entirely new appreciation of the clitoris. They claim that it is "both a receptor and transformer of sexual stimulation." When the clitoris is stroked gently the woman experiences sexual pleasure. However, it does not have to be touched to perform its function as a sexual transformer. When a woman is aroused by kissing, by the sight of the man she loves, by an erotic song or movie, she can feel sensation in the clitoris. Some describe a deep pelvic fullness, a warmth, need for release. Say Masters and Johnson, "Suffice it to say, that the clitoris, serving as a receptor and transformer organ, has a role as the center of female sensual focus, and the functional response it creates easily is identifiable by any sexually oriented woman."

If the clitoris is this important certainly the male should know how to reach it, manipulate it. He must be wary of overstimulation. "In direct manipulation of the clitoris there is a narrow margin between stimulation and irritation. If the unsuspecting male partner adheres strictly to the marriage manual dictum, he is placed in a most disadvantageous position," say Masters and Johnson. Most women like to have the entire *mons* area stimulated instead of just the clitoral body. When the level of female sexual tension is at its height the clitoris tends to retract. This frustrates the male who is trying to keep contact with it. He does not realize that the retracted clitoral body is still being stimulated by pressure on its protective hood.

Most men do not appreciate the role of the clitoris in arousing female sex desire. The advice given by a husband of some years' standing should be heeded. "If you don't know where it is, you'd better find out." Once you are familiar with the clitoris don't hesitate to bring your wife to the peak of sexual pleasure by manipulating it. At one time a group of psychoanalysts insisted that a clitoral orgasm was inferior to a vaginal orgasm. They tried to prove that a woman who could be aroused only by clitoral manipulation was somehow not "a real woman." This point of view can only be destructive to good marital relations. Help your wife enjoy herself in bed. If she likes clitoral stimulation give it to her. She will relax and expand her sexual responsiveness to include vaginal orgasm once she begins to appreciate her capacity for pleasure.

The *hymen* or "maidenhead" protects the opening to the *vagina*. It varies in shape, occasionally covering the entrance to the vagina almost completely. It is never completely closed, for menstrual blood must be able to pass through the hymen. In folk literature the husband broke the hymen on his wedding night causing pain and some bleeding. He was thus assured that his bride was a virgin. Today's bride has probably been using tampons since she began menstruating and her hymen has been gradually dilated.

The entrance to the vaginal canal is endowed with many nerve endings which will produce sexual pleasure when the penis is inserted. This sphincter muscle can be used to increase pleasure. A woman can exert pressure on the penis by contracting the muscle and give herself and her husband intense satisfaction.

These then are the external sex organs, capable of being stimulated to provide the female with intense pleasure, either for itself or as a prelude to intercourse.

The internal sex organs are primarily reproductive. The *vagina* is the canal linking the sensory external organs with the *womb* where the baby is developed during pregnancy.

The vaginal canal is about three to three and a half inches long. When the woman feels excited during intercouse it is primarily because she experiences a sense of fullness not because the penis is arousing any nerve endings within the vagina. The vaginal walls supply the lubricant for intercourse and facilitate the pleasurable friction which makes the sex act so enjoyable.

The *vagina* walls are very elastic and the canal can be easily distended. No penis is too small or too large to cause frustration or pain; the vagina can adapt to any size. Consider the size of a newborn baby which must travel down the vaginal canal and you can easily see how terrifically the vagina can expand when it has to.

The *vagina* ends at the *cervix,* or neck of the womb. During intercourse when sperm cells are ejaculated they are usually deposited near the cervix. Even though the head of the penis may press against the cervix during intercourse the woman will not feel any sensation except slight pressure. The cervix is not endowed with nerve endings.

The pear-shaped *uterus* or *womb* is about the size of a small fist normally. During pregnancy it can expand more than six hundred times this size. In the ninth month of pregnancy the *uterus* can measure twelve inches in length and eight inches in diameter. A few months after pregnancy the *womb,* or *uterus,* shrinks to its normal size.

The ovaries produce the eggs which are ultimately fertilized by male sperm. Located to either side of the uterus, the ovaries also manufacture vital female hormones. One mature egg cell is produced each month by one of the ovaries, and thrown free into the pelvic cavity for acceptance into the *Fallopian tubes.*

The fringelike ends of the tubes create a current which helps propel the egg into the *Fallopian tube.* The egg lies there waiting for the sperm. When the sperm swim up the tube they surround the egg and the millions of sperm together form a chemical substance which dissolves the covering of the egg to allow one sperm to enter. As soon as this sperm enters the egg all others are repelled. The egg is fertilized and begins to develop and roll down the side of the tube to the *uterus* to establish its dependent existence in the lining of the *uterus.*

Nature prepares to nourish the egg cell produced each month by supplying the walls of the *uterus* with additional nutrients. The *endometrium,* or lining of the *uterus,* thus becomes a rich source of blood sugar and essential minerals. If the egg is fertilized this lining supplies nourishment during the first weeks of life. If the egg is not fertilized, it will pass out of the body. This release of the *endometrium* is called menstruation.

Menstruation is said to occur every twenty-eight days and last for around four. Women do vary in their cycles, some for thirty days and others for twenty-seven. Many women, in excellent health, will menstruate for five or six days.

You are not sick during menstruation and can carry on any normal activities, including sexual relations if you and your husband so wish. Severe cramps may indicate trouble and you should see a gynecologist if they are severe. The female sex drive does vary with changes in hormone balance during each month. Some women feel very sexy just before menstruation. Others experience strong desire in the middle of the month. Accept these changes as normal and make the most of them.

Male Sex Organs

If you would understand the sex motivation of the human male you should certainly understand male anatomy. Most of your husband's sex organs are outside his body. No wonder he is easily stimulated.

The *penis* is composed of a shaft or body which is about three and a half inches long when relaxed. It develops into about six inches when erect. It is little more than an inch in diameter. The penis assumes a definite angle when erect and this is Nature's way of making sure it will fit the curve of the vaginal canal.

What causes the erection? The brain and nerve centers receive news of sexual excitement and this causes the central nervous system to signal for a rush of blood to the penis. The spongy tissues become engorged with blood, causing the penis to stiffen and become enlarged. As long as the male remains sexually excited he can maintain his erection. When orgasm occurs and ejaculation of the sperm takes place the blood vessels release the extra supply of blood and the penis once more becomes relaxed.

The shaft or body of the penis possesses very large blood vessels. The head, or *glans*, has smaller ones. The head then does not become as rigid as the shaft and it can enter the vagina without hurting the woman.

The head of the penis is somewhat larger than the diameter of the shaft. Sexual feeling is primarily located here. The head is covered with a foreskin at birth. This can be removed by circumcision and should be, not only for hygienic reasons but because the sensitive area of the head can then enjoy direct contact with the vagina during intercourse.

The *testicles* are two glands measuring about one inch in thickness. They are located outside the body in a skin sac called the *scrotum*. They hang in the sac, one lower than the other. Each testicle is made up of very fine tubules. Here the male sex hormones are manufactured and the sperm cells produced.

The sperm are manufactured in the tubules of the testicles and pushed up into the body and stored in seed sacs or seminal vesicles, where they absorb nourishment, grow in maturity and then are pushed down into the *prostate gland*.

The *prostate gland* contracts as if it were a bulb syringe being squeezed and this pushes the sperm out through the urethral canal in spurts. This is called ejaculation and consists of 200 to 500 million sperm, as well as seminal fluid, mucous cells and prostate fluid.

A man's sex organs are tangible evidence of his masculinity. He worries about his potency and virility. He knows that he is the one who must "perform" during the sex act. He has to take the initiative and carry through to a tremendously successful climax. Hopefully he can excite his wife so that she, too, will have orgasm. The responsibility for timing intercourse so that both have orgasm simultaneously goes to him. No one suggests that he should be stimulated to do his best because we assume the male is always ready for intercourse. This is not always true. He may lose his erection, have a premature ejaculation or simply not be able to satisfy his wife. There are countless reasons why a man can become impotent; most of them are psychological rather than physical. His wife has a great responsibility to make him feel like a man, to respect his physical nature and to show that she loves his masculinity. He responds to touch and fondling as much as she does and wants his wife to explore his body with pleasure, not distaste.

The Sex Act

Although the purpose of sexual activity is the culmination in intercourse and, hopefully, orgasm the preliminaries are as enjoyable as the resolution.

There are actually three stages in intercourse, the foreplay, the actual intercourse and the postintercourse period when you can enjoy being together in intimacy. You want to show affection and tenderness during all three of these periods. You like exploring your bodies, trying new positions, new erotic pleasures. There is nothing a husband and wife can do with each other that is "wrong." If it is agreeable to both then it is perfectly "normal." You can experiment to your hearts' content, using all the equipment Nature gave you and be perfectly certain that you are not "perverted." The point is that you should agree to whatever practice you like. It isn't fair and may be morally debatable whether one partner can coerce the other into doing something he (or she) feels is not right.

You set your own pattern for sex relations. If you want to do it twice a day and always in the morning then go to it. If you are showing each other affection and regard any time is a good time. You don't have to tear yourselves apart. You are married now. Within an hour or so you may be ready to try it again.

There is no "proper" number of times a couple should have intercourse in a given week or even on the same night. Do what you feel like doing. At first you may feel like twice a night, every night, but your ardor may cool after years of marriage.

The old Chinese proverb maintains that if a couple put a bean in the bottle every time they had intercourse during the first year of marriage and took a bean out of the bottle every time they had intercourse thereafter they would never empty the bottle.

Don't make the mistake of deciding that you will have sex every Saturday night or every Friday night and never on Sunday or Monday. Sex should be spontaneous and you should be ready for it on impulse. This means, of course, that you should be prepared with good contraceptive protection at all times so that you will not be obliged to put the damper on passion by "getting ready." The following chapter will outline the choices open to you in planning for parenthood. Sex is a reproductive function, but never forget that it is also meant to be enjoyed.

If there has been sufficient time for foreplay and fondling the actual sex act can be accomplished rather swiftly with great satisfaction on the part of both husband and wife. Actual intercourse can take only minutes, orgasm just seconds. What makes it pleasurable is the kissing, touching and stroking which takes place before actual penetration.

As soon as both partners are ready the wife guides her husband's penis into the vagina. Once the penis is in place instinct usually does the rest. The rocking motions of the female pelvis and the in-and-out movements of the penis should help both achieve orgasm.

It matters little which position is used. Generally the Western world prefers the man on top but this is known as "the missionary position" by amused natives of other lands. The man may be on the bottom and if he is his wife will enjoy more clitoral friction. Many couples use a side position with great success. Some have tried approaching the female from behind. You can have intercourse in bed, on the lawn, even in a chair. What matters is whether or not you find it enjoyable.

After orgasm both man and woman feel tremendously relaxed and pleasantly weary. Sometimes they fall asleep immediately. It is all-important that you stay in each other's arms after intercourse.

Sexual Problems

Probably the biggest problem you will have in sexual relations is responsiveness—lack of it or a mismating as far as sexual appetite goes. The inability to reach orgasm, premature ejaculation, frigidity, failure to maintain an erection are all signals that something is wrong with your sexual adjustment. More than that, however, you are probably anxious about any number of questions relating to sex. Although it takes time and experience to achieve a good sex life your progress toward this goal can be seriously hampered by unresolved fears.

That excellent bit of advice—"Relax and enjoy it"—could be revised to read, "If you don't always enjoy it, just relax." No man can be expected to perform like clockwork in bed. No woman is always in the mood for sex. If your timing is off don't feel that you are hurting the basic relationship. Don't feel put upon or rejected if you are ready and he is not, if she seems cold when you are fired up. If this happens all the time then, of course, you have problems and should see a professional about it. But if it is an

occasional disappointment learn to take it in your stride. Whatever you do, keep yourself from accusing your partner of sexual
inadequacy. Men, in particular, have enough self-doubt about
their sexual capacity. Don't compound their anxieties.

A man may wonder if his penis is large enough to achieve maximum pleasure. The authors of *Human Sexual Response* have discussed this issue at length. Their conclusions should certainly
allay any fears a man might have, calling this question "a phallic
fallacy." They add, "the delusion that penile size is related to
sexual adequacy has been founded in turn upon yet another phallic misconception. It has been presumed that full erection of the
larger penis provides a significantly greater penile size increase
than does erection of the smaller penis. . . . The difference in
average erective size increase between the smaller flaccid penis
and the larger flaccid penis is not significant."

What is the "normal" size penis? It can range from one and a
half inches to three and a half inches. Don't worry about the size.
It's what you do with it that counts. Remember, too, that the
vagina is "infinitely distensible." It can accommodate any size penis if the woman is ready to receive it and sexually excited.

True, a woman is not always ready for intercourse and will continue to be unresponsive even when her husband tries to stimulate her with tenderness and sexual foreplay. She worries that she
may be "frigid" and her husband may even accuse her of this,
thereby complicating the problem.

Sexual response cannot be divorced from other emotions. A
woman may be angry at her husband, despondent over some personal matter, feeling edgy because she is approaching menstruation. She isn't frigid, just conveying other emotions in this
frustrating manner. If it gets to be a habit she's in trouble (certainly her husband is!), but an occasional reaction like this isn't
going to destroy the marriage. If her husband is understanding,
if he seeks the true reasons behind her temporary disaffection for
sex, he can restore the relationship to harmony.

Some women do complain that they are willing to give their
husbands a chance at sexual intercourse but that they refuse to
become involved in it. This is a fine way to develop frigidity. You
owe it to yourself, as well as your husband, to participate fully
in the sex act. Don't just lie there, expecting him to work miracles.
Move toward him. Put your arms around him. Allow yourself to

be excited and do your best to help him achieve an erection. Once you develop a studied indifference toward sex you are going to lose something precious. Give your body the respect it deserves. If you don't feel like sex say so, say it with tact and love. Don't abuse your relationship by giving in and then feeling martyred.

There are times when nobody is satisfied. The man has a premature ejaculation and the woman feels cheated. He is working hard to arouse her but she complains that he is hurting her. No position they assume seems entirely satisfactory. These are very real problems and if they do not yield to the traditional solutions then you should certainly consult a gynecologist or get help with psychological barriers to a good sex life.

The male does have to develop a kind of discipline if he hopes to discover the subtler sides of sex. He has to restrain himself from plunging ahead to climax as soon as he enters the female. If he can learn to rest, stopping short of orgasm, while his wife enjoys the closeness and sensuality of their position, he can control his ejaculation. When both are ready he can bring himself to climax. His wife may have experienced one or more orgasms in the meantime. One marriage counselor prescribes frequent intercourse for the husband who has trouble controlling his ejaculation. He must learn how to handle his feelings and his physical powers so that his wife will not be disappointed and so that he will realize the full pleasure of intercourse.

The woman who complains that intercourse is painful may be suffering from a physical problem and should, of course, be checked by her doctor or gynecologist. She probably is fearful of being hurt by the penetration of the penis and it is worth repeating that this fear is groundless. Her vagina can accommodate itself to any enlargement of the penis. However, she needs to be soothed by the reassurances of her husband, gentle techniques of love-making. If she puts a pillow under her hips so that her sexual organs are elevated she will find that intercourse is easier. The use of vaginal jelly also facilitates entrance of the penis. Clearly, none of these aids will help if the wife is truly afraid of being hurt. She should explore her fears with a psychiatrist if they persist. The love and understanding of her husband, plus her own determination to enjoy the fruits of marriage, can do much to relieve her anxieties.

Remember, sexual fulfillment is not automatically conferred

upon you once you are married. You have to develop it. As you come to know one another intimately your desire to please the other person should flower. This, in itself, is the greatest thing you have going for you in the continuing sex life which is your marriage bond.

VI

PLANNING FOR PARENTHOOD

The sexual urge and the desire to be a parent are common to most couples. However, these two desires do not always coincide. A couple may wish to found a family but also enjoy sex relations without fear of pregnancy. A young couple might be advised to wait a year or two before beginning their family, to give themselves a little time to adjust to married life.

Naturally, a baby (or two or three) can elevate a marriage to its most harmonious state. When a man and woman are joined together in the rearing of children they feel immensely productive and worthwhile. Children are a joy; there's no doubt about it. However, every couple must decide quite seriously if the time has come when they are ready to become parents.

Parenthood is demanding and even though the challenge matures many it can bring others to a state of crisis. Some people are better able to cope with infants than with adolescents and vice versa, and there is no way of predicting how you will get along with your own children. You can't assume the path will be easy, because you have no idea of how they are going to turn out. This book cannot help you decide when to have children but it can give you information about the many ways open to you in planning your family. When you do embark upon parenthood you will need help of many kinds. Don't be afraid to seek it. Fortunately, there is a wealth of advice available. If you are not ready for parenthood then you need help in planning and controlling the size of your family.

Thanks to modern contraceptive methods you can be reasonably sure that you won't get pregnant until you are ready to be parents. Deciding to start a family is an important step. You must be able to take care of an infant, give him the physical and emotional help he needs. Remember, this tiny life will be completely dependent on you for everything.

Babies are expensive to have and to rear.

What It Costs in Cash to Have a Baby

Young couples who expect their first child are frequently unaware of all the expenses they will face. Most think only of the immediate medical bills. Considerably more is involved. A first child is usually the most costly in a family because clothing and other necessary equipment (crib, stroller, carriage, etc.) can be used for subsequent children. Too, the first child often means a family must find a larger home, particularly those couples who have been living in small apartments. At the same time they face these expenses, many families are losing the second income that a working wife provides. Consequently, planning and budgeting for the first baby is usually essential during the months of pregnancy, before if possible.

The costs of medical care and other expenses involved vary somewhat regionally and, of course, according to a family's standard of living. However, the costs cited in this article are representative of those prevailing in many areas and the kind that young couples in the $4,000 to $6,000 income bracket may face.

Medical expenses. The average for prenatal care and delivery, plus hospital charges, is $300, according to the Health Insurance Institute, an information agency for a number of health insurance companies. About one-half of this cost covers doctor fees and the other one-half hospital charges. These costs tend to be lower in smaller communities and higher in larger cities. In a 1961 survey, general practitioners' fees for complete care (prenatal, delivery and postpartum) ranged from $75 to $200 or higher and averaged $150 in the Far West, $125 in the Great Lakes region, $100 in the South Atlantic states and $125 in the Middle Atlantic states. Fees of obstetricians, specialists in maternal care and delivery, ranged from $125 to more than $275, with an average of $175, except in the Far West where it was $200.

Hospital charges include not only a room rate, but usually the use of the delivery room, drugs, tests and laboratory examinations. Although hospital costs have gone up, the average post-birth stay has been shortened to five days. If a private room is used, these charges may be $300 or more. An additional cost is any in-hospital visit ($5 to $10) by a pediatrician to start care of the infant.

More than one-half of the births in 1963 were covered by some form of health insurance. Insurance ranged from a $50 flat fee to full maternity coverage. The Health Insurance Institute says payments show that an average of $250 was paid by insurance for each of the 2.7 million births covered. In calculating the cost of having a baby, a family should find out what maternity benefits are paid by any health insurance plan which it may have, and the provisions for unusual expenses arising from premature birth, complication of pregnancy or cesarean section. For those who do not have insurance, a hospital may require a deposit. A father-to-be should learn what amount is required and be prepared to pay it before or when he takes his wife for her confinement.

Home costs. Gifts of outgrown baby equipment or even passed-along maternity clothes can be a major economy for a young couple on a tight budget. A maternity wardrobe, including two dresses, skirts, blouses and special supporting undergarments for late pregnancy, averages about $95, but the cost rises if the later stages of pregnancy are in the winter when heavier clothes are needed. Baby equipment costs can be kept to a minimum of $100, but can go up to $500 depending on how lavish parents want to be. In shopping for a layette (diapers, shirts, nightgowns, coats, caps, etc.) buy only what is needed for the first weeks. As the baby grows, larger sizes can then be purchased.

Diaper service is available in most cities and costs from $2.90 to $4 per week for 90 diapers. Costs decrease slightly as fewer diapers are used. According to figures compiled in a number of studies, first-year costs of food, clothing, personal care, medical care and a share of other family expenses will average from $375 to $490 for a new baby. A practical nurse costs from $12 to $22 a day if one is needed when the baby is brought home. A homemaker or houseworker costs less. Many new mothers have the help of relatives or even a husband who has arranged to take his vacation at this time. In buying baby equipment, such as a carriage which can cost from $25 to $130, consideration should be given to whether its use is planned for subsequent children. Sturdy equipment, which costs more, frequently can be used for several children and, in effect, may prove more economical than items whose initial cost is less.

Including an increase in rent of at least $25 a month for another room or a move to a house, a young couple may find a first-year baby budget climbing toward $1,000. A final expense that parents often overlook is that for baby-sitters. If a young couple plans to go out at least once a week, that cost can be about $150 to $175 during a year.

It is hard to visualize the impact a baby will have on your life until you are actually a parent. Let it be said that "baby makes three" quite literally. You and your husband will be part of an eternal triangle as soon as the children come. You can be driven apart or drawn together more securely, depending upon your capacity to be parents.

Even if you decide to wait for a few years before starting a family you should have a complete physical examination now to determine your biological capacity to have children. Some couples find that they are faced with physical obstacles to conception when they are finally ready to start a family. Had the problem been detected early in marriage it could have been treated. Consider, too, the fact that the older you are the harder it becomes to conceive. This goes for male fertility too. One survey indicated that 75 percent of husbands less than twenty-five years old were able to impregnate their wives in less than six months but only 23 percent of husbands forty and over were able to accomplish this.

The Importance of a Physical Examination

A married woman should have a gynecologist as well as a general practitioner to keep her in top physical health. She may decide to find a gynecologist before she is married so that she can be examined and obtain contraceptive information.

In most states a premarital blood test for venereal disease is required. Many doctors also do a physical examination at the time of that test.

Dr. Goodrich C. Schauffler, associate professor of obstetrics and gynecology at the University of Oregon Medical School, says that a young woman about to be married should not be fearful or distressed about a physical examination or premarital consultation. As a wife and mother-to-be, he says, she should begin to establish her own doctor-patient relationship with "eager inquiry and intelligent cooperation." Dr. Schauffler says three steps are included in the premarital process—a physical examination, any necessary medical treatment and counseling.

Many doctors believe a physical examination, not just a blood test for venereal disease, is important. Physical conditions may be present which should be corrected before the wedding day. An examination usually requires about one-half hour. It includes particular attention to the pelvic area and the breasts. In addition to blood tests, a chest X-ray, urinalysis and a Papanicolaou (Pap) test for cervical cancer may be made.

At this time the bride may ask the doctor to stretch the hymen so that first intercourse will not be painful. He does this using his lubricated, gloved finger. When the opening is large enough to fit and insert a birth control device called a diaphragm, it will be able to receive an erect penis without pain or bleeding.

The doctor also takes a history of previous illnesses and reviews family background which can be important as far as the couple's fitness for parenthood is concerned.

Discussion of inherited traits is called *genetic counseling*. For example, hemophilia, a blood condition in which blood clotting does not readily occur, can be transmitted by heredity, usually through mothers to sons. A family history of diabetes, club feet, harelip and other conditions also may be of concern. In many cases, doctors can reassure a young couple about the chances of such defects or conditions appearing in their children. Or special precautions may be advised for prevention or control.

How the Rh Factor in Blood Affects Babies

Women who are pregnant for the first time occasionally are concerned about a blood condition which can adversely affect their child. This concern usually stems from the fact that many people discuss the problem—which involves the *Rh factor* in blood—without really knowing much about it. Understanding the basic facts about this condition can eliminate much needless worry. The problem itself is a comparatively infrequent one—about one in two hundred pregnancies. In these, disease symptoms of varying severity appear in an unborn or newborn baby, which are caused by a difference in blood factors between the mother and child. This is one of the main reasons a blood test is made on the mother early in pregnancy.

If doctors know that a blood difference may be possible between mother and baby, they can treat the condition and, in most cases, save the child. Modern medicine has even found a way to treat an affected *unborn* baby by giving him blood transfusions (also called *infusions*) while he is in the mother's womb.

These blood differences are caused by a protein—the Rh factor —in red blood cells. It is an inherited condition, but is uncommon in nonwhite races. About 85 percent of the people in the United States have this factor. They are called *Rh positive*. The 15 percent who do *not* have it are *Rh negative*. In the main, problems arise when a husband is Rh positive and his wife is Rh negative. If a baby inherits his father's Rh factor and his mother is Rh negative, blood disease *may* develop in the child.

Blood disease, it should be emphasized, does not *always* occur in these cases. For the disease to develop, the Rh negative mother must become sensitized to the Rh factor by exposure to it, much the same way allergies are developed. This may occur either through the mother having received a blood transfusion of Rh positive blood or through an exchange of blood with an Rh positive baby she was carrying. Because of the body's natural defenses against foreign elements, the mother's system makes *antibodies* to combat the Rh factor when it enters her bloodstream. Normally, the placenta acts as a barrier to any exchange of blood between the mother and baby, but sensitization can occur when there is a leak in this barrier.

First babies of an Rh negative mother and Rh positive father are unlikely to develop blood disease because the mother has not become sensitized. Problems may not even occur in the second baby, but they are more likely to develop in subsequent children because of the increasing chance that some of an Rh positive baby's blood has sensitized the mother. Tests are made during pregnancy to see if an Rh negative mother has become sensitized and is producing antibodies. These antibodies can cross the placental barrier and enter the baby's circulatory system. This causes destruction of the baby's red blood cells, resulting in anemia. Brain damage can also occur if jaundice, which develops after birth, is not treated.

When a mother is producing antibodies, it is necessary to learn as much as possible about the condition of the baby. One test, done when Rh factor problems are suspected, is to insert a needle through the mother's abdomen into the sac enclosing the baby and to take a sample of the surrounding (amniotic) fluid. By analyzing the sample, it is possible to tell how anemic the baby has become. On the basis of this and other information, doctors decide how to protect the baby.

A major question is whether the baby can survive blood disease until birth. If a doctor believes that the baby can survive the full term of pregnancy, the disease can be treated at birth by giving an *exchange transfusion*. In this procedure, the baby's blood supply is replaced with Rh negative blood which will not react to the antibodies which he got from his mother. Exchange transfusions have been used successfully for about twenty years to overcome blood disease caused by the Rh factor.

Where the baby is believed not able to survive to full term, a doctor may induce labor or do a cesarean section (delivery by abdominal operation) while the baby is premature. Dr. Charles F. Gillespie, chairman of the obstetrics and gynecology department at Marion County General Hospital in Indianapolis, says the risks of prematurity must be weighed carefully with the risks of blood disease. In about 10 percent of the babies afflicted with Rh problems, there is a question of whether they can survive even to the thirty-fourth week of pregnancy when a safe premature delivery is feasible. Most of these babies previously were stillborn. Recently, though, a method was devised to treat even these babies. In 1963, Dr. A. W. Liley, a New Zealand obstetrician, developed a way to give a baby a blood transfusion *before* birth. Babies with severe blood disease were able to survive with these transfusions to a time when live delivery was possible. Dr. Liley, who is on a research fellowship at Columbia University's College of Physicians and Surgeons, estimates 3,500 babies among the four million born yearly in the U.S. could be saved by this method, called an *intrauterine* transfusion.

Dr. Liley's technique is not without risk and he has limited its use to babies who doctors believe would die of blood disease before the thirty-fifth week of pregnancy. Essentially, the technique determines by X-rays the position of the baby and the location of the abdominal cavity. Then a long needle is inserted through the mother's abdomen and into the baby's abdominal cavity. A transfusion of concentrated red blood cells of the Rh negative type is given. This is absorbed into the baby's circulation system to give him a supply of blood which is not affected by the mother's antibodies. Sometimes, Dr. Liley says, two or three such transfusions are needed to keep the baby alive until birth is accomplished.

Such prebirth transfusions using Dr. Liley's technique are done in major medical centers in this country. Dr. Clyde L. Randall, chairman of the obstetrics and gynecology department, State University of New York at Buffalo, says use of such prebirth infusions of blood provides an Rh negative woman who has never been able to have a live baby the possibility she now can do so.

Authorities on marriage relations say that doctors should talk to young couples about the meaning of sex and family relationships. No information should be withheld. Many brides take their husbands along for counseling when they seek help from doctors or birth control clinics. Certainly the question of contraception concerns both husband and wife. Together they must take the responsibility for bringing up a family; together they must control its size.

Which Contraceptive?

Dr. Alan F. Guttmacher, who is president of the Planned Parenthood Federation, cites thirteen different methods of birth control in his excellent paperback book *The Complete Book of Birth Control.* Each one has its assets and its liabilities. Some have been practiced for centuries; others are as new as space travel and cybernetics.

You have a choice. Your problem is making the best choice, and that will depend upon personal preference and experience.

Dr. Guttmacher advises newlyweds to "be experimental. Try several methods before you decide which comes closest to being best in all ways for you as a couple. Learn as much as you can about the different techniques, and discuss them with a knowledgeable physician or visit a Planned Parenthood center.

"You will never know if one technique functions better for you than another unless you can judge from personal experience. Experimentation in sex is good, not only with different positions for intercourse, but also with different methods of birth control."

Dr. Guttmacher does rank the known contraceptive methods in order of their effectiveness, pointing out that no method can be called 100 percent safe. He has set up several groupings with the most reliable heading the list, least reliable at the bottom. Here is his evaluation.

Group I	Oral pills.
Group II	Diaphragm plus jelly or cream. Condom. Cervical cap.
Group III	Aerosol vaginal cream.
Group IV	Jelly or cream alone. Rhythm. Withdrawal.
Group V	Suppositories. Vaginal tablets.
Group VI	Douche.

Oral Contraceptive—the Pill

An estimated five million American women are now taking oral contraceptives with great success. They are particularly appealing to the new bride who likes the ease with which she can protect herself. She may not be ready to be fitted for a diaphragm, nor does she always want to be. When taken as directed they are the most effective contraceptive known to us at present.

They must, however, be taken on schedule. This means that you start taking the pills on the fifth day of the menstrual cycle (the day menstruation begins is the first day) and take one a day for twenty days. If you miss even one day you may get pregnant.

How does the pill work? It seems to suppress ovulation; under the influence of the medication the ovary does not release its egg and so there is nothing for the sperm to fertilize.

Oral contraceptives contain synthetic hormones (those manufactured rather than produced naturally) which act in similar fashion to the female sex hormones estrogen and progesterone. A woman taking an oral contraceptive experiences some conditions usually associated with pregnancy, including the inhibition of ovulation. These conditions, some doctors point out, are natural. Women who have had large numbers of children have experienced such conditions during most of their childbearing years. During pregnancy, progesterone and estrogen levels are raised. This signals the pituitary gland, sometimes called the body's master gland, that no more egg cells are needed. The pituitary withholds stimulation of the ovaries to produce such cells. Oral contraceptives are believed to accomplish the same responses.

A rise in estrogen and progesterone levels—whether during pregnancy or when taking contraceptive pills—also affects other mechanisms of body chemistry. This is what may cause the side effects some pill users experience.

Some women complain of mild nausea and a bloated feeling when taking the pills. Others say they tend to gain weight. One in five may find the pills produce side effects which counterbalance their assets. Besides controlling conception the pills reduce premenstrual tension, contribute to regularity of cycle and freedom from pain.

More serious than the side effects (which can be minimized with other medications) is the fear that the pills may produce certain unknown adverse reactions. In 1962 it was disclosed that blood clotting, fatal in some cases, had occurred among a number of women who, perhaps coincidentally, were using the pills. In 1965 fears about the pills' safety were raised by a medical journal report that detailed damage to eyes and the central nervous system in some women taking the drug.

The government is keeping oral contraceptives under close surveillance and at this writing the Federal Drug Administration reports that tests have not established a "cause-and-effect relationship" between the pills and the "adverse experiences" of some women.

Doctors have been advised to be cautious in prescribing them for patients with case histories of breast tumors, heart trouble, migraine headaches, liver disease, kidney ailments or inflammation of the veins caused by blood clotting. The doctor should examine his pill-taking patient regularly to make sure she is able to take the medication. She should, of course, immediately report any unusual reactions to the pills. Patients should stop using the pill if there is a sudden onset of severe headache or dizziness, blurred vision, or if examination reveals eye nerve, retinal or vision defects.

Significantly, Dr. Guttmacher says the pills "are safe for the overwhelming majority of women."

Diaphragm

Until the development of the Pill, this was the most effective method of birth control. A diaphragm is a thin sheet of rubber stretched over a collapsible metal ring. It is placed in the birth canal and covers the entrance to the womb. The diaphragm comes in many different sizes and must be fitted to the woman by a trained doctor. He shows her how to insert the device. This can be done with the fingers or with an inserter especially designed for this purpose.

The diaphragm must always be used with a contraceptive jelly or cream, both for added protection and as a lubricant. The chemicals in the lubricant will kill sperm, thereby insuring full protection. You don't use much of the cream or jelly, just about a teaspoonful which is placed inside the diaphragm and spread around the rim.

If the diaphragm is properly inserted you are not conscious of it. You should insert the diaphragm before going to bed; some doctors say this ought to be a regular nightly procedure whether you can accurately anticipate intercourse or not. In other words, you might as well be prepared so there will be no interruption in the love-making. You should leave it in place for at least six hours after the last sex relations. It is possible to wear a diaphragm constantly for twenty-four hours but after that time you should take it out, wash and dry it. If you want to douche you can do so then.

Condom

This is doubtless the most popular contraceptive device in use today. You can buy them without prescription in any drugstore. They are easy to use; the male simply slips this thin rubber protection over his penis. They are safe unless defective to begin with or unless the rubber breaks during intercourse. Their safety has been improved because the United States Food and Drug Administration has been supervising the quality of condoms since 1938. Only one in 350 is found defective. However, if the condom slips off when the penis is being withdrawn some sperm may spill into the vagina.

The case against the condom is best expressed by men who claim that it interferes with sensation. Also, they may experience premature ejaculation while putting on the condom.

Cervical Cap or IUD

Intrauterine devices have become important as recently as 1965 as contraceptive aids. A doctor must insert the plastic or stainless steel device but once it is in its proper position the wearer has no further responsibility. The device is removed by the doctor when the woman wants to conceive. Insertion is no more painful than menstrual cramps. Neither the woman nor her husband is aware of the device during intercourse. There is only one problem; the device may be pushed out of position by the womb. Expulsion occurs most frequently in the young married group. Women who have not had children are less able to tolerate the IUD.

Foam, Jelly or Cream; Tablets, Suppositories

You can buy these contraceptive aids without a doctor's prescription. Although they are most effective used in conjunction with a mechanical device, the chemicals in these products do kill sperm. Special applicators come with each product so you are never in doubt about how much to use. Follow directions on the package carefully. These products must be used properly or they will not work. For example, they cannot be used more than an hour before intercourse; douching must be delayed for six hours after the last sex act.

Vaginal tablets and suppositories are easy to use. They become effective when their chemical properties are released by contact with body moisture. Therefore, you will have to allow some time to elapse after inserting them. They are less effective than the jelly or cream, and much less than the foam.

Rhythm

This is the method approved by the Catholic Church. It is also known as the "safe method" because you are safe from conception if you can figure out just exactly when you are ovulating. There are only a few days each month when a woman is fertile. The rest are the safe days. How can you identify them?

Success with the rhythm method depends on the regularity of the menstrual cycles, the care with which the record of them is kept and on a willingness not to take chances when there is any possibility you are fertile.

You must keep a written record of the day when each menstrual period begins. When the record has been kept for at least eight months and preferably twelve, it can be used as a guide to Safe Periods. Only when this record is accurately kept can rhythm be used effectively. Women who "think" their cycles are regular often find surprising variations when they keep track.

Here is how to find the length of each menstrual cycle.

Count the days from the first day of one menstrual period to the first day of the next period. For instance, if bleeding started October 3 and again on October 30, the cycle that began on October 3 was twenty-seven days long.

Record the length of each menstrual cycle on a list. If a list of at least eight cycles is not available begin the list with two "make-believe" cycles 33 and 23. These numbers should stay on the list until at least eight actual cycles are listed.

The lengths of the most recent cycles are added to the bottom of the list, removing the older cycles at the top, so that at least eight and preferably twelve cycles are always available for figuring the Safe Period.

To find when sex relations should be *avoided*:

Choose the shortest cycle in the list and subtract 18. For instance, if the shortest cycle were twenty-five days, 25 minus 18 is Day 7 which would be the day of the cycle when sex relations should be stopped. The first day of bleeding is always Day 1 of each cycle.

To find when sex relations *can be resumed*:

Choose the longest cycle in the list and subtract 11. For instance, if the longest cycle were thirty-three days, 33 minus 11 is Day 22, which is the day of the cycle when sex relations can safely be resumed.

The safe and fertile days for the present cycle should then be clearly marked on a calendar. To make rhythm work, you cannot have sex on the fertile days. Of course, the shortest cycle may not be twenty-five days or the longest cycle thirty-three days; these figures are only examples. But whatever the lengths of the cycles may be, and regardless of how many days bleeding may last, the two italicized figures must always be used:

18 is subtracted from the shortest cycle to find the day sex relations are stopped.

11 is subtracted from the longest cycle to find the day sex relations may be resumed.

Worry, illness or unusual excitement may change the length of the menstrual cycle; the Safe Period method will be less reliable as long as the unusual conditions last.

The Safe Period cannot be used during the times between childbirth and the first menstrual period. Sex relations during this time may result in pregnancy even if the mother is nursing the baby.

The Margaret Sanger Research Bureau, 17 West 16th Street, New York, N.Y. 10011, offers a Safe Period Service at an annual fee of $5.00. Monthly personal consultations by mail or by an appointment at the Bureau can help you use the Rhythm Method with confidence.

Withdrawal

This is probably the oldest contraceptive method known to man. It couldn't be simpler. The male withdraws his penis from the female's vagina as soon as he feels he might ejaculate sperm.

If he has control over himself he will withdraw in time; if not he may easily make his wife pregnant. The first few drops of the ejaculate are blessed with the greatest concentration of sperm.

There are other reasons why withdrawal is not considered a very good method of birth control. Intercourse must be interrupted at the very moment when it should be its most pleasurable. Both partners can suffer. The wife who has not yet achieved orgasm will feel cheated. The male cannot relax and enjoy sex because the responsibility is his to withdraw in good time.

Some authorities claim that chronic pelvic pain and other complaints in women can be traced to their husband's withdrawal technique. The male who relies on this method may develop the pattern of premature ejaculation. However, the most damning argument against withdrawal is that it frustrates the close relationship which should characterize good sexual relations. At the moment when man and wife want to be near each other, clasped in each other's arms, they are obliged to draw apart.

Douche

Despite what you have heard about the efficacy of the French bidet, douching is a very poor method of birth control. Besides, the woman is asked to jump out of bed the minute intercourse has been effected and douche herself. What could be less conducive to warm, gratifying postsexual experience?

Experts on contraceptive methods are amazed that the douche works at all. According to research at the Sanger Bureau the mucus within the opening of the cervix is already swarming with sperm just three minutes after intercourse. Some have even penetrated up the cervical canal.

Dr. Abraham Stone's advice should be followed explicitly if you do decide to douche.

Use a nonirritating but highly spermicidal solution.

Distend the vagina by slight pressure.

Flush with a gush.

Douche *immediately* after intercourse.

The Infertility Problem

Even though the emphasis seems to be on helping young couples plan their families and regulate the size, you cannot ignore the possibility that you may not be able to conceive. Some 15 to 20 percent of married couples are infertile or subfertile. Happily, they can be helped toward parenthood. Some are simply uneducated in productive sexual relations. Without realizing it, they are frustrating their chances to become natural parents.

Others are limited by physical disabilities that can be corrected. If a man's sperm count is low (the case in 40 percent of those who seek help) it can be built up through proper medical treatment. A woman who is unable to conceive may be suffering from some problem which prevents the sperm from traveling up through the vagina and cervix to the womb. She can be relieved of whatever is obstructing the passage of the sperm.

Sometimes a woman is unable to conceive because, although ovulation has occurred, the egg is not being delivered down the Fallopian tubes because either or both are blocked. There are many ways in which modern medicine can relieve this problem.

The new so-called "fertility drugs" have been hailed as "the most important breakthrough in the last twenty years," by one medical researcher who works with childless couples. However, the multiple births resulting from this type of therapy has created concern in medical circles. The drugs are still in the experimental stage and should be administered with caution.

Young couples are advised not to be alarmed if they have not conceived a child after six months to a year of good sex relations. After that period has elapsed they should certainly seek professional help. They may find that the very act of seeking help is a kind of therapy. More than one woman has found herself pregnant after a few weeks of intensive medical or psychiatric probing of the problem.

If you and your husband cannot have children, then you may want to consider adopting one. Do it while you are young. The adopted child can make you as happy and fulfilled as your own if you welcome him with love.

Pregnancy: Its Problems and the Importance of Prenatal Care

Despite the increasing availability of factual information about pregnancy and childbirth, various old wives' tales still persist about these natural procedures. Such myths may be harmful if they create needless anxieties and problems. Women who have few fears and doubts about pregnancy usually are those who have the easiest time in delivery. Some typical persistent myths:

Myth: You should eat for two when you are pregnant. Fact: Women should eat about the same amount as usual, but should improve the quality of their diet to include all the important food ingredients and emphasize high-protein, low-carbohydrate food. Women are usually less able to assist in labor if overweight. Other risks may also be increased.

Myth: The fetus robs its mother of calcium and causes increased tooth decay. Hence the saying, "A tooth lost for every child." *Fact:* Enamel on teeth is permanent and is unaffected by the amount of calcium in a diet. However, the tooth formation of the fetus can be helped by increasing a mother's calcium intake.

Myth: Teen-agers have the healthiest pregnancies. Fact: The best age for normal pregnancies and deliveries is between twenty and thirty years. Complications occur more often in women under twenty and over forty.

Because of the wide circulation of those and many other wrong beliefs and misconceptions about pregnancy, any questions or doubts that a woman may have should be discussed fully with a doctor. In addition to giving authoritative medical advice, the physician can play an important role in providing the mother-to-be with psychological support during pregnancy. This frank exchange between patient and doctor should begin when a woman first believes she is pregnant. A missed menstrual period usually indicates pregnancy, but this is not always the case. Emotional factors or medical conditions may cause a missed period. If a need exists—either for medical, psychological or legal reasons—to know for sure whether a woman is pregnant, certain laboratory tests can confirm pregnancy several weeks before it can be determined by a physical examination. The most common tests are based on a hormone produced in pregnancy which shows up in blood or urine samples. These tests—in some the results are available in less than an hour—are not used as a matter of routine by most doctors. Although the tests have a high degree of accuracy, errors do occur. Most women wait until after a second missed period before being examined by a doctor, who can usually diagnose a pregnancy by physical means after eight weeks. Obviously, a woman is extremely interested in knowing for certain whether she is pregnant, but she should let her physician decide whether a test is necessary.

Medical care during pregnancy is important to both the mother and the baby. Illness or permanent damage to the baby may result from conditions which can be prevented by proper care. A woman should have a gynecological examination at her initial visit to a doctor, as well as giving her medical history and having a general exam. She should see the doctor regularly, usually about once a month for the first six months and more often as the delivery date approaches.

Because X-rays can have serious effects on the embryo in the first stages of pregnancy, many obstetricians recommend that women of childbearing age have routine pelvic or abdominal X-rays only during the first ten days from the start of her menstrual period when pregnancy is improbable. During pregnancy, the doctor can advise when it is medically necessary and safe for a woman to be X-rayed. Another risk to the unborn baby in the first few months of pregnancy is the danger of the mother contracting contagious diseases, especially German measles. Pregnant women should avoid places where they might be exposed to such diseases.

Proper diet is a basic element in prenatal care. It should include the essential food elements—proteins, carbohydrates, fats, minerals and vitamins. Doctors prefer that an expectant mother gain not more than twenty pounds over her normal weight. The size of the baby is determined mostly by heredity. Overeating does not produce a large baby or undereating a small one. Doctors may prescribe vitamins, iron, calcium or other supplements if they are needed. Salt intake may be restricted to cut down on fluid retention.

Many doctors advocate special exercises for pregnant women. They believe exercises condition the muscles for delivery and combat daily fatigue. Classes in exercises and other prenatal instructions are given at hospitals and various community agencies. Booklets are also available for home instruction, but any program should be undertaken only on the advice of a physician.

During pregnancy, a patient should report immediately to her doctor any symptoms such as vaginal bleeding, swelling or pain. Vaginal bleeding is a cause for concern at any time during pregnancy. Although there are other causes, it may mean the loss of a pregnancy. A doctor may want to do a pelvic examination to find the cause of bleeding. The examination will not stimulate a spontaneous abortion and should not be feared. Of the estimated 20 percent of pregnant women who have some spotting or bleeding, half of them do miscarry. To save the baby, bed rest may be prescribed and hormone drugs may be used. Bleeding in the last three months can be dangerous to both mother and child. Among causes are separation of the placenta from the wall of the uterus and improper position of the placenta. This is an obstetrical emergency and probably will require hospitalization. A *cesarean section* —birth by an abdominal operation—may be necessary.

Swelling or pain in the latter months (after twenty-eight weeks) may indicate a condition known as *toxemia* of pregnancy. It is not connected with an infection, but can be accompanied by high blood pressure, swelling (*edema*) and faulty elimination from the kidneys. (Other symptoms to report to a doctor are rapid weight gain, headache or visual disturbances.) Convulsions and coma can result from toxemia. Fortunately, with modern prenatal care, this serious advanced stage is seldom reached. Although the cause of toxemia is not specifically known, early control of weight increase, salt intake and blood pressure can prevent it from becoming serious.

A full-term, nine-month pregnancy consists of three general periods (*trimesters*). In the first trimester, about one out of two women experience some nausea, usually in the sixth to tenth week. Most doctors advise frequent small meals during this period. Although the nausea is commonly called morning sickness, it can occur at any time and may come and go in an irregular way. To combat it, a small, dry snack high in carbohydrate content (e.g., a cookie or a cracker with jelly) is recommended. Nausea can be increased by lack of sufficient food. No drug for nausea—or, for that matter, *any* prescription or over-the-counter medication—

should be taken unless prescribed by a physician. Too, no treatment for other discomforts associated with pregnancy should be undertaken without checking with a physician. Other discomforts include:

Back pains. These may be caused by a change in posture or walking habits and usually can be corrected by proper maternity girdles, shoes and exercise.

Indigestion. Medical treatment or a change in diet can correct indigestion. Over-the-counter remedies should not be taken because they may contain sodium (salt).

Leg cramps. These may be helped by an adjustment in calcium intake or by placing weight on the foot or putting it on a cold surface.

Varicose veins. Surgical stockings or other supportive devices can help.

Constipation. Some cathartics are habit forming and should not be used. Fruit and liquids will help.

Insomnia. Less tea and coffee and drinking a glass of warm milk before bedtime contribute to relaxation.

Childbirth, What Is Done in Routine and Complicated Births

Most babies are born without complications. However, knowing exactly what happens in childbirth and the measures a doctor can use to minimize problems which might arise can be reassuring to the expectant mother.

As a woman's delivery date approaches, her doctor will examine her cervix, which is elongated and thick during pregnancy but thins and shortens as delivery time approaches. Most women do not give birth on the exact date calculated and delivery normally varies from two weeks before to two weeks after.

Stages of labor. The birth of a baby involves three stages of labor. In the first, contractions start and when they become regular the doctor should be called promptly. This stage of labor may last for as long as eighteen hours for mothers having their first child. The *bag of waters*, the membrane around the baby in the uterus, may rupture at this point, although it also may break before labor begins. With subsequent babies, labor may last only two or three hours or even less. At first, contractions are mild and irregular—from ten to twenty minutes apart—or may stop temporarily. As the cervix opens, contractions increase until they come at two- to three-minute intervals. In the second stage of labor, the cervix is completely dilated, allowing the baby to move through the vaginal tract to be born. The third stage is the expulsion of the *placenta*, the round, flat structure on the uterine wall through which the baby receives nourishment by way of the umbilical cord. This usually takes five to ten minutes, sometimes as long as thirty. Some bleeding occurs at this time. It subsides with the shrinking of the uterus as labor is completed. The umbilical cord is tied and cut two to four inches from the baby's navel.

Cesarean section. A baby is delivered this way by an abdominal incision through the uterine wall. The baby is lifted out. The main reasons for this operation are:

The mother's pelvis is too small to permit the child to pass through.

The placenta is between the baby and the entrance to the birth canal blocking passage or causing bleeding.

There is prolonged or difficult labor due to the size or position of the baby, deformities within the mother or her failure to have effective contractions.

Early detachment of the placenta from the uterine wall causes bleeding and threatens the baby's oxygen supply.

In some cases of toxemia or blood incompatibility and in certain diseases such as diabetes or cancer of the cervix a cesarean is necessary.

As in any abdominal operation, some risk is present in a cesarean section. Recovery is longer and it is not known for sure how many cesareans a woman can undergo and continue to have children safely. The conditions which require a cesarean section and how many a woman can have are individual to each mother. With a first child, medical authorities recommend that a second doctor be consulted for a confirming opinion when a cesarean section is advised, if time permits.

Induced labor. Labor can be started by artificial means. Authorities, though, stress that induction should not be used merely for the convenience of either the patient or the doctor. Labor can be induced by breaking the membranes which surround the baby in the uterus or by use of a hormonal drug to start labor contractions. Because both methods raise the possibilities of some risk, their use has been controversial in medical circles. In general, a doctor induces labor only if the woman is physically ready to deliver. When the drug *oxytocin* is used to start contractions, they may become severe or prolonged, thus threatening the oxygen supply of the baby. Breaking the membranes runs the risk of inducing a baby prematurely. However, used under proper conditions, it can be advantageous as opposed to an emergency birth.

Forceps. Many doctors use this instrument to guide and control passage of the baby through the birth canal. The dangerous type of forceps delivery where damage to the baby could result has largely been abandoned in recent years because of the increasing use of cesarean section. When forceps are used today, it may only be for slight assistance or adjustment of the baby's head. As a rule, doctors try to limit the use of forceps, pain killers and anesthesia in childbirth. But even for those women who have been trained in "natural childbirth" techniques, drugs and pain killers are used if needed.

Rh factor. When a mother has a blood incompatibility with the baby due to the Rh factor, the baby may be affected. This is tested for early in pregnancy. If the baby can survive until birth, he can be given an immediate *exchange transfusion,* in which his blood supply is replaced. A relatively new technique gives the baby a transfusion *before* birth. A concentration of red blood cells is transfused into the baby's abdominal cavity by use of a long needle inserted through the mother's abdomen. Sometimes two or three such transfusions are given to keep the baby alive until birth. (A similar technique—using a long needle to tap the amniotic fluid surrounding the baby—has been used to tell in advance the sex of a child by analysis of the cells from the fluid. However, this procedure is reserved *only* for medical reasons such as testing for Rh problem severity or genetic aberration. It is *not* used simply to satisfy a parent's curiosity.)

Multiple births. These can pose additional medical problems. The danger of stillbirths is higher and most multiple births are premature. As a result, doctors may ask a patient to come more frequently for examination and they keep closer watch on the mother's diet. A doctor's examination during pregnancy can reveal whether more than one child is expected. An X-ray usually is taken in the eighth month to confirm and provide specific information on position of the infants. When multiple births occur, the babies—once past the critical first weeks—usually enjoy the same health outlook as other children.

Baby blues. Many women experience a feeling of sadness within the first week after giving birth. Medically known as *postpartum depression,* these feelings are commonly called "childbirth or baby blues." A mother may not be able to explain why she feels sad. She may cry and yet laugh through her tears. Doctors feel that the psychological and physical stresses of childbirth are the cause. Some believe that preparation for labor by exercises and instruction classes and by presence of the father in the labor room or even the delivery room will minimize a woman's emotional upset following childbirth. In most cases, childbirth blues are temporary and disappear after a night's sleep, having a good cry or after a discussion with a physician.

Breast feeding. A woman who wants to nurse her baby should visit during pregnancy the pediatrician who will care for her child following birth. Physicians are generally agreed that nursing is a mother's responsibility and her choice, while the doctor's job is to relieve any doubts she may have. It usually requires about two weeks of nursing to learn the best technique. Some mothers have difficulty and cannot nurse. Nursing, of course, has distinct advantages of personal satisfaction, convenience and supplying the baby with a food exactly suited to him. But women who cannot or do not want to nurse should understand that bottle-fed babies also thrive.

VII

RUNNING YOUR OWN SHOW

As soon as you marry you will be expected to create your own style as a couple. Everything you do, buy, consume will contribute to it. You will have a new "look" appropriate to your status as a husband and wife team. Individual styles will blend into a composite one and, in turn, that marital style you develop will influence each of you more than you know.

The greatest tribute a wife can earn from a husband was summed up in an artist's accolade to his mate. "She has," he said, "made us a life of considerable beauty."

"Style—The quality which gives distinctive excellence." This is Webster's definition. Style, then, means more than fashion, more than keeping up with the Joneses, much more than conspicuous consumption. It means, simply, a kind of achievement open to all, even to those young marrieds who must evolve a style while they sort out what is important to them.

The kind of housing you pick; the food you eat; the way you spend your leisure hours will influence that style. Much of your development will be accomplished in private but not all. If you like to entertain you will be known as a young couple who can throw a party with grace. If you become influential in your community your reputation will grow accordingly. You are being watched, you know, to see how marriage and all the responsibilities it entails will change you.

You need the courage of your convictions. If you decide to forego possessions and save every cent toward a year abroad that will, of course, be your style and people will respect it. Enjoy the choices that are yours and never be afraid to change your mind. Now is the time to experiment, to try on a variety of roles, to let yourself grow as you experience adulthood.

You aren't alone even though the final decisions will be yours. Your parents are standing by, ready with advice and help. As a matter of fact, you will be offered more help than ever before. Don't be afraid to use it.

Picking the Pros: Your Doctor, Lawyer, etc.

Once you are married a new set of professionals will enter your life. You'll need a lawyer to make a will, handle property purchases. If you start an investment program a broker, banker, mutual funds agent will be working for you. If you decide to build a house you'll need an architect and contractor, not to mention a host of specialists in lighting, kitchen design, plumbing, heating, decorating. You'll be buying insurance and will need to pick a company and agent. Now that you're making out a joint income tax the services of a public accountant may save you money.

You may have been lucky enough to have known only one good family doctor all your life. If you move away from his practice area you'll have to make a switch. Or you decide you want your own doctor, someone younger perhaps or someone who is more of a specialist. You will certainly want to visit a gynecologist and when the family is on the way you will have to pick an obstetrician. Your husband needs his own physician too. He may be exposed to good medical services in his job; many factories and businesses provide annual checkups for their workers. But you both want to have someone you can call in case of emergency.

How should you pick a professional? You can get names from friends you trust, use experts they enthusiastically endorse. When moving to a new town you will have to rely on professional organizations to supply you with names. Call the County Medical Society, for example, and ask them to suggest specialists practicing in your area. The Bar Association can furnish you with the names of lawyers. Other professional groups will offer the same service.

Getting the name is only the beginning. You will have to make a choice between several personalities and, in the case of investment companies, banks, insurance agents, several organizations. How can you make the right decision?

Look for someone compatible who is already on your side. If you don't trust your lawyer to look after your interests, then he isn't right for you. If you can't bring yourself to tell your doctor about all your symptoms, you need a new one. Social friendship and professional respect do not always go hand in hand. You don't necessarily have to approve the way your tax man dresses or want to play bridge with your insurance agent to like the way he does business. Some people, as a matter of fact, want to keep a certain distance from their professional advisers.

Be sure to talk money right away. Your doctor won't be able to tell you with any certainty how much he'll charge for a week's worth of the virus. But he ought to be frank about fees for office visits, home calls, simple surgery. Most obstetricians have flat rates for delivering a baby. Be equally direct about your own personal finances. He has a right to know if you intend to pay him over a period of months.

Get your money's worth. If you feel you can get a better deal on insurance don't hesitate to shop around and compare offers. When you're building a house you have every right to ask for bids and pick the lowest one. You may, of course, decide to take a slightly higher offer because you think you'll get more in craftsmanship, attention, resourcefulness. Ask questions. Your youth and inexperience can stand you in good stead. Nobody expects you to know all the answers and the experts may be more than willing to give you an assist.

When Your Doctor Is Part of a Group Practice

The tremendous advances in medical knowledge during the past twenty-five years have been accompanied by a significant change for millions of families involving who is their family physician. Most families still rely on a single doctor, either a general practitioner or an internist (a diagnostician) who refers patients to specialists as the need arises. However, in many communities, *group medical practices* have been established. These usually consist of three or more physicians, each with a different specialty, who form a professional partnership. The idea is to provide families with comprehensive diagnosis and treatment (aside from hospital and home care) in a single building. Some of these practices are huge, including many doctors (one hundred or more) and are called clinics. Some even have hospital facilities. The most famous is the Mayo Clinic in Rochester, Minnesota.

The basic unit for family care in a group practice usually consists of a surgeon, internist, obstetrician and pediatrician. General practitioners often are included in a group and may be the first to see a new patient before any specialists are involved. Large groups may include specialists in radiology, orthopedics, ophthalmology, urology, and ear, nose and throat. Many provide X-ray, laboratory tests and pharmacy services.

Doctors in group practice believe they provide patients with certain advantages. Among them:

Specialists are readily available for consultation on a patient's related medical problems.

A detailed up-to-date medical record is kept in a single file with reports from all doctors consulted.

X-ray and laboratory test results can be obtained faster.

A doctor is always available, whether at night or on a weekend, who has quick access to a patient's complete medical history.

Despite these claimed advantages, other doctors question whether such practices provide patients with the same intimate doctor-patient relationships which exist with an individual family physician. Even some physicians in groups believe there is a degree of less-personal relationship. For instance, a doctor in one large clinic told editors that patients sometimes feel they are being shunted from one specialist to another. Mac F. Cahal, executive director of the American Academy of General Practice, says, "Individual family physicians often have an intimate knowledge of family relationships, which do not appear on medical records, that is useful in diagnosis and treatment."

Most groups or clinics try to cope with this vital problem of human relationships by having a patient consider one doctor as his *personal* physician. But if that doctor is away or tied up with an emergency, another doctor is available. Dr. G. Freeman Brooks, a founder of the Rye Medical Group in Rye, New York, says this availability is considered a community asset.

An example of how a large group practice functions is that of the Palo Alto Medical Clinic in Palo Alto, California, a town about thirty-five miles south of San Francisco. One of the largest groups in the country, it has 120 doctors and its own modern, three-story building. A new patient, such as a housewife, most likely will be seen on her first visit to the clinic by a general practitioner. He takes her medical history and treats any complaints not requiring specialists. Laboratory tests or X-rays are made in the same building. She can pick up any prescribed medicine at a pharmacy in the building.

If a patient of the clinic becomes pregnant, she is transferred to an obstetrician for prenatal care. He has her previous medical record to refer to on her first visit to him. Any complications of pregnancy can be discussed with specialists in related fields. Her baby will be delivered at the Palo Alto-Stanford Hospital Center. When her child is born, he may become a patient of one of the clinic's pediatricians.

Fees for medical treatment are comparable to those of other doctors in the same region. Some groups maintain hospitals or hospital-bed facilities, while others hospitalize patients at the community hospital with which their doctors are affiliated, as is the case in Palo Alto.

Dr. Russel V. Lee, founder of the Palo Alto Medical Clinic and a pioneer in establishing this type of practice, says informal consultations in the clinic with other doctors are quicker and more economical for a patient. A patient, he says, sometimes may see six doctors within an hour. These informal consultations, says Dr. Lee, may save a patient a considerable amount of money in fees over a period of years compared to what he would pay for outside, formal consultations. Dr. Lee believes patients also profit from what he calls "curbstone" consultations where doctors discuss cases among themselves at lunch or at other times. Although a patient is not aware of these "curbstone" consultations, says Dr. Lee, he benefits enormously.

On the average, most groups have more non-physician employees than doctors. This means a doctor does not have to bother with much of the paper work he might have to handle in practice by himself and enables him to see more patients. When a group has more than seven or eight doctors, a business manager usually supervises the business affairs of the clinic. Although the heaviest concentration of group practices has been in the Midwest and on the Pacific coast, their number is increasing in all sections of the country. A 1962 survey showed that more than 12 percent of all physicians were in group practice and that number has been growing. Dr. Lee predicts that the number will rise to 20 percent within a few years.

Some groups have been formed to give medical coverage to persons within an industry or profession on a *prepayment* basis. Teachers, factory workers, policemen and students are given comprehensive medical coverage by these groups for a fee paid in advance. For instance, the Palo Alto Medical Clinic has a contract with Stanford University to provide medical coverage for students for a prepaid fee of $11 a quarter (three months) for each student. One of the largest prepayment plans is the Health Insurance Plan of Greater New York, which has enrolled more than 700,000 persons who obtain care through thirty-two affiliated groups of doctors. Another large plan is the Kaiser Foundation Health Plan of California, Oregon and Hawaii.

A Roof Over Your Head

Before marriage you probably lived with your parents, shared a small apartment, rented a room or, if you were still in school, you led the dormitory life. Now, it would seem, the sky is the limit, particularly if you have two paychecks to use. You might put a down payment on a house, using the wedding checks. Or buy a mobile home. You can settle in the heart of a city or decide to commute from a garden apartment in the suburbs. If you move in with in-laws you can even save a good chunk of rent money. As a matter of fact, you have so much choice you may have a hard time making up your mind. So you settle on the first thing that's offered, living to regret it. Unless you are pressed to make a major move, hold off until you have considered all your options.

Here are some pointers on picking your home. They may save you time, trouble and expense.

If each of you already rents an apartment why not consolidate your belongings in the biggest and best. This may be only a temporary solution but it will give you time to look for your dream place. Meantime, you'll get a line on the kind of life you're going to be living together, and plan more realistically for it. If you like to entertain a lot you're going to want an apartment with a good kitchen and a big living room. If you both crave privacy you'll sacrifice the entertainment room for an extra bedroom which can be turned into a study. If you need to be close to job or school you can do without a car and spend the money saved on better housing.

Or if you can't wait to settle down in the kind of suburb you knew as a child you may be willing to spend more on housing to get the kind of life you enjoy most.

As newlyweds you can make the decision about commuting free from such considerations as "fresh air and good schools for the children." You don't have to commute. You can come to your own personal conclusions on whether you'd like to do it. Here are some pros and cons to help you make up your mind.

You can buy more space with your housing dollar in the suburbs. There are garden apartments as well as houses to be had and generally the rentals become cheaper as you move out.

You can start paying on a house, preparing a homestead for the children when they come. You won't have to uproot yourself and search hysterically for the right neighborhood when the time to settle down finally comes.

Your leisure problems are solved if you live near a golf course, tennis court, beach.

You want to become part of a community, join a church, run for office, serve on committees and boards. You are eager to find your own "hometown."

In your part of the world city living is either too expensive or too dreary. Comfort and fresh air are possible only outside the business district.

So much for the advantages of suburban or residential living. What can be said for big-city life?

You see more of each other in the city. You can get home at night in record time, meet for lunch or cocktails on short notice. That extra hour for a leisurely breakfast certainly beats the commuter hustle.

There's more opportunity for culture, intellectual stimulation, in the city—theater, museums, music, dancing, college courses, lectures.

Commuting costs money, outweighs the savings you may achieve when you own your own home.

You have to maintain a car in the suburbs; public transportation is fast and cheap in most cities.

Once you have decided where you will live you must then estimate your income and come to some conclusion on the amount you can afford to spend on shelter.

Most family money experts estimate that a quarter of your income will go for housing and they think that is about right. You, however, may be shocked at the dollars housing takes away from your income. If you make one hundred dollars a week after taxes you will wince at paying twenty-five dollars of that for shelter. Most people face two choices when they try to cut down on housing expenses. They can rent an apartment with everything included or buy a house, pay less per month but find themselves saddled with additional homeowner expenses. Of course, the homeowner is, in a sense, investing his monthly payments. He will get them back when he sells the house, except for whacking interest charges on the mortgage which can never be recovered. The apartment dweller, however, can point to substantial savings when he measures his monthly expense against that of the homeowner.

House or Apartment?

Everything that can be said in favor of apartment living goes for renting a house. Besides, you get more space in a house rental and if you like working around the place you will appreciate the chance to practice your gardening and do-it-yourself skills.

When you rent you get a complete package for your housing dollar. The monthly rent may well include utilities (electricity and/or gas). Certainly water (hot and cold) is included, along with heat and, possibly, air conditioning. You are entitled to services—garbage disposal, elevator service and superintendent protection—without charge. Many big apartment complexes have their own shopping centers, amusement and recreation facilities, such as swimming pools and tennis courts. You can garage your car free, or at a modest monthly rental, on the premises. Even an unfurnished apartment comes with kitchen equipment, stove and refrigerator, possibly a dishwasher and garbage disposal. The building probably contains a laundry room for tenants. Best of all, apartment living is designed for mobile couples. If you get tired of the neighborhood, if a new job beckons, if you need more space, you can move on when the lease expires. Or sublet if you must pull up stakes in a hurry.

When you rent you don't pay real estate taxes. You aren't obliged to carry insurance on your quarters or your possessions. You use the streets outside the building without paying a home-owner's assessment on maintaining them. Snow removal is the building's responsibility, not yours.

Obviously, you aren't paying interest charges when you rent and they can come to a sizable amount over the life of a mortgage. Nor must you pay the lawyer's fees, closing costs, title insurance, fee for a credit check, which must be counted into the price of home ownership.

You will be advised by older and wiser hands not to invest in a house until you have saved up enough for a down payment, usually a fourth to a third of the total cost. If you borrow the money for a down payment as well as assume monthly mortgage charges, the chances are your debt load will be unrealistic and insupportable. However, suppose you have enough for the down payment, thanks to wedding checks, savings and a windfall from your rich uncle. Should you tie it up in a down payment? Or wouldn't you be better off investing it so it can produce income and increase in value? If you keep it invested for five years you can then make a larger down payment and reduce your mortgage payments by a few years. And this, if you soberly consider the interest on an average mortgage, is well worth doing.

You will pay less money but more interest per month on a long-run mortgage. For example: a $20,000 mortgage at 5½ percent will cost you additional $13,018.60 interest if you assume it for twenty years and $16,846 if it is extended to twenty-five years. Look at the amount you pay in interest for the privilege of borrowing!

When you are young you are likely to think that the low monthly payments are cheaper than rent for equivalent space and that since you have years to pay off the mortgage you can take the long-term offer. Resist this temptation unless you don't mind paying nearly double the cost of your house, money you will not get back unless property values skyrocket. Instead, put as big a down payment as you can on the house, opt for the shortest mortgage you can manage without real suffering each month. And be sure you get an estimate of the other costs involved in buying a house.

Suppose you do decide that you want to buy a house. How can you be sure of getting your money's worth if it's your first buy?

You can ask someone who knows—a contractor-builder or your father-in-law (if he's knowledgeable) or the bank's building inspector. Let an expert go over the house to make sure construction is sound. You may have to make repairs but you ought to know what they are going to be before you decide it's a good buy.

Consider the neighborhood. Is it going up or down? Your bargain house may be just that simply because everybody is moving out of the area. Perhaps a new superhighway is going through your part of town or it is about to be rezoned for industrial use. Or suppose it is slated for urban renewal. You may decide you want to buy anyway but before you sign anything check out the neighborhood.

You should be able to think of your house as space that will grow and adapt to family needs. That is, if you intend living in it for a number of years. If it's purely a temporary investment then you can just enjoy it as is. Ideally a house, particularly a small one, should have expansion potential. Does it have an unfinished attic you can convert into extra bedrooms? Can you build a wing on one of the sides without destroying the lines of the house? Is the basement big enough to house a family room, workshop or home office?

If you can rent part of your house then it will indeed cost less than an apartment rental. You might rent out a room or two. Or look for a two-family house. Or fix up an apartment over the garage to serve as a rental unit. If your property brings in some income you can write off home improvements and maintenance as a business expense on your income tax.

Clearly a good case can be made for ownership. Otherwise, it would not be so popular. Even newlyweds may, if they possess certain assets besides the price of a down payment, find that buying is better than renting.

Consider your "equity," or value, in the property. With every monthly mortgage payment you are building up your family worth. True, you pay interest but that can be deducted from income on your tax return. If you maintain your property it should increase in value over the years, giving you more for your investment. In the meantime you are living "rent free." Obviously, you have to consider certain homeowner expenses before you can really judge whether you come out ahead as a buyer rather than renter.

Add up the mortgage payments for a year.

Estimate the cost of utilities for a given year.

Figure out how much insurance and taxes will cost.

Get an estimate on the heating bills.

Try to anticipate the cost of maintenance—painting the house, planting the grounds, repairs you can't do yourself. If the house needs drastic work—rewiring, major plumbing, a new furnace, a roof—then you should compute such initial renovation over a five- or ten-year period.

What will it cost to furnish the house with refrigerator, stove, dishwasher, etc. Figure out the life of these appliances, generally ten years, and divide to get a yearly figure.

Add all of these expenses and divide by 12. This is the figure you use to compare with the cost of apartment rental. Don't forget to take into consideration the intangibles, however. If owning your own home means a lot then it will be worth the extra expense. You may even save on entertainment expense because you'll be so busy running up curtains and planting a garden.

Facts about Mortgages

Knowing the basic facts about mortgages can be helpful when buying a home. Mortgage loans are made by various sources, including banks, savings and loan associations, insurance companies and mortgage companies. Before deciding on which to use, check them all to get the best terms available in your area.

Terms of mortgages vary not only by region but by policies of the lenders. Early this year, for instance, highest interest rates were in the West and Southwest. Lenders that require a higher down payment may have lower interest rates. For example, although their down-payment requirements are high, insurance companies generally charge less interest on the loan but have a shorter term and higher monthly payments. Lenders requiring less than a 20 percent down payment have higher interest rates.

Mortgages may either be a conventional loan, guaranteed by the

Veterans Administration or insured by the Federal Housing Administration. Most lenders handle all three types. But when lenders can get higher rates on conventional loans, it may be difficult to find one willing to write an FHA or VA mortgage with the government-imposed limit of 6 percent interest. (FHA loans have an additional ½ percent insurance charge.) Some lenders *discount* VA and FHA mortgages, that is, charge a premium to increase the return on a loan. Conventional mortgage rates averaged 6.70 percent interest on existing homes and 6.65 on new ones in January. A fraction of a percentage point can mean considerable difference in the total interest paid during the life of a mortgage. On a $10,000, 20-year mortgage, the interest would total $7,195 at 6 percent, $7,894 at 6½ percent and $8,608 at 7 percent. In addition, conventional loans usually require a larger down payment—at least 20 to 25 percent of the purchase price. VA loans obtained by a qualified veteran may be made for the *full* appraised value of a house. FHA requires down payments of 3 up to 14.3 percent on a $35,000 house, but lenders may ask more.

In considering a mortgage, other features should also be compared, including: *Prepayment privilege.* This allows the borrower to pay all or part of the mortgage in advance without penalty, a feature useful if there is a chance the house might be sold before the mortgage ends or for refinancing it if interest rates drop significantly. Conventional loans may have restrictions, such as allowing prepayment of 10 to 20 percent without penalty in any one year, but charge one-half year's interest on any amount of prepayment over that. FHA limits prepayment to 15 percent in any one year without penalty and charges 1 percent on any amount more than that, except in special circumstances. VA mortgages permit prepayment without penalty.

Open-end mortgage. When part of a mortgage has been paid off, this feature, in states allowing it, permits reborrowing that amount. The most advantageous open-end mortgages permit reborrowing at the original interest rate. Some apply a new rate to the amount reborrowed and others set a new rate for the whole mortgage. Using an open-end clause can save much of the service charges on a new mortgage, which may be up to 3 percent.

The length, or term, of a mortgage also affects interest costs. Conventional mortgages customarily run from 20 to 25 years. VA and FHA mortgages run up to 35 years. Interest paid on a 7 percent $10,000 mortgage would total $6,179 over 15 years, $8,608 over 20 years and $13,951 over 30 years. You can reduce the overall cost of the house by using a shorter-term mortgage. This, of course, raises monthly mortgage payments.

Some families find that today's high down-payment requirement makes it difficult to buy a house. It is not advisable to use all of a family's available cash for a down payment. Some funds should be saved for moving expenses, closing costs, service charges and any immediate repairs the house may require. If a down payment is beyond a family's means, consideration can be given to obtaining a *second mortgage*. This may be offered by a seller to complete a sale or it may be available from mortgage lenders. Interest rates, however, are high on such mortgages and the FHA does not permit them. Additional financing is also possible by using a contract with the seller to repay a loan in monthly installments.

If the first-mortgage loan is not large enough to complete purchase of the home, another or *second mortgage* may be required. This mortgage is issued on the house and property beyond the amount owed in the first mortgage. The second loan, sometimes called a junior mortgage, is almost always for a smaller amount than the first. Like a first mortgage, it generally calls for monthly installments, but over a much shorter period. Its interest rate generally is higher because it is a more speculative loan. In the event of foreclosure, the first mortgage must be paid in full *before* the second mortgage can be settled.

Second-mortgage loans are used most frequently by businessmen seeking to raise money using their commercial property as collateral. Many reputable firms and individuals make these loans to homeowners as well. However, an unscrupulous second-mortgage firm or broker—an agent who arranges a second mortgage for the borrower—can take advantage of an unsuspecting homeowner by providing a second mortgage with hidden costs beyond the legal interest charge. For instance, a widow in Ohio borrowed $3,000 for a five-year period and was charged $775 in interest *and* $2,075 for various costs, chief among them a $1,735 "placement fee" for the broker who arranged the mortgage.

The major targets for such operators are property owners burdened by heavy debts or large pending expenses. The homeowner is attracted by advertisements that promise the money he needs. The loan, say the ads, can be repaid in a specified time, most commonly three to ten years. The repayments appear small and the amount owed is not apparent unless *all* the payments are totaled. Inquiries about interest receive a truthful answer based on the rate permitted in that state. But a borrower should ask about *all* charges before he signs a contract.

Interest charges on all loans, it should be realized, are regulated by most states. Charges usually range from 6 to 8 percent *true* annual interest although in some states they are as high as 12 percent and in one, 30 percent. A lender who wants to exploit a homeowner will set an interest rate *within* the legal limit but will *add* a number of fees or assessments.

"Beyond the interest limitation on loans, there is no regulation in the great majority of states against those who would charge exorbitant, hidden fees or other costs in second-mortgage transactions," says Allan E. Bachman, executive vice-president of the National Better Business Bureau. "Unfortunately, this kind of activity is increasing. In most cases, the only protection against questionable companies or brokers is the individual's willingness and determination to investigate thoroughly before he signs any contract." Companies that engage in this kind of dealing frequently lead "precarious" existences, says the NBBB. They may operate in one area for a short time and then move a distance away.

Consumer finance authorities generally agree that a debt-ridden family should consider alternatives before seeking a second mortgage. "As a general rule of thumb, a second mortgage is not the most economical way for the average homeowner to borrow," says Dr. Saul B. Klaman, director of research for the National Association of Mutual Savings Banks. The homeowner should first consult officials of the institution holding the first mortgage. The major sources of first mortgages generally are barred by law from handling second mortgages. However, they may suggest refinancing the first mortgage, that is, arranging a new and larger mortgage to supply the cash needed. This can usually be done if the house is not already mortgaged to its limit and if the homeowner is considered a good credit risk. Although interest rates now are lower than five years ago, these rates usually rise over the years. Therefore, the refinanced mortgage probably would carry a higher rate than the original mortgage. Too, closing costs usually are assessed again.

A personal loan, though, may be better for the homeowner if he can qualify. If he cannot, the institution may refer him to a reliable source for a second mortgage.

Anyone seeking a second mortgage should use professional assistance—an attorney or an accountant. If this is not possible, a potential borrower should ask his local Better Business Bureau or bank for information about the lender he is considering.

Homes You Can Buy from the VA

House-hunting can be a problem, especially for young families unable to make a large down payment. One small source of homes for such families is not widely known. It involves homes repossessed by the Veterans Administration from owners who were unable to continue mortgage payments. These houses, originally sold only to veterans, are resold to anyone who has a good credit standing. Buyers get the same financial terms once available only to veterans.

Since the VA began guaranteeing home mortgages for veterans in 1944, more than 6.2 million loans have been guaranteed. Most of the borrowers are meeting their obligations. But about 150,000 homes have been repossessed. About 30,000 houses, a record number, were sold during the twelve-month period ending last June. Almost 17,000 homes are now on sale in every state except Hawaii and in the District of Columbia.

Most of the houses range in price from $8,000 to $20,000, although some have been sold for as little as $3,000 or as much as $35,000. These houses are generally in good condition, comparable to other houses in the area.

Prices and locations of homes available depend upon local real estate conditions. But the VA financing terms are usually better than obtainable from a commercial lending institution. These are major advantages:

Low down payment. This varies according to the policy of the regional VA office listing the home. Many areas require less than 1 percent down or, occasionally, no down payment at all. In other regions, purchasers may be asked to provide 10 percent as down payment. The average minimum down payment required for these homes is 2 percent of the purchase price.

This contrasts with the minimum 3 percent down payment required for homes valued up to $15,000 with mortgages insured by the Federal Housing Administration. For a $20,000 home, FHA-insured mortgages require a minimum 5 percent down payment. Down payments for homes financed conventionally are usually higher.

Low interest rate. Mortgages are available in most VA regions at an interest rate of 5¼ or 5½ percent. The rate is usually lower than rates charged by commercial lenders in the area. Repayment period can be as long as thirty years with prepayment privileges.

No closing costs. All legal and financial details are handled by the VA. The VA says it has clear title for every house it sells. As a result, most of the closing costs, which can be as high as $800 for a $20,000 home, are eliminated. In many cases, the VA will allow a buyer to rent the house until sale is completed.

Home inspection and utility repair. Every home is inspected by the VA before it is sold. Utilities, if damaged, are repaired. Structural repairs also are made.

Although the houses are sold and financed by the VA, all transactions are handled by local real estate agents. The houses are advertised in newspapers. In most cases, the homes are identified as VA repossessions. Information concerning these homes in your area can be obtained from the nearest VA office or from the Loan Guaranty Service, 263, Veterans Administration, Washington, D.C. 20420.

A Checklist for Apartment Hunters

In many areas, apartment hunters today are offered a variety of attractive inducements to rent in a particular building. For example, some buildings offer free occupancy for several months. Many have swimming pools or other recreational facilities. Some have private patios or balconies for individual apartments. These should be considered when renting an apartment but other basic factors should never be overlooked.

Location. Consider the availability of schools, playgrounds, parks, shopping areas and churches. Is the building removed from noise-producing sources such as industrial centers or major highways, yet close enough to the highways for easy access when required?

Building and grounds. The building's design and maintenance are key factors. The building and landscaping should be attractive. The grounds and lobby often are good indications of the management's attitude toward maintenance. Grounds should be neat and trim. If lobby furniture, carpeting and furnishing accessories are clean, if smoking receptacles are relatively empty and if the area generally is well kept, maintenance throughout the building usually is good. As you walk through the building, look for attempts to improve interior appearance. Has attention been paid to eye-pleasing decorating effects or was the decorating merely a minimal effort? Are corridors long, dark tunnels? Or has the builder lighted them sufficiently? Did the builder vary their monotonous length in some fashion, perhaps decoratively or with small vestibules at apartment doors? Was an attempt made to provide for the heavy traffic all corridors must bear, e.g., carpeting to soak up footfalls?

The apartment. Ask the rental agent for a floor plan or draw up one yourself to trace traffic flow and to place the major furniture items. Do you have to walk through the living room to get from the entrance to the kitchen? Will someone walking from a bedroom be seen from the living room? Are walls broken into short stretches or is there length for proper furniture arrangement?

Consider noise volume. Can bathroom plumbing be heard in the living room? Also, to check soundproofing, have a companion go into another room, close the door and talk normally. In the kitchen, go through motions of preparing a meal to determine whether space and layout are adequate. A closet should be fairly close to the entrance door. Other closets should be large enough for family needs. Doors and sliding panels should open easily and windows move freely. Look for evidence of good workmanship. Is the trim neat and are fixtures hung properly?

Services. Can you control heating or cooling to your satisfaction or must you depend on a building-wide setting? Many new buildings provide individual heating and cooling controls. Check services such as trash collection, janitorial work, garages or parking space and laundry facilities.

Lease. Be sure inducements offered are in the lease. Before you sign a lease, understand provisions such as payment of security and privileges of decorating and subleasing.

Coops and Condominiums

Owning a home without the responsibility of taking care of lawn, garden, outside painting and the like is an appealing idea to some families. It *can* be done and methods of such ownership are available in many parts of the country through *condominiums* and *cooperatives*. In both, the occupants—usually of an apartment building—have a form of ownership of their units and join together to pay for certain operational features. Cooperatives and condominiums range from low-income projects to luxury dwellings. They are being built around urban areas mainly because of the rising cost of land in suburban areas and the higher rents of apartments in cities.

Condominiums are relatively new to the United States, but they have been popular in Europe for many years. Basically, a condominium owner has *individual* title to the apartment or building unit he occupies and *common* ownership of the land, hallways, elevators, stairways, yards, basements, floors and foundations of the structure. He obtains a mortgage on his unit in the same way as one for a house is arranged. Size and duration of the mortgage are negotiated with a lending institution. Closing costs such as title search, broker, lawyer and mortgage fees are paid by the condominium buyer. With the other owners, he belongs to an association and makes regular payments for services and maintenance of the commonly held property. Each owner pays individual real estate taxes usually based on the size of his unit and makes his own payments on his mortgage.

In a cooperative, tenants hold shares in a corporation which owns and operates the property. The apartments are not individually owned and each cooperative shareholder has a lease agreement with the corporation. Members of a cooperative elect a board from among themselves to run the corporation. Maintenance costs, real estate taxes and mortgage payments are paid by the corporation. A member pays a carrying charge to the corporation based on the size of his unit.

A common advantage condominiums and cooperatives have

over rented homes is that mortgage interest and real estate taxes can be deducted from income taxes. Monthly charges are usually less than rents for comparable housing. Although charges may increase with rising maintenance costs, these increases have frequently been less than rent advances in the same area.

Condominiums and cooperatives are more alike than unlike, but they do have some differences which should be considered by a prospective buyer:

A condominium owner may usually sell, rent or alter his unit without consulting other owners. (In some cases, the condominium association has right of first refusal on a sale.) Cooperatives are usually more restrictive. A member may have to get approval from the cooperative corporation to rent or alter his apartment. Many cooperatives require that the unit be sold back to the corporation or a purchaser be approved.

Individually arranged condominium mortgages usually carry a higher interest rate than the single, overall mortgage on a cooperative.

Another point to consider when thinking about becoming a cooperative or condominium owner is what happens when other owners do not pay their share of the joint expenses. In a *new* cooperative or condominium, it is wise to find out how many units have been contracted for and what the provisions are to maintain the property until enough units are sold to produce income to cover operating costs. Only a few cooperatives have failed in recent years. But if a number of members do not pay their carrying charges, other tenants may have to make up the difference or the corporation may go bankrupt. In that case a cooperative member may lose his equity in the corporation, even if he had continued to pay his own carrying charges. A condominium owner also may face additional costs if other association members fail to pay maintenance charges. However, because of his individual ownership, he does not lose his equity as long as he pays his own costs.

Cooperatives and condominiums can be formed by tenants who join in buying the buildings they occupy. Such ownership is also available in new housing, including high-rise apartment houses, garden apartments, row houses or semiattached houses. The Federal Housing Administration insures mortgages for both condominiums and cooperatives which meet its requirements. Prices for cooperatives or condominiums range widely. In some federally aided cooperatives the down payment is from $120 to $325 and carrying charges are less than $100 a month. On the other hand privately sponsored cooperatives and condominiums range in price from $5,000 to $60,000. Some sell for over $100,000. In many state or federally aided cooperatives a family's income must be below a certain figure for eligibility and there may be limitations on the sale price. In a private cooperative or condominium, the units can be sold at the market price.

Possessions—How Many? How Soon?

You need more than a roof over your head to start housekeeping. Something to sleep on, eat on, sit on, is called for. Unhappily, the all-purpose bed-table-chair has yet to be designed although before long someone will doubtless invent it. Newlyweds can, however, profit from a trend toward convertible furniture —the coffee table that can be raised to serve as a dining table, the sofa that turns into a bed, the bed that can be converted into a table.

These are called "starter sets" and specifically designed for young, mobile couples who do not want to invest too heavily in furniture until they know how and where they will live. If your life is bound to be transient for a spell because of college, the army, a business training program, you should put off making major purchases. Otherwise, your precious furniture will run up bills in storage and you'll never have the pleasure of using your prized possessions. Some designers are working on disposable furniture, which can simply be chucked out when you want to move on. The heavy cardboard child's chair will soon have its grown-up playmate. However, until that day comes when furniture will be acquired and disposed of as freely as clothing you are going to be confronted with decisions common to every married couple since Adam and Eve. One supposes that they too were worried about outgrowing a particular stump or rock, wondered whether it was worth dragging into the cave or not.

You hate to commit yourself to a period, a color, wallpaper, rug before your taste is formed. After all, you have to live with that dining room furniture for years to come. If it does not wear well aesthetically you will be loath to let it go. After all, the chairs are still "perfectly good." Nothing is more discouragingly durable than good furniture. So you want to make sure you are buying not only the best quality but the most lasting as far as your personal taste and style goes.

Is there any sure-fire formula for furnishing a room? The answer is an unsatisfactory "no." But you can keep from making big mistakes if you go slow. You can develop a sense of what is appropriate to your way of life, but it takes time and training. Relax, you don't have to have everything pulled together right now, this minute. Suppose, in an excess of enthusiasm, you decide that everything is going to be contemporary, all oiled walnut and Danish design. Then, five years later you develop an intense craving for Early American. Had you acquired a few pieces of the contemporary, lived with them, evaluated them, your investment would not be so great. You could make the switch more easily, without a guilty feeling that you should have known better. It will be less expensive to change if you don't go all out for one style or another.

While you are deciding what you like, what goes with your house or apartment, you can educate yourself on decorating. Learn all you can about furniture, period pieces, accessories, fabrics, colors, scale, good design. Visit museums which have period rooms of antiques, go on house tours, see the major reconstructions like Williamsburg and Winterthur, scout the furniture sections of good stores, make notes on ideas which appeal to you, read the decorating magazines and clip pictures and advice you think you can use.

Of course you can't wait forever. You still have to have a bed, table, chairs. You can invest in the inexpensive starter sets and acquire the basic furniture without too heavy an outlay. Unpainted furniture is usually a good buy. You owe it to yourself to visit the furniture outlets for such charities as Goodwill, Salvation Army. Once you have developed an eye for bargains you'll find them there. Go to auctions and antique shops; piecing out your furniture wardrobe with amusing lamps, end tables, bibelots.

Learn some of the do-it-yourself skills. Discover the fun—and profit—in furniture refinishing. Strip a table of its old varnish and bring it back to life with a rubbing of linseed oil and turpentine. You will have a handsome piece at half the price you would pay for it new.

If you can reweb a couch, replace the caning in a chair, run up a slipcover, recover a headboard, stain a chest, make a needlepoint or crewel seat, you are going to be able to furnish your new home for very little real cash. With such modest investment at stake you can afford to experiment with color and scale. You can mix periods and patterns, use effects boldly. Naturally it takes some creative flair or just plain brass to bring it off. If you are the timid type you might well hire a decorator to show you the ropes. It would be the best investment you ever made. The home furnishings department in most stores usually provides a decorating consultant for customers. You can get free advice on decorating a room if you buy some material or a piece of furniture. Home furnishing magazines maintain a reader service to help their subscribers. Don't hesitate to ask for advice. It's the only way to learn.

Beg or borrow the necessities from your family. Ask permission to rummage through the basement or garage, looking for castoffs. Ingratiate yourself with Aunt Emily and maybe she will part with her Victoriana. She's tired of it, but on you it will look great.

Invest in one beautiful piece. Look until you find it. Whether it's a Queen Anne table, a Hudson River chair, a splendid hunt table, or just a magnificent clock it will give you courage and set the tone you want.

So much for the soul. What about the equipment you need to set up real, everyday housekeeping?

The sensible acquisition of kitchen gadgets can mean the difference between household drudgery and an optimistic approach to vital living. They can be borrowed, bought secondhand or acquired as wedding presents but no "homemaker" should be without the following:

A lightweight vacuum cleaner.

A blender. Get the heavy-duty kind with all the attachments. You can make hollandaise, mayonnaise, chop and grind with ease.

A mixer. The hand type will do as a starter.

A dishwasher. Start married life off right. This is the greatest invention since the wheel. Not only does it eliminate the after dinner conflicts over who will clean up, but you can store dirties in it all day, thereby keeping the kitchen reasonably neat.

A small freezer or refrigerator with freezer compartment. Admittedly this sounds extravagant but is it really? When you cook for two you will be swamped with leftovers or you will spend a fortune on small steaks and chops. If you can tuck the extra spaghetti sauce, half a cake, meat loaf, lamb curry, into the freezer for another meal, the savings add up. Also, you can have enormous menu variety with a minimum of preparation.

You can skip the clothes washer and dryer until the children come. There is a laundromat on almost every corner and for a quarter you can do the week's wash. Most apartment buildings have laundry facilities in the basement. If washing and ironing (most particularly men's shirts) fills you with dread, then you should earmark some household money for professional service. It's worth it. Otherwise you'll feel like Cinderella.

Getting Your Dollar's Worth

If you want to make a lifetime study of consumer-manship (and you could spend time less profitably) there is a mountain of advice to lean on. The U.S. Government publishes dozens of booklets on every consumer decision. Write the Superintendent of Documents for a list. *Consumer Reports* is a fine guide to comparative shopping.

We are all bargain hunters but do we really know what we're looking for? A bargain is not ten sheets for the price of eight which will lie unused in your linen closet. Beware of buying more than you need at the moment. Don't be tempted to invest in a case of tomato juice even if the price is low. It may take a year to drink it up, and you and your husband will be weary of the obligation long before the year is up.

Unless you have the spare cash for impulse buying you should try to estimate—before you leave the house—how much the shopping expedition is likely to cost.

If you want to make your buying power go far don't travel with more money in your pocket than you want to spend. For some reason we often feel an obligation to come home with empty pockets. Another tip—pay everything by check and you will not be tempted to turn jingling change into purchases. A bargain is something you *need*, found at a lower price. It must also work.

If you buy a secondhand article—car, piano, television, refrigerator—be sure it carries some kind of guarantee. Don't assume that because it runs today it will perform tomorrow. You will be wise to invest a small sum in getting it checked over by a reputable garage or repairman. If the owner objects to this, then take your business elsewhere. The seller doesn't have to guarantee that everything is perfect but he ought to level with you ("you may have to replace the clutch") so that the price can be adjusted.

Rent, don't buy, equipment you will use only once or twice a year like a floor sander, power saw, painter's spray gun. It also makes sense to rent before you buy so you can get the feel of different brands. Renting a car or trailer or boat can help you decide which one you want.

Ask questions when you buy, especially about something relatively complicated as far as the choices go. You have every right to an explanation of, say, why a hair mattress is better than foam rubber.

Think ahead to the use you will make of your new possessions.

When you buy linens for the first time you might as well save yourself future headaches. Get fitted sheets, by all means. You will save on laundry bills—they don't need ironing—and even a bed made by a tyro looks neat.

If you have a guest bed in a different size by all means buy colored sheets for it. If all the single sheets are blue and the double bed white, sorting the laundry will be a cinch.

If you can pay cash for your new possessions you'll be way ahead. Beware of high finance charges. Don't be so taken in by the glories of a furniture bargain, the gloss of a new car, the efficiencies of kitchen equipment that you throw caution to the winds and sign up for thirty-six "painless" payments. You will be thoroughly sick of your bargain by the time you've run through only twelve payments. And if you calculate the cost of interest you may discover that your bargain is double the price you signed up to pay. Ask the seller to give you a breakdown of the principal and interest when he tries to talk you into time payments. He may be reluctant to do so but it is the only way you can decide whether the item in question is worth going into hock or whether you can resist. You are better off resisting except for one case. Buy a new car or one that is only a year old if you must have a car. The high cost of repairing a used car may well offset the higher price of the new one.

Consumer Frauds

Each year the public is victimized by a wide variety of schemes and outright frauds. These range from a growing number of various home-improvement rackets to the sale of worthless—sometimes dangerous—medicines promoted as "cures" for a long list of serious chronic ailments. The annual cost to the public is untold, but it is undoubtedly in the hundreds of millions of dollars. Some schemes, it must be noted, operate within the law. Your only protection is knowing how they work and the precautions to take when you have questions about a product or service.

In consulting official consumer-protection agencies and authorities, investigators have repeatedly found how many schemes are based on certain types of misleading advertising and referral selling. The unethical advertiser offers a brand-name product or service at a very low price—one at which he does not intend to sell. He immediately tries to switch the customer attracted by the ad to a higher-priced, off-brand item. The customer may be told that the advertised merchandise has been sold out or is defective. The National Better Business Bureau says the products most often involved are meats for freezer food plans, sewing machines and appliances.

In referral selling, a salesman tells the buyer he can earn the cost of a product and more by giving him the names of friends, relatives or neighbors. He is promised a commission for each person who buys the product. Of course, he must also sign a contract to purchase the product himself. It is rare that he ever gets any commissions. The method has been used to sell all sorts of products, ranging from TV sets to carpeting.

The most frequently cited frauds involve these areas:

Home improvements. Each year thousands of homeowners are victimized by shoddy work done in kitchen or bathroom renovations, installation of aluminum siding or storm windows, chimney or roof repairs and pest control. Most firms in this field are reputable. However, the dishonest operators, says the NBBB, defraud the public of more than $500 million a year. Common complaints include overcharging, poor materials, incompetent work and failure to fulfill contract terms. To protect against these schemes never allow unrequested free inspections of furnaces, wiring and gas lines. A salesman may try to frighten you by warning of possible fires or leaking gas or fumes from what he claims is faulty equipment. If you are not familiar with a company, check with the local BBB or chamber of commerce *before* signing any contract.

Health quackery. Elderly persons in particular, looking desperately for cures to serious chronic illnesses, spend millions of dollars on worthless and often dangerous medicines or therapeutic devices. Aside from the sheer economic waste, such promotions have caused the deaths of seriously ill persons who delayed seeing physicians.

Repair services. Although the majority of home-appliance and auto repairmen are honest, some states report an increased number of unethical and dishonest practices in these fields. The complaints center on actual costs running substantially higher than estimates, charges for work not done and poor workmanship. If you are not familiar with a garage or other repair service, check with the local BBB or chamber of commerce on its reputation.

Charity rackets. The public loses millions of dollars a year contributing to outright fraudulent charities and to those in which only a few cents of every dollar collected go to charity. If you are not sure about the legitimacy of a group soliciting contributions, check with the local BBB.

Work-at-home schemes. There are many legitimate work-at-home opportunities. The U.S. Post Office Department warns, however, that women should be suspicious of work-at-home plans that demand money be sent immediately for information. Some are outright frauds. The advertiser may ask for a dollar or more and have no intention of sending anything in return.

Debt pooling. Homeowners should be aware of unlicensed lenders who promise easy solutions to financial problems. They may say that they can reduce monthly debt payments by 50 percent or more. Actually, the individual pays back twice—or even more—the amount borrowed. Families in financial trouble should seek advice from banks or agencies such as those affiliated with the Family Service Association of America.

Insurance. A handful of dishonest companies in this field defraud thousands of persons a year by offering worthless protection, says the Post Office Department. Insurance frauds occur most commonly in health care, especially for persons over sixty-five, and auto insurance. If you have any doubts about a company and the policies it offers, check with your state insurance department.

Key rules to follow in avoiding consumer frauds are:

Get guarantees in writing.

Never sign a blank contract or blank paper. Read and understand everything in the contract before signing it and keep a copy. If you have any doubts, consult a lawyer.

Clothing: Staying in Fashion on a Modest Budget

The challenge of keeping a family well dressed on a modest clothing budget can be one of the most difficult homemaking problems. But it *can* be done. The Good Housekeeping Fashion Department and clothing specialists at the U.S. Department of Agriculture believe these suggestions can be valuable in getting the most for your clothing dollar:

Make a wardrobe inventory. Instead of shopping on a sporadic, unorganized basis, list completely the clothing each family member has and decide what is needed. Estimate how much you can spend on each item. Tour stores—from budget to expensive departments—at the beginning of each season, if possible, to get an idea of which has the best values. Before you purchase anything, try to remember mistakes (e.g., buying items you never or rarely wear) you have made previously. Shop at stores that have a reputation for good quality and service but always *shop* and compare quality and price. You can get good buys by shopping out of season and at sales. However, be careful when considering sales of high-fashion clothing or millinery. Items at these sales may be those that soon will be out of style or those that nobody wanted. Sales usually provide good values on stockings, underwear, gloves and basic clothing that remain in good fashion year after year. In particular men should shop carefully at clothing sales, usually in January and July, when good-quality suits are frequently reduced 20 percent or more.

Determine your needs. Begin with basics—the clothing you expect to wear several seasons. Basics should be simple enough to wear almost anywhere and in colors that blend. USDA clothing specialists say that coordinating colors is an excellent way to save money. Buy colors that are complementary to the main colors in your wardrobe. For example, if you have brown in your wardrobe, choose beige, gray and orange.

Do not buy all major items the same year. Buy a suit one year and a coat the next. Choose a suit that can be worn in the spring and fall. One coat may be able to serve as a sport and a dress coat. (Example: a bright green, simple classic coat goes well with black, brown and blue accessories and can be worn in the day and evening.) An untrimmed cloth coat is a good choice because fur trim usually limits the use of accessories and may look "dated" before an untrimmed coat will.

Well-made clothing is a money-saver. Signs of good workmanship include seams wide enough to let out and finished to prevent fraying; garments cut with the grain of the goods; even machine stitching; hems, facing and buttons firmly attached; and patterns that match (check the back center seam, side seams and armhole seams for matching patterns).

Buy garments that fit correctly. Never buy anything without trying it on. Do not buy clothes for future fit. If you are dieting, do not buy clothing in the size you *expect* to become. Extensive alterations are costly if you guess wrong.

Small-size women can shop in junior departments for casual wear. They have sportswear that is basic enough for most ages and usually less expensive than clothing in comparable dress departments. If you have occasional use for a party dress, do not wait until just before you need it to shop for it. Be price conscious, in such clothing. Try to *anticipate* this and other dress needs so that you can shop for clothing carefully and be more likely to get something you like and will wear more often. Also remember a high-fashion garment may give you only one or two seasons wear.

You can get many variations from your basic clothing with carefully chosen accessories. Do not buy shoes to go with one particular coat or suit. Chances are they will not look right with other things. Simple blue, black and brown shoes should go well with most basic clothing. Plain silk dress shoes can be used for several outfits by changing ornaments on them.

Children's clothing. Do not buy too many clothes for children at one time because they outgrow clothing relatively quickly.

Look for sturdy workmanship and growth features such as expandable waistbands and deep hems and cuffs. Children's clothing takes a lot of rough wear, so select fabrics that clean easily. Polyester-cotton blends usually look well after frequent cleaning. Durable Press fabrics can be time- and money-savers. Children's clothing can be passed along from one child to another, but it is possible to freshen it up by adding something new like new buttons or ribbons.

Medical Expenses: Key Ways to Reduce Them

Families are spending more on medical care each year and these costs are expected to continue to rise for at least fifteen years. In recent years, costs for physicians, dentists, hospitals and health insurance have increased more rapidly than other expenses such as for food, clothing and transportation. And, additionally, patients use doctors and hospitals more than they ever did. The average expenditure for medical care per person in the U.S. rose from $104 in 1960 to $142 in 1965. Many people believe this reflects an increase in the quality of health care.

Although four out of five Americans have some form of health insurance, heavy medical expenses can put an enormous strain on a family's resources. However, medical costs can be cut—without lowering the quality of medical care—by proper planning and best use of medical services.

Your family physician is the key to lowering annual medical expenses. Any attempt to cut costs should begin with a frank discussion between you and him about his fees. He is also important in determining the extent of other medical bills you face because he decides on specialists to see, the length of any hospital stay and the prescription drugs you use. In addition:

If you go to a specialist, move or change doctors, ask your doctor to supply medical records, test results and X-rays to save duplication.

When sick, visit your doctor in his office, if possible. Home visits are more expensive and treatment can be more complete in his office.

Find out about available community medical services, such as free chest X-rays, mass vaccination programs or low-cost laboratory tests.

Have an annual physical examination. Many diseases detected in early stages can be treated more successfully and at substantially less cost.

Prevention of disease is also important. Children and adults should have recommended immunization shots. Regular visits, at least every six months, should be made to a dentist. Accident prevention also can reduce medical and dental costs. Homes should be kept in safe repair and hazardous conditions should be corrected. Guidance on home safety is available from local fire and safety organizations, the U.S. Public Health Service and the National Safety Council.

The cost of drugs can sometimes be reduced. When your doctor writes a prescription for a drug, he has the choice of either using its *generic* (or general) name or its trademark name. You can ask him to prescribe drugs generically. If he agrees, ask the pharmacist for the lowest-priced generic drug available. However, a physician may have good reason to use the trademark name and his decision should be accepted. Following a doctor's orders and using prescription drugs *as directed* are essential to speedy recovery. Prolonged illnesses are more costly.

Although a majority of Americans are covered by some form of health insurance, its proper purchase and use can lessen medical costs. Group health insurance offered to employees by companies costs less than individual policies. The terms of such policies should be studied so that full benefits can be applied for when needed. It may be that a group policy needs supplementing with, for example, major medical insurance, which covers long-term, serious illnesses. However, duplication of coverage or overlapping policies should be avoided to save on premium costs. Records should be kept of all medical expenses, not only to be able to apply for insurance benefits, but for possible use in taking medical deductions on income tax returns.

Even with insurance, not all hospital charges are always covered. If no hospital insurance is carried or in cases where benefit limits are reached, hospital costs can be cut in these ways:

Use a semiprivate or ward room unless your doctor advises otherwise.

Use private-duty nurses only when a physician orders them.

However, it may be less costly to have private nursing at home rather than stay in a hospital. A practical nurse or homemaker is even more economical.

Investigate nursing homes or hospital self-service arrangements for illnesses requiring long recuperation or less medical care.

Check if community health agencies, such as the Visiting Nurse Association, are available for part-time home care.

Food: How to Cut Costs but Maintain Quality

Saving money on food expenses does not have to mean serving less food or food of inferior quality. Meaningful economies are possible if you spend more time in meal planning and shopping. For many years the Good Housekeeping Foods and Cookery Department has regularly advised on how to trim food bills. It believes that the following have been among its most useful and helpful suggestions:

Before going shopping check newspaper ads closely for special sales. Prepare a day-by-day list of menus and then a shopping list.

Organize the list by the location of items in the store. You will save time and avoid buying unnecessary items. However, although you should generally stick to your shopping list, don't overlook unadvertised specials or possible thrifty substitutions for items on your list while in the store.

Plan to buy most groceries over weekends when there are more sales.

Check prices in neighborhood stores as well as supermarkets. Occasionally try to allow time for reading labels and comparing costs among brands.

Serve more of the foods that are in season. They usually cost less than out-of-season ones, which may have to be shipped into your area.

A larger can or package may be less expensive per unit than the same item in smaller quantities. But do not buy the large size unless it is a food you use regularly, and will not result in leftovers which are wasted. Small-size cans are a wise buy for two people. They eliminate leftovers and allow variety.

Canned meat can save money and waste because trimming and boning has already been done.

Here is a breakdown of the many different types of food available with helpful things to know about each variety.

Beef. You can save time and money by buying a meat cut that will serve your family for two or more meals. For instance, if you have freezer space, it pays to buy a whole rump of beef and divide it for a roast, casserole dishes, stews and hash.

Pork. Pork shoulder cuts usually cost less than the loin and leg cuts. End-cut pork loin roasts are just as tender and easy to roast as center loin roasts, but cost less. Choose a whole or half ham instead of the butt or shank end to get at the meaty center slices. Planning a meal around sausages is a good way to add interest at budget prices.

Lamb. Lamb (and beef or pork) liver gives you the same nutritional value as calf liver and costs less. Two grades of ground lamb are often available. The less expensive, from the breast or neck, has more fat. The leaner comes from shanks, chuck or shoulder.

Chicken. Chicken is a high-protein, low-calorie favorite that is versatile and inexpensive. You can save two to four pennies a pound by buying whole chickens and cutting them up yourself.

Fish. Certain fresh, frozen or canned fish (such as cod, ocean perch and haddock) is quick to cook and low in calories and cost. Frozen fish, such as fish sticks and breaded fillet, is generally less expensive than fresh fish. Canned tuna comes in several styles (chunk, solid, grated or flaked) which differ in price but not in food value. Therefore, consider how you are going to use it before you choose the type to buy.

Vegetables and fruits. Look for fruits and vegetables that are plentiful nationally or grown in season nearby. These are likely to be of good quality but lower in price than scarcer foods or ones that are out of season. Carrots, cabbage and onions are nutritious and always a food bargain. Watch for sales on frozen or canned fruits and vegetables which can be stored.

Bread and cereal. Some stores sell day-old bread, rolls and other bakery products at discount prices. These can be used immediately or stored in a freezer where they stay fresh for several weeks. Ready-to-serve cereals, packed in multipacks of small boxes, are convenient and provide variety, particularly for children. However, they may also cost more per serving than the same cereals in larger boxes. Packaged hot cereals that must be heated are generally less expensive than ready-to-serve ones. Too, sugar-coated, ready-to-serve cereals usually cost more than regular ready-to-serves.

Dairy. Substitute milk for cream on cereal. It is less expensive and has higher food value. In some cities you can save on milk bills by buying it at a store instead of having it delivered. The difference in cost may not be worthwhile, however, if it means extra auto trips to the store just to buy milk. Too, you may be able to get a discount by ordering more milk delivered at a time. Milk in two-quart or gallon containers is frequently lower priced than milk in quarts.

Nonfat dry milk is nearly half the cost of whole skim milk. Try using evaporated milk in recipes instead of more costly whole milk. Try substituting ice milk for ice cream—it is cheaper and has fewer calories per serving.

Cheese that is cut and wrapped in the store may cost less per pound than similar prepackaged cheeses. Cheese which is sliced, cubed or shredded for convenience may cost more per pound than blocks or wedges. Also, mild Cheddar cheese costs less than sharp Cheddar.

Convenience foods. Convenience foods are products such as cake mixes and prepared casseroles which have been prepared by the manufacturer and require little work to serve. Consider both your time and the quality of the finished product in deciding whether to buy or to make the dish yourself from basic ingredients. Remember that if a reasonable value were put on your time as a homemaker, a number of convenience foods cost less than home-made ones.

Obviously, any money-saving food measure that leaves your family dissatisfied with the meals you prepare really isn't a saving. Consequently, it may be necessary for you to familiarize yourself with the many ways that budget meals can be attractive and nutritious. Some ideas:

For supper, serve hot toasted sandwiches of canned roast-beef hash, adding a little catchup or chopped pickle.

Flank steak is all meat and a good buy. Quickly broil it, then thinly slice it on the diagonal. Add flavor with meat marinade.

Stews made with yesterday's roast or an inexpensive meat cut are flavorful as well as economical, and, in fact, taste better when prepared well in advance.

Frankfurters can be used in main dishes, casseroles, pizzas and hors d'oeuvres as well as on a bun.

Pork sausage links, sautéed with canned pineapple chunks or rings, make a delicious supper dish.

Blend bits of canned tuna with sour cream or mayonnaise for sandwiches, dips or salads.

When you are planning a casserole, pie, stew or soup, it is often more economical to buy a lower grade of canned vegetables or fruits. They are just as good in nutritional value but are less attractive.

Trim cabbage and lettuce sparingly. The dark outer leaves are rich in iron, calcium and vitamin A.

For an inexpensive sauce, heat cans of celery, chicken, Cheddar cheese, tomato or cream of vegetable soup with enough milk to make the soup of sauce consistency.

Try beginning meals with soup. It is inexpensive and nutritious.

Combine any cooked vegetable with rice for vegetable Jambalaya.

Buying a New Car

The kind of new car a family buys is a personal decision usually based on what an auto means to it. Many people are interested only in getting comfortable, dependable transportation at the lowest price. Others are willing to pay considerably more for an auto for a variety of reasons, including the desire for better styling, more performance ability, or simply that a more expensive car represents *status* to them. However, if your new-car buying decision must be based to a large degree on actual family needs and financial limitations, here are key points to consider:

Size. A family of four can get around comfortably in a *compact*. Among American-made cars, compacts are usually the least expensive to operate and maintain. The next size, the *intermediate* provides more interior and trunk room and usually a quieter, smoother ride. A *full-size* car with bench-type seats can accommodate six people. For large families, though, a station wagon may be the most suitable buy. Automobile experts at *Popular Mechanics* say the four-door sedan is probably the most practical body type for family use. It permits easier entry and, say those authorities, is less prone to rattles and squeaks. One drawback is that it generally brings less money on resale.

Engine. An eight-cylinder engine costs more, but has a higher resale value. Although it is more expensive to operate than a six-cylinder engine, it is preferred if most of your driving covers long distances on superhighway-type roads and if higher performance (more power, quicker acceleration, etc.) is desired. For around-town, mainly short-trip driving, the six-cylinder engine is recommended.

Transmission. Unless you have specific reasons for wanting a manual transmission (e.g., some authorities believe it's preferable if you regularly tow a trailer), an automatic transmission will probably be more satisfying. It costs more but provides much easier driving for most people and adds to the car's resale value.

Accessories. Buy only those you believe you need and will *use*. For example, a stereo tape player may be appealing, but will you and your family really use it after its novelty fades? Certain options, though, add to driving safety and pleasure. These include oversized tires and, if you do much driving on snow and ice, a limited slip differential that improves a car's traction.

How much to spend. Determine what you can make as a down payment. (Include the trade-in value of your old car.) Decide how long you want to take to repay the loan needed to complete the purchase. Estimate monthly payments for it, the needed auto insurance *and* car upkeep expenses. That total monthly figure should fit *comfortably* within your budget. If it doesn't, you may have to reconsider the kind of car to buy, possibly lengthen the term of the loan, or even delay buying a car.

Where to buy. Many people prefer to go to several dealers and get prices on the particular model they want. They then buy from the one who quotes the lowest price. Price, though, should not be the sole factor in deciding where to buy. If a dealer in your community has provided you with good servicing and promptly handled complaints (or if he has the reputation of doing so), you probably would be wise to continue doing business with him. In any case, if you plan to buy from a dealer whom you know little about, first check with the local Better Business Bureau (or chamber of commerce). It will tell you whether his past policies have created a number of buyer complaints.

When to buy. When new models are introduced, usually in

September and October, good savings can be realized by buying one of the unsold cars of the previous model year. The savings frequently depend on how many unsold new cars are left. (A dealer pays for the cars he gets from the factory and can't return unsold ones.) Also watch for manufacturers' sales contests when some dealers may give additional discounts.

How often to buy. If you view a car strictly as transportation, the most economical approach is probably to keep it until repairs become frequent and costly. (The key to long-term use of an auto is *regular* maintenance by a *qualified* mechanic.) If you prefer to get a new car every two or three years, be prepared for sizable depreciation losses on trade-ins. A car loses about half of its initial value during its first three years.

Financing. Auto loans are available from banks, credit unions and finance companies and through dealers. *Shop for financing carefully.* If such terms as discount interest and add-on interest are confusing, simply figure the cost of the loan in terms of dollars. Then add the cost of any life insurance provided on the loan. If auto insurance is offered as part of the financing package, be sure the lender tells you exactly what it includes. Then compare it with rates for the same insurance offered elsewhere. Don't be rushed into any final buying decision. Carefully shopping for the loan and insurance can save money, sometimes hundreds of dollars.

Finally, drive the car before accepting final delivery. Be sure you are satisfied. And understand the warranty on the car—just what is and what is not covered.

Good driving habits and attention to preventive maintenance can produce substantial savings in daily operation of your family car and reduce likelihood of major repair bills.

Maintenance. Follow car manufacturer's recommendations for servicing. The motor should be tuned and its ignition timing checked every 8,000 to 10,000 miles. Replace necessary parts. Have brake linings and fluid cylinders inspected if the brake pedal has too much play, sinks too low or the car does not stop properly. If the temperature gauge indicates boiling, stop immediately and have the radiator checked. Frequent extreme temperature rises indicate need for servicing.

Have fluid levels in the radiator and battery and oil level in the motor checked frequently. The Rubber Manufacturers Association recommends that tires be rotated every 5,000 miles according to a regular plan that includes the spare. Inspect tires regularly for sidewall blisters or bruises and for sharp materials that may be imbedded in the tread. Keep tires inflated to at least pressure recommended by the manufacturer. This improves mileage and tire life. Check the tires (when they are cold) for pressure regularly and before and during long trips. Wheels should be checked for alignment, loose play and balance at least once a year. If there is uneven tread wear in the front tires, get an alignment check. Have minor damage to the car body repaired as soon as possible to prevent rusting. Correct mechanical problems as they occur.

Driving habits. Cost of fuel for two comparable cars can vary by 50 percent, says the American Automobile Association. Do not idle a motor unnecessarily. In cold weather, drive off as soon as the motor is turning over properly. Drive slowly until the temperature gauge shows the motor has warmed. Avoid high-speed starts. Best mileage is obtained between 30 and 40 miles per hour.

Plan routes to forestall unnecessary stops. Watch developing traffic patterns to avoid small jams. Observe changing lights. You can often miss a red signal by dropping speed slightly a block or two away. Try various gasoline octanes to determine which is best for your car. Many cars, particularly compacts, run well on regular-grade gas. Use good-quality oil.

Insurance. Compare rates of several companies. Many offer discounts in most states to drivers with accident-free records, owners of compacts and drivers under twenty-one who have had accredited driver education training. Some companies also sell package coverage at a lower cost than policies with individually selected items.

Before Calling a Repairman, Check This List

Many house calls made by appliance repairmen are unnecessary. This is because the appliance owner does not know how to operate the unit or assumes, without investigating, that sudden failure of an appliance can only mean a breakdown. Any appliance can fail because of a number of minor, *easily* corrected causes. These routine checks before you call a serviceman sometimes can save you needless expense:

See if the appliance cord is properly plugged into the outlet. Try another appliance or lamp in the same outlet. If it does not work, the fault may be in the outlet, not the appliance. If you are using an extension cord, try another on which an appliance is working. (Be sure any extension cord is suited to the appliance it serves. For example, a lamp extension cord is a fire hazard if used with a broiler.) The trouble may be with the cord, not the appliance.

If other appliances or lights in the same room or adjacent rooms have gone out, a fuse may have blown or a circuit breaker may have been tripped. A circuit breaker is a device used instead of a fuse to break an electrical circuit when an overload occurs. Should fuses continue to blow out or the circuit breaker keep tripping, call an electrician. Do not insert a more powerful fuse or try to wedge the circuit breaker closed. Fire can result. Some appliances have their own circuit breakers. They usually resemble a small, protruding button. The manual will state where the circuit breaker is. If the appliance has one, push it in once and release.

On appliances that have several controls, make sure the proper ones are on fully. For example, an "on" button may not be completely depressed.

Refer to the operating and maintenance instructions in the owners manual which came with the appliance. Keep such manuals where you can find them quickly. For these large appliances, check the following points:

Refrigerator/freezer combination. If it has stopped, see whether the temperature-control dial is on and properly set. Should the unit be too warm, it may be that shelves are so crowded that air does not circulate or a temperature control may be set improperly. The cold control should be set for a lower temperature when a refrigerator is heavily loaded or opened frequently. Units that need manual defrosting should be defrosted before ice reaches one-quarter-inch thickness. Noisy models may have a loose grille or drain pan. (If your unit has condenser coils at the bottom, remove the grille and vacuum or brush dust from the coils according to the maker's directions.)

Range. Set the timer on "manual" operation, not "automatic," if the oven does not heat. Check the controls for proper setting. Press control buttons firmly in. Be sure any removable elements are firmly plugged in. Replace the range fuse should the range's appliance outlet stop or the control lights work intermittently or quit altogether. (Oven or range must be off.) The manual indicates where the fuse is if your range has one.

Automatic washer. If the unit has stopped, follow the manual's directions to make certain that the controls have been turned on properly. Some washers will not start if two cycles have been pushed. Are the water faucets, hot and cold, turned on? Are the water hoses kinked or the hose strainers clogged? Is the loading door open? Some washers have a safety mechanism that will stop the machine if it is open. An out-of-balance load or one that is too heavy can stop a machine. Some units have overload reset buttons which must then be pushed in to start the machine again. Too many suds or a twisted hose are frequent causes of improper draining. Vibration noise often is a result of poor load balance or a very heavy piece in the machine. Many common problems can be prevented by turning off water faucets between washings, emptying pockets and cleaning the lint trap after use.

Automatic dryer. In case of stoppage, check the controls for proper setting. The door should be closed tightly. Be sure the main valve and pilot light are fully on if the dryer is a gas unit. If the clothes take too long to dry or are wet at the end of the cycle, the lint trap may be clogged or the exhaust vent blocked. (The lint screen in most units should be cleaned after each use.) The timer may have to be set for a longer period. Clothing unusually wet or bulky or temperature colder than usual in the dryer room could delay drying.

Television. Do not attempt to repair a set. Television receivers operate with high-voltage electrical circuits. However, some minor checks can be made safely. Be sure the wall switch is on if it controls the plug. If the sound is normal and the picture gone, turn the brightness control on fully. If there is a picture but no sound, adjust the fine-tuning control with the volume control at maximum. Try other channels. Should only one channel be affected, allow the station time to announce technical difficulties. If sound is weak and distorted and if the picture is fogged with "snow," see whether the antenna is still facing in its original position with antenna wires intact. Be sure the antenna wires are connected to the set and that the bare ends are not touching each other.

Housekeeping Tips

The trouble with possessions is . . . you have to take care of them. The more you have the more complicated your household duties become. It behooves you then to decide straight off which matters more, the valance over the window which must be put up, slip-covered, and cleaned, or time to read a book. If you get a kick out of polishing and dusting, then you certainly won't mind the maintenance work. If, however, you were a girl who could never find her bedroom slippers because they had somehow slipped down under the blanket and the blanket belonged to a bed that hadn't been made in forty-eight hours, then "homemaking" is not going to be your strong suit. You can learn to do it with dispatch, however, and you had best get started learning all the tricks in the trade. You're going to need them.

There are two schools of thought on housecleaning. One group believes in a thorough scrubbing once a week or so. The other finds that a daily pickup works best. If you are the type who likes to make a mess and then clean it all up, you will probably go in for the big cleaning on weekends and be a slob the rest of the time. Let's hope your husband shares your point of view. If you can't stand mess, then you will be wiping surfaces from morning to night for fear the house "will get away from me." (P.S. It won't.)

Housekeeping (or homemaking if you like) is hard work. There's no getting around it. Even women who really like to clean ovens, wash windows, scrub the floor, wax the cabinets, polish silver, don't deny that this is real exercise. Comfort yourself with the knowledge that it is good for the figure as well as the house. And remember, too, that the immaculate housekeeper is not the saint she once was. We are more casual about cleaning and dusting. You can get away with more than your mother could. And if you're holding down a job as well nobody expects you to be perfect. All you need to do is put first things first and decide how much housecleaning you have to do and how little you can get away with.

Here are some tips from new brides who learned from experience. They may start you thinking in the right direction.

"Decide which room means most to you and keep that room immaculate. When I come home from work I like the living room to be presentable. The kitchen is usually a mess but if I can have a few minutes in the living room, then I pull myself together and do the rest of the place."

"When you live in a one-room apartment you simply have to keep the place picked up. I go around sorting magazines, emptying ashtrays, putting away glasses until my husband goes mad but it's the only way to keep ahead of it."

"This is a terrible admission but I do the dishes in the morning. After dinner I stack them in the sink so they can soak overnight. Maybe I like the illusion that some good fairy will do them. I do like to relax after dinner and feel taken care of. But by morning the job doesn't look so terrible."

"I do believe that you should have a place for everything and keep it there. It has been a battle with myself to remember to put the umbrella in the same place, stack the papers in a holder, keep the empty bottles under the sink."

"The main thing is to keep the surfaces clean and polished. If all the tables are bare except for essentials, the whole room looks better."

"Fresh flowers can make a room looked pulled together even if it could use a scrub from top to bottom."

"Don't hide things under beds, in the back of the closet, behind a bureau. Get rid of it or use it. Out-of-season things, like blankets and overcoats, bathing suits and skis, should be stored in one place. When you clutter up space under, behind and on top of things you'll never be able to clean properly. And, the room will feel like a warehouse."

"If it offends you, pick it up. Don't wait until you can do the job properly. You may never get around to it. Instead, tuck that sweater under your arm as you sail through the room. You're passing by anyway; might as well put it in the bureau where it belongs. Grab an empty glass when you're en route to the kitchen and you're that much ahead."

Schedules and Lists

There was a time when each household chore had its appointed day. You washed on Monday, ironed on Tuesday, cleaned on Wednesday, baked on Thursday, collapsed on Friday. You don't

have to follow a schedule unless it helps to have the jobs lined
up so you won't forget. Even if your husband suggests a schedule
you are under no obligation to set one up. After all, you are the
one who has to get the laundry done.

Men may be more schedule- and list-prone than women. At
any rate they are frequently overheard giving advice: "If you
would just write it down . . . do the same thing at the same
time . . ." Such efficiency expertise is well meant and it may
work for some, but a more relaxed kind of scheduling seems to
appeal to the young homemaker.

Of course, you are going to have to conform to some schedules
out of your control. If the milkman comes on Tuesday and Saturday, you had better get the bottles out in time for him. If you fail
to remember that the laundry picks up on Wednesday, your husband will go without a clean shirt that week.

The real moment of truth for the wife who detests schedules
and lists comes when she confronts the yards and yards of produce
laid out at the supermarket. A list may save the day. Organize it
according to known sources of supply. Put all the dairy products
in one section, meat in another, vegetables and fruits, etc. Don't
worry if you forget the list. One housewife said she always ended
up leaving it on the kitchen table but "by the time I made it out
I'd memorized it."

Try to shop when the traffic is light. Admittedly this isn't easy
when you work. You have to devote Saturday to stocking up. But
must you go to the supermarket at the rush hours when everybody else has the same idea? Try going at the noon hour when the
mothers are home feeding their young.

Buy the necessities first. Don't let yourself be seduced by the
"free" encyclopedia, the jumbo olives, the nylons which are cun-
ningly displayed along your route. Pick up the milk, butter, eggs,
meat, vegetables, fruit, cereal, bread, coffee, first. Then, and only
then, look at the change you have left and decide if you really
want or need the frosting on the cake. One young wife claims that
a small gadget called "a checker" has saved her untold dollars at
the market. You click off the prices of the items as you tuck them
into your shopping cart and are constantly aware of just how
much you have spent. This way you know how you are doing as
you move through the aisles and you can adjust your spending
accordingly.

If You Like to Cook

You may truly adore cooking. You can hardly wait to try out your "crepes suzette," "beef Strogonoff," "Shrimp Indienne" on a captive guest, i.e., your husband. You've made it for the family on weekends at home or in the apartment and the applause was heady stuff. Won't it be wonderful to be able to cook every day and dream up inspired recipes to tempt your husband out of his pizza-hamburger-milk shake routine? Will it? Maybe for the first month or so, but you'll soon get tired of putting on a production every day. And one of these days your husband will hurt your feelings by asking, "Can't we ever just have meat and potatoes."

So-called "gourmet cooking" is fine for weekend binges, company dinner, those low days when nothing is more soothing than meticulously skimming a *boeuf à la mode*. But there's something to be said for meat loaf, stuffed peppers, plain broiled chicken. You don't have to live up to such food; it is pure sustenance and leaves you free for other endeavors such as listening to records, going out for a drive. You can become satiated with *hollandaise, béarnaise* and *soubise*.

Also "classic French cuisine" is really an art. Each dish must be prepared the classic way. There are no shortcuts to this kind of perfection (no matter what the quick-and-easy experts tell you). If the recipe insists that butter must be added a bit at a time while the sauce simmers, you can be certain there is a reason for it. If you put all the butter in at once you won't achieve that smooth, glossy look the great chefs produce. This kind of cooking takes time, and if you love doing it then it is time well spent but if not then you are better off with a less exotic diet.

If you do love doing it by all means invest in Julia Child, Michael Field and Elizabeth David. Their books are easy to follow and give you the feel of doing the thing properly.

Advice to a Noncook

On the other side of the coin we have the wife who hates to cook and says so. Can she survive by opening cans, using frozen goodies, eating out when she can manage? Probably, but it's dangerous, not only for the family budget but for the family digestion and temper. Like it or not, most men marry women with the expectation that their appetites will be satisfied by a built-in cook.

Rather than depend wholly on convenience foods (you can certainly lean on them and cut down on expenses elsewhere), you would do well to build a small repertory of meals you can cook blindfolded. For example:

It takes no great skill to roast a piece of meat, be it ham, turkey, chicken, duck, lamb, pork or beef. Buy yourself a meat thermometer so you won't have to guess when it's done. Invest in a shallow roasting pan with a rack. (If it's Teflon-coated so much the better, then you won't hate the roast because you have to clean a sticky pan.) One tip, do your cleanup and make a pan gravy at the same time. When the roast is done, put it on a carving board, and pour the fat out of the pan. Then add some stock (gourmet parlance for consommé, bouillon, vegetable juice —all of which you can acquire by way of your canned goods shelf) or wine or water, scrape up the browned bits, boil the whole thing down using the top of the stove. Or you can put it back in the oven and forget it for ten minutes or so while it reduces. If your husband likes thick gravy, you can add a tablespoon of cornstarch mixed with a small amount of water to the pan juices, let it simmer for about ten minutes, stirring occasionally.

For the noncook a largish piece of roasted meat offers one great advantage; you can eat it for several more meals and do no more cooking. The disadvantage lies, of course, in the boredom of the same meat day after day. However, your husband could do worse than know there is a slab of beef in the icebox ready for him to nibble on when he's hungry. The problems of lunch boxes are neatly taken care of with a ham. You can make countless chef's salads for yourself with turkey and veal tidbits. And, if you master one or two leftover recipes, generally made with a cream sauce, you won't have to develop another cooking skill.

How about the rest of the meal? How can the noncook cope?

Fix salads instead of elaborate vegetables. You can always broil a tomato, bake a potato, heat a can of macaroni and cheese—can't you? For dessert there's ice cream, fruit, cheese and crackers. Garlic or herb bread is easily made with heat-and-serve ingredients. Nothing makes more of an impression.

Every cook should have at least one "glup" recipe on hand. Start with a pound of hamburger and glup it up with canned kidney beans, stewed tomatoes. Let it simmer for an hour or two. Glup is known by many other names, the most inspired being "Frugally." Not only does this kind of crazy mixed-up meal fill the stomach, it requires no accessories—only some bread to sop up the juice. Peg Bracken's *I Hate to Cook Book* offers endless variations on glup, all of them edible.

Certainly every first cook should master the basics. Learn to make a really good cup of coffee, even if it means experimenting with percolators, electric, drip, vacuum pots. The drip pot is the surefire one.

Be confident about salad dressing. The purists make the simplest kind—two parts oil to one part vinegar or lemon. Always use the best oil you can afford and the strongest vinegar.

Achieve a light hand with vegetables; don't overcook or boil the vitamins away in a bath of water.

Anybody can broil a chop but it's amazing how few people can cook a decent hamburger. Pan broiling is the answer. Salt a heavy pan, heat until a drop of water sizzles when dropped in. Then put in the hamburger patty. Turn after five minutes. It will be crusty brown, the juices sealed in. Keep the fire high. Cook another five minutes.

If you have time, learn to make at least one hot bread (from a mix if need be) and a good pie crust. Nothing impresses the male more than a plate of biscuits, rolls or buttery buns.

Questions Young Cooks Ask

Must I plan a week's menus ahead? I won't know what we'll feel like next Thursday.

Back in the days of "chicken-every-Sunday" the week had a predictable rhythm as far as menus went. It was leftovers on Monday. Lamb chops on Tuesday. Meat loaf on Wednesday, etc. But that was when somebody was around to do the short-order broiling and frying every night. When the chief cook must also look pretty, hold a job, please her husband with attentions and conversations, there is something to be said for cooking ahead. Besides, you can vary the menus from week to week. It doesn't have to be stew on Thursday. Surprise him with a steak and have baked beans on Saturday.

It does help to make a plan, albeit a rough one, for the week's menus. Said one young wife, "It's not the actual cooking that's hard but the figuring out what to have. If I don't plan it out very carefully I find that I am wasting the food money. I will go shopping in a very careless way—lots of potato chips, cakes, things like that. There won't be enough vegetables. When I go at it sensibly I have food left over."

You don't have to pin yourself down to veal on Thursday but you should have enough green vegetables, milk, fruit, cereal, bread, coffee and at least one roast and some hamburger in the house for the week. You can supplement this basic larder as the week wears on.

"What do you do with a husband who has very definite—and queer—tastes in food? Mine could live on chocolate milk and well-done beef."

Be glad he doesn't crave lobster and champagne. You can plan many a meal around stew, goulash, hamburger, chipped beef. You might even be able to ease him into lasagna and spaghetti, macaroni and manicotti by making a strong hamburger base for these one-dish meals.

"My husband wants to eat exactly the way he did at home. His mother was a terrific cook—made her own bread and cakes and pies. I can't bake and don't want to learn. Besides, I don't think all those desserts are good for us."

Taper him off his mother's desserts by making a speciality of salads after the meat course. You might even start the meal with soup or appetizer. Flatter his figure so he'll want to keep it. Once or twice a week you might splurge at the pastry shop but chances are he'll wince at the expense and claim "not as good as Mother makes." When he does don't bridle. Just agree and say sweetly, "Maybe we better do without and fill up when we go to her house for dinner."

"What about breakfast? That's the only meal that really throws me."

Breakfast is the real crisis meal. If you are used to a glass of juice and coffee (no matter what the dieticians tell you), you will be repelled by your husband's appetite for eggs and bacon first thing in the morning. Even if you know intellectually that he's bigger, needs the calories, the sight of that running yolk can be unsettling. He may agree happily to fix his own breakfast if you set everything out and clean up afterward. Or you can grin and bear it, switching from soft-boiled to scrambled eggs. One wife solved her problem by cooking her husband a small hamburger every morning and it smelled so delicious she broke down and had one too. Says she never felt so well.

The real problem with breakfast is the timing. You have to juggle more disparate elements with their own intricate timing than at any other meal. The toast and eggs have to be done at precisely the right moment, the coffee must be fresh and hot, the juice freshly squeezed. All this, at a time when you are at your worst as far as coordination goes.

Get everything out the night before—the coffepot, egg poacher, skillet. Put butter and eggs where you can see them in the front of the refrigerator. Squeeze the juice but cover it so vitamins won't escape. Defrost whatever is going to need it. Put a lazy Susan on the table, loaded with jams and jellies, so he can help himself. Then go back to bed.

Keeping Yourself and Your Husband Healthy

Women are more inclined to look after their health than are men. A man will think it's "sissy" to be concerned with diet, exercise, symptoms. A young man is inclined to believe that his rosy glow and excellent muscle tone will last forever. It won't unless he keeps in shape while young. A few years of sedentary office work and wild weekend exercising will do a lot to wear him down. If he snatches a coffee and doughnut breakfast, eats lunch with the gang at a spaghetti joint every day, his physical condition is bound to deteriorate. This is where wifely prevention is worth years of cure.

The first thing you can do as a wife is to see that breakfast is hot and ready for your husband. It should contain fruit or juice, milk and cereal, or bacon and eggs. Toast, pancakes, waffles are fine energy extras. Make sure there is a sizable portion of protein in the meal—milk, eggs, meat. He needs real food to do his best on the job. It won't hurt you or your diet to eat along with him.

Your portions may be smaller. You might elect to skip the toast and jelly but you need a good start on the day too.

If your husband takes his lunch to work (a fine way to make sure his diet is adequate and the food budget kept in trim) you can put it up while he eats breakfast. Again, be sure you pack in some protein. Leftover meat loaf, roasts, chicken give sandwiches the proper heft. Include some raw vegetables—carrots, celery, tomatoes. A thermos of soup will give him a real break midmorning or afternoon.

Many physicians are concerned about the rich diet Americans have come to enjoy. They worry, too, that young men will put on poundage that will plague them in middle age and affect their chances for a long and disease-free life.

You can do a lot to keep your husband (and incidentally yourself) healthy if you make sure your family diet is high in lean meats, oleomargarine, salad oils, fruits, vegetables, whole grains. Be reasonable in your consumption of meats and animal fats. If your husband shows a tendency to gain weight, then the family menus should be trimmed.

What You Can Do to Help Your Husband Avoid a Heart Attack

Most wives in the United States outlive their husbands. A key reason for this is that men, up to the age of fifty have a five-times higher death rate from heart attacks than women have. Consequently, many wives are concerned about whether they can help their husbands avoid a heart attack. For example, more than 10,000 women recently attended a program in Portland, Oregon, to hear noted Boston cardiologist Dr. Paul Dudley White speak on that subject. As more research data accumulate, a number of authorities are more convinced that a wife can play a vital role in maintaining her husband's health and reducing the likelihood of a heart attack. At the same time, the good nutrition and other health measures she helps him observe will be of substantial benefit to her entire family.

Coronary heart disease, the major cause of heart attacks, occurs more often in people who have a combination of two or more risk factors. These include a history of early heart disease in the family, high blood pressure, high fat levels in the blood, overweight, diabetes, lack of exercise, heavy cigarette smoking and constant emotional strain. Medical conditions cited can only be diagnosed by a physician, and it is essential to have an annual physical examination. To determine whether a person may be prone to a heart attack, factors are evaluated to show his *coronary profile*. Doctors do not predict heart attacks, but when some of these risk conditions are present the physician can recommend ways to correct them, possibly heading off a heart attack. Authorities consulted by editors believe that women are in a key position to help husbands in these important areas:

Diet. Most wives are proud of their cooking ability and try to feed their families well. To many doctors, an overabundance of well-cooked food can be an embarrassment of riches in two ways. First, they are concerned about the high fat content and the kind of fat in the food some families eat. Second, they warn against overweight, particularly the substantial gains that occur in many men from young adulthood to middle age.

The role that fats in a diet play in contributing to coronary heart disease is still not absolutely determined. Nevertheless, the American Heart Association says that most leading heart disease researchers now believe that the level of *cholesterol* in the blood is a major factor in heart disease. Cholesterol is a fatty substance which can be manufactured by the body or absorbed into the blood from food of animal sources. Many leading researchers believe that a high level of cholesterol in the blood is associated with the development of *atherosclerosis*, a thickening of the walls of arteries which is the underlying cause of most heart attacks. Cholesterol is particularly high in egg yolks, liver and other organ meats. It is also found in meats and animal fats, such as butterfats of cheese, whole milk, ice cream and other dairy products. The American diet contains an average of from 40 to 45 percent fat, much of it *saturated* fat from animal sources. Blood cholesterol increases with a high saturated-fat diet. Studies have shown there is a lower rate of heart attacks in countries where less saturated fat and more *polyunsaturated* fat from vegetable and fish oil are consumed. (The terms saturated and polyunsaturated refer to the chemical structure of the fatty acid in the fat molecule.) Other studies have shown that blood levels of cholesterol can be reduced in most people by substituting polyunsaturated for saturated fats.

The American Heart Association has advised the public to reduce fat consumption as a possible means of decreasing the risk of heart attacks by reducing the blood levels of cholesterol. It also recommends the "reasonable" substitution of vegetable oils and other polyunsaturated fats for saturated animal fats in the diet *under medical supervision*. Other medical groups have not recommended a change in diet for the general public. The Heart Disease Control Program of the U.S. Public Health Service recommends that individual diet changes should be made only under the guidance of the personal physician. The American Medical Association's Council on Nutrition said in 1962 that doctors might logically attempt to reduce high cholesterol levels in patients, but that it did not recommend a general change in the American diet. However, at the time this article went to press, the AMA was reviewing its previous stand.

Dr. Irvine H. Page, director of research at the Cleveland Clinic and chairman of the National Diet-Heart Study financed by the federal government, says he believes the relationship between high blood cholesterol and the incidence of atherosclerotic heart disease has been demonstrated repeatedly. If a person wants to substitute polyunsaturated fat for saturated fat in his diet, Dr. Page says there is no reason why he should not do so. But, he cautions, there is no *direct* evidence that this will *prevent* a heart attack. Dr. Jeremiah Stamler, director of the heart disease control program of the Chicago Board of Health, believes that an overwhelming part of the population risks having heart disease because of the present American diet.

If a doctor tells your husband to change his diet or to lose weight, meals can be prepared which are both attractive, appetizing and yet low in fats and calories. Dr. Fredrick J. Stare, chairman of the department of nutrition at the Harvard School of Public Health, says a man is not fat because his wife is a good cook, but because he overeats. Three-fourths of the people who lose five to ten pounds, Dr. Stare says, have a modest reduction in blood pressure and cholesterol.

Exercise. Dr. Paul Dudley White says regular exercise aids circulation, is a good antidote for fatigue and stress, and causes an apparent delay in the onset of *arteriosclerosis* (hardening of the arteries). Consistent exercise is reported to improve the network of blood vessels which nourish the heart muscle. Studies have also shown that exercise lowers cholesterol levels in some cases. Dr. Herman K. Hellerstein, assistant professor of medicine at Western Reserve University School of Medicine, says exercise should start gradually and work up to a point where full effort is expended. He suggests regular one-hour workouts three to five times a week when a man has become conditioned to exercise.

Before an exercise program begins, it is wise to have a medical checkup. A start on a program might be for a husband to walk—at least part way—to work. His wife can join him in weekend walks or exercise programs and thereby benefit herself.

Smoking. Studies have linked heart disease with cigarette smoking. The American Heart Association says the death rates from heart attacks in middle-aged men are from 50 to 150 percent higher among heavy (more than one pack a day) cigarette smokers than among those who do not smoke. Dr. Stare recommends that women urge their husbands to stop smoking, a recommendation emphatically endorsed by Dr. White.

Stress. The relationship between emotional stress and coronary heart disease has not been definitely established. However, some researchers believe that the hard-driving, competitive man who works and lives under deadline pressure has a greater proneness to an early heart attack. Doctors say excitement tends to raise blood pressure and make extra demands on the heart. Dr. J. Scott Butterworth, a former president of the AHA, says such men need relaxation away from work and a tranquil home. Dr. Stare says sleep is an important part of relaxation. If a husband needs eight or nine hours sleep a night, he says a wife should see that her husband gets them.

Physical Exams for Women

The key to maintaining good health is to detect and prevent illness *before* it becomes serious. The best way this can be done is by having regular physical examinations. This applies to both men and women. Periodically, every woman should have a *general physical examination* and a *gynecological examination.* And, before she marries, she should have a *premarital examination.* Some aspects of these exams are the same. In general they include these basic procedures:

General physical examination. This is a complete physical checkup that usually takes about an hour. How frequently you should have a complete physical depends on your age and general health. Many authorities suggest that women, aged eighteen to forty should have a thorough checkup at least every two years; after age 40, every year. The checkup includes a *medical history* to find out about your past illnesses and any conditions that may still be affecting your health. The doctor examines your heart and lungs with a stethoscope and by tapping the chest and back. He records your temperature, pulse, height, weight and blood pressure; looks closely at your eyes, ears, mouth, teeth, throat and nasal passages (and may do routine tests of vision and hearing); feels for enlargement of liver and spleen and for signs of hernia; and checks your reflexes. He may do a rectal and vaginal examination to detect tumors which can be early signs of cancer. Routine laboratory tests usually include an analysis of urine and blood and possibly a chest X-ray.

Gynecological examination. This is a careful examination of female reproductive organs, breasts, abdomen and other parts of the body. Many gynecologists say that such exams should be conducted annually and should start at about age eighteen. One of the most pressing reasons why women should have such examinations is to rule out—or detect early—the presence of such serious diseases as cancer, a major killer of women. The examination may also enable the physician to diagnose less serious but distressing conditions, including vaginal infections, hormone deficiencies or menstrual irregularities.

Unfortunately, most women do not have regular gynecological exams. Some women simply do not realize their importance, while others are excessively modest, embarrassed or afraid that the examination will be painful. Too, some mothers fear such an examination will change their daughters' virginal state. Dr. Jerome A. Dolan, associate professor of clinical obstetrics and gynecology at the New Jersey College of Medicine, says, "None of these fears is justified. A woman should not wait until she is married or pregnant or has some serious complaint before she visits a gynecologist. Such diseases as cancer can occur regardless of a woman's age, modesty or virginity."

The gynecological checkup may start with an examination of breasts. If the doctor discovers any unusual mass, lump or discharge, it is investigated further because of the possibility of breast cancer. This check generally is followed by an examination of the abdomen to detect any evidence of tenderness, hernia or unusual masses. Finally, the doctor conducts a thorough examination of reproductive organs. A nurse or doctor's assistant, who is always present during such an exam, helps the patient into the proper position for the internal examination. The legs are usually placed in holders or *stirrups* which support them comfortably. The doctor examines the external genital organs for any evidence of irritation, infection or tumor. He explores the wall of the vagina and checks the condition of the cervix, uterus, ovaries and Fallopian tubes to determine that they are normal.

One of the most important parts of the gynecological examination is the simple, painless, but vital Pap (for Papanicolaou) test. This test can detect the earliest stage of uterine cancer with almost complete accuracy. Most gynecologists use a cotton swab, wooden applicator or syringe which is simply touched to the cervix to obtain a small amount of surface material.

Symptoms and Treatment of the Most Common Female Disorders

Mrs. Mary Watson was troubled. For two months she had noticed irregular bleeding between her menstrual periods. Occasionally she was also bothered by an unusual kind of whitish vaginal discharge. As months passed and the symptoms continued to occur, Mary Watson grew increasingly anxious. But she delayed seeing her doctor. Finally, after about eight months, she went to see him.

At about the same time in another city, Mrs. Elizabeth Carson had noticed the same kinds of symptoms. She wasted no time in going to a doctor. His examination revealed that she had uterine cancer. Fortunately, the disease was in an early stage and was treated successfully.

Mrs. Watson, it turned out, did not have cancer. Her symptoms were caused by a common type of vaginal infection. The doctor was able to clear it up in a few months. She was fortunate. If her symptoms had been of cancer, her long delay in having them checked would have permitted the disease to reach a dangerously late stage. As it was, Mary Watson would have been spared months of needless anxiety and distress by consulting her doctor early.

As these two cases show, the same symptoms may be caused by very serious diseases or by those that are far less urgent. There are many such female diseases. Even the most serious ones of those discussed below are often curable if they are detected and treated *early*.

Cancer. This disease, an abnormal growth and spread of body cells, is the leading cause of death among women aged thirty to fifty-four. (Cancer may strike at any age, but in most cases it occurs with increasing frequency with advancing age.) The malignant process may start in any of various parts of the body. If the process is not checked, the patient may die. But many cancers *can* be controlled or cured if detected early enough. Treatment may involve surgery, X-rays, radioactive substances, chemicals or hormones. In women, the most common and most serious types of cancer include:

Breast cancer. This is the leading cause of cancer death in women today. This year there will be an estimated 64,000 new cases of breast cancer and the disease will cause some 27,000 deaths. Most cases of breast cancer occur in women past forty. Many cases could be prevented, says the American Cancer Society, if more women practiced monthly self-examination of breasts and went to a physician at the first signs of any unusual lump or thickening or any unusual nipple discharge. A physician can instruct a woman in the proper method of examining breasts—a procedure that can be a lifesaving health habit. Because the death rate from breast cancer remains high, much research is being done to develop techniques that can aid in early detection of the disease. One technique is *mammography*, the use of X-rays which can discover growths in the breast *before* they are apparent to the touch. Another is *thermography*, a method which uses infrared rays to help localize tumor sites by detecting areas of unusual heat. Widespread clinical studies of these techniques are being conducted or supported by the U.S. Public Health Service and the American Cancer Society. The primary treatment of breast cancer is surgery. An operation known as a *mastectomy* (removal of the breast) may save a woman's life by preventing or arresting the spread of the disease. In addition to surgery, a doctor may use radiation therapy (treatment by X-rays or other radiation).

Uterine cancer. The most encouraging progress in detecting and preventing cancer has occurred regarding cancer of the *cervix* or neck of the uterus. In the last thirty years, deaths from this disease—once the chief cause of cancer death in women—have declined almost 50 percent. This decrease is attributed in large part to increasing use of the Pap test, a simple and painless technique which can uncover precancerous conditions as much as several years before cancer symptoms appear. (Warning signals are unusual bleeding or discharge.) Although the incidence of cervical cancer has declined, it remains a serious form of cancer. Health authorities estimate that about 44,000 new cases of the disease will be diagnosed this year, and that some 14,000 women will die of it. These figures could be dramatically reduced if *every* woman would have a Pap test as part of her annual health checkup. Once detected, cervical cancer is treated by surgery or radiation therapy, or a combination of both. One form of treatment is *conization,* removal of a cone of tissue from the cervix. If the cancer is advanced, a *radical hysterectomy* (removal of the uterus and cervix) is required. Hysterectomy, also used for other uterine diseases, is unnecessarily feared by many women. Although it does end childbearing and menstruation, removal of the uterus alone (without removing the ovaries) does not hasten the menopause or eliminate production of feminizing sex hormones. It also does not interfere with marital relations.

Another serious form of uterine cancer, called *cancer of the endometrium,* affects the body of the uterus. This disease has become more common in the last twenty-five years and occurs most frequently in women who have passed the menopause. Postmenopausal bleeding is the most common symptom. Endometrial cancer is usually treated by a combination of radiation therapy and surgery.

Several other kinds of cancer peculiar to women include cancer of the ovaries and, much more rarely, of the Fallopian tubes and vagina. To help detect *any* kind of cancer early, every woman should be familiar with these warning signals:

Unusual bleeding or discharge.

A lump or thickening in the breast or elsewhere.

Change in bowel or bladder habits.

A sore that does not heal.

Indigestion or difficulty in swallowing.

Hoarseness or cough.

Change in a wart or mole.

If any of these symptoms lasts longer than two weeks, see a doctor.

Endometriosis. The *endometrium* is the mucous tissue which lines the uterus. Each month, starting just after menstruation, this tissue grows and after ovulation is prepared to receive and nourish a fertilized female egg cell. If the egg is not fertilized, the endometrium disintegrates and is discharged in menstruation. In a significant number of women, endometrial tissue is found growing *outside* the uterus or in the uterine muscle. It may be found at any of a dozen possible sites, including on the ovaries, cervix, abdominal wall or bladder. This abnormal and baffling disorder is *endometriosis.* Gynecologists believe it is occurring with increasing frequency. Most cases occur in women thirty to forty years of age, and the disease seems to be more common in women who marry late. Endometriosis may cause pelvic pain, infertility and abnormal uterine bleeding. Symptoms usually (but not always) include premenstrual pain and painful menstruation. Although a number of theories have been advanced, the cause or causes of endometriosis is not known with certainty. In some cases the disease may be relatively mild and require no treatment. In these cases, though, it is important for a women to have follow-up examinations once or twice a year to determine whether the disease has become more advanced. In more serious cases, endometriosis may be treated by surgery or use of hormones.

Vaginal infections. Women are susceptible to a number of vaginal infections that can cause acute discomfort, irritation, itching and often a malodorous vaginal discharge. Because of the personal nature of these diseases, they are rarely discussed in public. But since these disorders are so common and usually *can* be treated successfully, women should know about them and should promptly seek treatment. The most common vaginal infections include:

Trichomoniasis. Public health experts estimate that 75 to 90 percent of all women will have this disease at some time during their lives. Trichomoniasis is caused by a microscopic organism which can be easily identified by a doctor. The infection produces a typically white or yellow-brown thin discharge which is very irritating. Burning and itching of the vulva and vagina are usually associated with the infection. In the past, doctors have used various medications to control the symptoms of this disease. While these medications (creams, jellies and suppositories) may bring relief, they do not necessarily cure the disease. Now, though, a drug is available that has proved highly effective against trichomoniasis and may provide a cure in virtually all patients who use it. The drug, *metronidazole*, is usually taken orally and generally clears up trichomoniasis within two weeks. The husband, some authorities say, should also be treated to eliminate the possibility of cross-infection. No serious side effects have been reported from use of the drug.

Candidiasis. This is a vaginal infection (also called *moniliasis*) caused by a fungus, *Candida albicans*. The infection is usually characterized by intense itching and swelling. These symptoms may be accompanied by a secondary inflammation of the vulva and by a cheesy, whitish discharge. Some researchers have found that candidiasis is more likely to develop when a patient is treated with a broad-spectrum antibiotic drug. It may be that elimination of other organisms gives the fungus a chance to flourish in the vagina. Fortunately, candidiasis usually can be treated successfully by use of a local medication.

Cystitis. At one time or other many women develop an attack of cystitis, an inflammation of the bladder. It may occur in children as well as adults. Symptoms may include abdominal pain, painful or "burning" urination, frequent urination and the presence of blood and pus in the urine. In mild cases, symptoms may be vague and difficult to diagnose unless a urinalysis is done. They can include a sense of discomfort low in the abdomen or sensations of pressure or heaviness in the groin. Cystitis may be caused by bacterial infection or by improper drainage of the bladder. Bacteria can enter the tract from the bloodstream, the kidneys or other organs or through the *urethra*, the tube leading to the bladder from the outside. Or the urethra may be blocked by a constriction or congestion. Bladder stones or tumors may cause this kind of blockage and interfere with proper urination. This can cause infection.

Some cases of cystitis are *acute*; the attack is sudden and symptoms tend to be severe. However, such attacks usually subside within a few days and the infection can be controlled by medications, such as sulfa drugs. Other cases of cystitis are *chronic*. Symptoms may be less severe but the infection usually lasts longer and eventually may have serious complications. For example, the kidneys may become involved, leading a woman to develop high blood pressure. Thus, symptoms of chronic cystitis should never be ignored. The treatment a physician prescribes depends on the severity and cause of the disease. Drugs, special diets or surgery may be required.

Tumors of ovary and uterus. A tumor is an abnormal or unusual growth of cells. Many different kinds of tumors may develop in the ovary or uterus, which are the two main reproductive organs of women. Although some tumors are *malignant* (caused by some form of cancer), the vast majority occurring in the uterus and ovary are *benign*, or noncancerous, and may not even cause distress or require surgery. However, it must be stressed that even benign tumors need to be watched carefully, since they may grow large and cause pressure or infection in the abdomen or malfunction of other organs. Some tumors cause pain or unusual menstrual bleeding. Many, though, present no symptoms and are only detected in a physical examination of the pelvic area. These are the most common kinds of female tumors:

Ovarian tumors. Many of these are *cysts*, capsule-like structures containing fluid or other material. In women under forty, ovarian cysts usually are not malignant, but in some cases they may become unusually large. Such cysts have been known to grow to the size of a basketball or even larger. Most gynecologists believe that any persistent ovarian cyst larger than a lime should be removed. It should be understood that removal of a cyst does not always mean that the ovary also must be removed. Gynecologists sometimes can perform a *cystectomy*, which removes the cyst and leaves the ovary or part of it to function normally.

Uterine tumors. The most common type of tumor of the uterus is called a *fibroid*. About four out of ten women eventually develop fibroid tumors. They are rarely malignant and often do not require surgical removal. Again, if surgery is required, a fibroid tumor sometimes can be removed without loss of the uterus. The operation to remove only the fibroid tumor is called a *myomectomy* and is generally done for younger women who still want to have children. In many cases, though, particularly in older women, removal of the uterus is required.

Polyps. These are small tumors on the inner lining of the uterus or cervix. They are usually not malignant, but can cause bleeding. Polyps can be removed by an operation commonly called a "D&C," or *dilatation and curettage.* The doctor scrapes the endometrial or cervical lining without damage to the uterus.

Gynecological backache. Backache is one of the most common complaints of women treated by gynecologists. This syptom has many possible causes. It is particularly common during pregnancy, before menstruation and after childbirth. In some cases the backache is indeed caused by a gynecologic disease or disorder, such as endometriosis or tumors. More frequently it is caused by poor posture, anxiety or tension, or by an extra workload, such as frequently bending over a crib and lifting the baby. Backaches during pregnancy can often be helped by use of a proper corset and by posture exercises. Since a backache *can* be caused by a serious condition, doctors recommend a pelvic examination to rule out the possibility of gynecologic disease.

A Guide to Using Medications Safely

Almost every woman is likely to use drugs of some kind, ranging from common aspirin to antibiotics or birth control pills. The use of drugs is so widespread in modern medical treatment that many people have adopted almost a casual attitude about them. This can be dangerous. Virtually all drugs, including those available without a prescription, can be toxic *if misused.* To find out what is a sensible attitude for women regarding use of drugs, editors consulted one of the nation's most noted authorities on drugs, Dr. Walter Modell, associate professor of pharmacology at the New York Hospital-Cornell Medical Center.

It needs to be emphasized, says Dr. Modell, that almost all drugs have more than one kind of effect on the body. One type of effect may be highly beneficial for treating a specific ailment. But other effects—*side effects*—of the same drug may range from mildly distressing to severe or even life-threatening. This is why so many potent drugs may be used only under a doctor's careful supervision and why directions for use should be followed precisely. Even nonprescription drugs may be seriously harmful to persons with certain medical conditions. For example, aspirin and other common pain-relievers which are often useful and have relatively few serious side effects may cause dangerous intestinal bleeding in persons with ulcers. Likewise, in persons with kidney, liver and heart disease, drugs may have serious effects that would not occur in healthy persons.

Pregnant women must be particularly careful about use of drugs. The need for such caution was demonstrated tragically several years ago, when a supposedly safe and effective European sleeping pill, *thalidomide*, produced terrible deformities in babies. It is also known that in some periods during pregnancy certain hormones are not desirable for some women. On the other hand, they may be needed by others. Thus, drugs for pregnant women must be prescribed by a physician on the basis of his detailed knowledge of the individual patient. *All* women should realize that oral contraceptive pills should not be used by women with certain medical conditions. In general, says Dr. Modell, the fewer drugs a pregnant woman takes, the better.

Many drugs deteriorate with the passage of time, sometimes within a few months. Although a drug may simply lose its potency and become ineffective, some drugs become *more* toxic when they deteriorate. Every person who buys a prescription drug, says Dr. Modell, should ask the pharmacist to indicate its *expiration date* on the label. Prescription drugs left over from a previous illness should be discarded if an expiration date is not indicated. In addition, Dr. Modell suggests:

Never take a drug prescribed for someone else without first consulting your physician. What is good for your friend may be the very worst thing for you.

Do not ask your doctor to prescribe a tranquilizer, hormone, antibiotic or any other drug you may have read about. *He* is the one best qualified to decide which drugs are most likely to be of benefit to you.

Exercise That's Fun

Exercise is as important as good diet for health. But who has time for it? You may have to make time for it. The weekend touch football game is apt to be scrubbed in favor of homeowner chores. The man who worked out in the gym every afternoon or who made it a point to hike home in the evening may decide to skip it after marriage. He wants to get home to his bride. You may have to meet him halfway to make certain he gets the exercise he needs.

One bride always walks to the bus stop to join her husband for his homecoming half a mile hike. She gets the benefit of the jaunt down and back but he walks down by himself in the morning, so they are even.

Another couple have become passionate cyclists. They are both students and use their bikes instead of a car to get around the campus. On weekends they pack a picnic lunch and cycle out of town to historic or scenic points of interest.

Daily exercise of some sort, even if it is only walking to the store instead of driving the car, keeps you in tone. Some people find it easiest to run through fifteen minutes of calisthenics every morning to keep in trim. The Royal Canadian Air Force Exercise Plans for Physical Fitness are designed for both His and Her needs and capabilities.

Young couples generally share a common interest in one or more sports—surfing, swimming, tennis, skiing, golf, riding. By all means pursue your favorite after marriage. Make time for it in your budget. An investment in good health will pay lasting dividends.

Fighting Fatigue

The usual picture of the fatigued housewife is one of mother beset by four children, all preschool. The young married who has no children can match her in sheer exhaustion, particularly if she is a working wife. Adding to the fatigue is a sneaking suspicion that this is all wrong. Shouldn't she be able to sail through a day at the office, whisk up the apartment, cook a gourmet dinner for her husband, entertain on weekends? After all, she doesn't have four preschool kiddies.

Part of her fatigue may well come from the sense that she should be able to do all she's doing. A good part of the load will lift once she can see that she really is attempting to do quite a lot. And if she insists upon perfection she is only burdening herself still further. Nobody, no matter how energetic, can run a house, hold down a job and cook to perfection. Maybe it's possible after you've been at it for twenty years or more but not right off the bat.

Try to eliminate the things you don't like to do, the expendables. If you hate cleaning silver put your wedding presents away and use the stainless steel. If you really aren't up to do-it-yourself and home maintenance then spend a little more for housing and live in an up-to-date apartment.

Know your limitations and take them into account. "I think Wednesday is the low point of the week," says a working wife. "I just don't schedule anything for Wednesday. The rest of the week I can manage a household quite easily. On Monday I sort the laundry so it can be picked up next day. Somehow I always seem to clean out the icebox on Friday, getting ready for the week-end load of groceries, I guess. But on Wednesday I couldn't put myself into anything domestic. Sometimes I feel like it and then, okay, I do it but if I'm obligated I would dread the whole week."

Indulge yourself on purpose. One young bride discovered the perfect way to slip out of her working girl life and into the role of pampered wife when she bought a bottle of bath oil. "When I come home after work I head right for that tub. I soak for about half an hour, using a lot of bath oil. Then I get out feeling relaxed and quite able to get dinner going without any sense of pressure. If I had to plunge right into the kitchen department without this break I think I'd crack up."

Another young wife says that she and her husband make it a point to sit down together for a drink as soon as they get home. "We talk about what's happened and we unwind. Maybe it's not even a drink, just a cup of coffee or a Coke. The important thing is to shift from work into home life. If I felt I had to get right to the next job without a break I would feel terribly put upon."

Make your free time count for fun but try to avoid that morning-after feeling. One couple claim they made a significant decision early in their marriage. "We used to go out on Friday night because we kept to our schedule all week. We were really ready for a night out then. But we found out that if we did blow ourselves on Friday we were all done in Saturday. That's the day when we have to do the week's shopping, clean the house because we both work. Now we go out on Saturday night and because we

feel fresh Saturday morning we can get all the chores done and
really enjoy the evening."

Pamper each other. "I get breakfast in bed on Sunday morning,"
says a young wife, "but after I've eaten it I get up and get his
breakfast."

Entertaining

One standard complaint of young marrieds (after the first
bloom of being together in private has worn off) is that "we
never have any fun any more." By "fun" they mean the care-
free good times of the dating period. The ski weekends, beach
parties, dancing and folksinging. You don't have to cut out the
fun once you're married but inevitably your perspective changes.
It isn't as much fun as it used to be just to kick around. You
wonder why.

One reason has to do with motives. Before you were married
your goal was to get married. Free time was taken up with the
chase. Although you may love the beach life it had an extra
dimension as the scene where you could meet someone important. Now that you've met and married that someone the beach
is just a beach once more.

Now that you are on your way as a couple you want more adult
fun. The trouble is, that costs money. You'd like to join a club,
say, but can't afford it yet. You are interested in the theater, concerts, travel, but the cost is high. Even bowling is a high-ticket
game when you're paying for two instead of one.

Clearly you will have to find a low-cost, pleasurable way of
spending your free time. You'll want to get out of the house once
in a while. Weekends can be a drag if nothing is planned. You
need to make new friends and cultivate old ones. Most important,
you'll be establishing now the leisure pattern which will see you
through the years when children are going to take up most of your
free time. Make the most of those golden hours. They will be
gone soon enough.

Keep up with your favorite sport and find one you can both
enjoy. Public tennis courts, pools, golf courses offer a chance to
play at low cost.

Use your job as a springboard to leisure activity. Most businesses encourage employees to form sports teams, discussion groups, travel deals. If yours doesn't have such a setup, get one started.

Volunteer for community action. Hospitals, youth groups, social agencies, good works of all kinds, need bright, able volunteers. You won't get paid but you'll make new friends, feel alive and connected to the real world.

Join a church. Most congregations go all out to attract young members. They will invite you to special young-marrieds discussions and service meetings.

Become a politico. Who knows you may end up running for office. Meantime there's no better way to get to know the powers that be.

Take a course. There is no reason why education should stop when you get a degree. If both of you take the same course you may find it wholly stimulating to carry on discussion at home, do your reading together.

Visit the museums. Every city has one. You can develop taste for fine art on your own by just looking as well as attending the free lectures most museums offer. Museums of science and industry, historic reconstructions, are equally fascinating.

Become an expert. On local history, antiques, folk music, fine guns, herbs, old prints, whatever strikes your fancy. Collecting—information or tangible evidence—can be a lifetime pursuit.

Use your apartment or house as the center for fun. You don't have to go out to have a good time. Home entertaining is an economical way to see people and enjoy yourself in the bargain. Bargain it is too, once you get the hang of it.

The Hang of Being a Hostess

Some girls discover, with just a twinge of guilt, that they really don't like entertaining after marriage. They may have looked forward to showing off the new apartment, proving that they could cook and serve a dinner for eight, but soon the novelty wears off. One young bride explains why.

"When the guests have more than you do they look down on your furniture and housekeeping and when they have less they are too impressed. We never seem to be able to entertain couples who are on our wave length and it just isn't much fun."

One could observe that this bride misses the whole point of entertaining. It is not (or shouldn't be at any rate) to impress friends or neighbors but to satisfy the basic need for companionship. Moreover, her reasons sound unconvincing. More likely, she resents the extra work entertaining involves. Probably she looks back with longing to the time when pizza and a can of beer constituted "a party." Once married she feels she has to live up to the entertaining standards set by her mother at home. This is only one of several misconceptions which hamper the efforts of young hostesses.

"I don't really know the ropes," said one. "Which forks to use, how to introduce people, the whole business of RSVP." Well, you can learn easily enough. Invest in a good etiquette book like Amy Vanderbilt's and you'll find answers to every conceivable question. Practice does make perfect and if you delay taking your place in the social swim you'll be left out by the time you are thirty. Come on in. Just relax and you have it made.

"I don't like to be tied down," complains another wife when the subject of entertaining comes up. "Maybe I won't feel like having four for dinner next Saturday but I have to ask them now just in case I do feel like it. Before I was married I could invite people on the spur of the moment." You can still do that. There's no law that says your entertaining can't be impromptu if you like it that way. Maybe you'll be happy running a salon where conversation and cheap wine are the main attraction.

The easy, relaxed hostess is the one who does what comes naturally. If she thoroughly detests outdoor cooking she doesn't go near the barbecue. Instead, she becomes known for her French cuisine and handsome table settings.

She uses her mother's recipes if she likes them, feeling that she might as well take advantage of a good thing. If she likes regional food—Boston beans, Texas stew, West Coast salads—she offers them proudly even though she may be living a thousand miles away from their origin. Her guests are happy enough to sample a new and, to them, exotic menu.

She asks for help when she needs it. If she feels she really can't cope with thirty people for cocktails she earmarks part of the food money for maid service. Better that she should be free to mingle with the guests.

She is a good provider, having learned to serve sour-cream-onion-soup dip with a lavish hand rather than parcel out the caviar.

She doesn't think of parties in terms of a "payback." She asks the people she likes and if they've had her she's happy to reciprocate. However, she wouldn't have anybody over she doesn't really like even if she does "owe them."

She believes that well-loved family fare is good enough for guests. It doesn't have to be steak; that great meat loaf is appreciated fully as much if served with love and confidence.

She uses her wedding china and silver instead of storing it against the day when she will really throw a party. If she doesn't have all the equipment she needs she pieces out with what she does have and doesn't worry that her table looks a bit informal.

She doesn't apologize for simplicity. Some hostesses, unwittingly, make their guests feel unwanted because they protest too much. "I haven't done a thing about dinner," they giggle nervously at the front door. Who can blame a guest for wishing she had gone to the nearest hamburger stand? By the time dinner is served the damage has been done; they expect the worst.

She practices on family, not guests, when experimenting with a new dish. Then, when her fabulous mocha mousse finally does go public, she is sure it will be a success.

One triumph is enough for a meal. She doesn't fall into the trap of grande cuisine. Not for her the Beef Wellington followed by braised endive and chocolate soufflé. If she manages to pull off an "important" dish she is content to let frozen peas and fruit compote carry the rest of the meal.

If she's not sure of a dish she doesn't hedge her bets by buying a tremendous wine or an expensive cheese. She takes a calculated risk that it will work out. If it doesn't at least she hasn't ruined the family budget.

Never complain, never explain, is her motto. If she forgot the chives or rolls or shrimp sauce she carries it off with aplomb. Many a hostess makes guests feel it was all their fault for coming; she wouldn't have forgotten the chocolate sauce had they not been there.

Before the party she makes her battle plan. But part of the plan involves her own relaxation. If she has to figure out a schedule forty-eight hours in advance—at 3 P.M. do the radish roses; at four whip the cream, she will have battle fatigue by the time the guests arrive. So, sensibly, she does everything she can do ahead of time—makes the casserole, washes the lettuce, puts the wine on ice, fixes dessert—then she looks out for herself. She takes a nap, then a long, perfumed bath and gets into her prettiest dress.

She knows that the whole point of a party is the people. Not the food, the flowers, the service, the music, dancing or even the cocktails. The point is to be with people, enjoy them, make them feel good. And so she never, never falls into the absentee hostess habit. Some young wives disappear into the kitchen as soon as the guests come, either because they are nervous about the food or because they don't believe the company comes to see them. They become cook-maid-bottlewasher-barkeep instead of a charming hostess. The anxious guest concludes that (a) he isn't worth being with or (b) there's something dreadfully wrong in the kitchen.

When she's with her guests she gives them her full attention. The cook who keeps one ear cocked on the kitchen, waiting for the dessert to bomb out, is bound to miss the fun.

The happy hostess is always the one who has the best time at her own party.

VIII

CAN COLLEGE AND MARRIAGE MIX?

GI Joe, who went on to become your father, made it possible for you to combine college and marriage. After World War II thousands of veterans took advantage of the GI Bill to finish their education. Financed by a grateful government, encouraged by college administrators to make up for time lost in the service, they were, often enough, accompanied back to the campus by the wife and kids. Colleges were obliged to improvise young-married housing units to accommodate the families which descended on them. Quonset huts hastily converted to domesticity dotted the campus. Inside, the student-veteran managed to plow through his accelerated courses, only momentarily distracted by diapers and formula-making. He was older than his classmates, anxious to catch up and move out in the great world where business was eager for his services (once he captured that degree). He was in a hurry and short of cash. His family responsibilities were shared by his wife but she, too, was eager to be done with campus life and move to the suburbs.

In spite of the odds against him he did well enough to make cynics think twice about the merits of combining college and marriage. The next great wave of student-veterans which came in the 1950's after the Korean War cinched the argument. Yes, college and marriage can mix, decided the academic world. Whereupon colleges began to build housing for married couples, help them with grants and loans, provide part-time jobs for both husbands and wives. Who knows how influential this supportive treatment has been in accelerating the number of college marriages. "Do we house them because we have them or do we have them because we house them?" asks Kate Hevner Mueller of the University of Indiana.

Although many college marriages have rough going because of the financial pressures, academic obligations and basic adjustments to marriage, marriage as subsidized by the colleges is something of a bargain.

Mrs. Mueller points out, "Any coeducational campus enjoys high priority as a marriage market and the inexpensive housing can raise a simmering romance to the boiling point. On a state campus where the cost of an average double room in a residence hall is $530 for the year ($265 for each) the cost of a married couple in a one-room efficiency apartment is $596. This, of course, is a somewhat larger space and for the additional $65 this couple gets a stove, refrigerator, private bathroom, built-in cupboards, closets, a table, but no counseling or supervision and no cleaning service or linens."

At the University of Illinois married students pay $40 to $60 a month for "barracks" accommodations. However, the University is building new quarters for married students and here the rent will range from $60 to $105 a month. At Illinois only 18 percent of the married students live in University-provided housing ($85 a month is the average rental for an off-campus three-room apartment). But the University is rapidly providing more rental units to meet the need. President David Henry expresses the protective attitude of the colleges toward married students when he says, "We feel we have an obligation to be sure that students can get good housing, and, to the extent to which it is not available, we feel obliged to build it."

Married students tend to be found in quantity in the large state universities which provide special services for them or in city colleges where they can easily find outside employment, a cheap apartment and a social life which is not dependent upon undergraduate activities. The small, sequestered colleges and the Ivy League group have been slow to recognize the needs of married students or to cater to them. However, even colleges which were sternly opposed to married students a decade ago have begun to provide housing for married seniors and graduate students.

At Princeton, for example, the University has built a "Barracks" with more than two hundred units to house married students.

These small apartments consist of two bedrooms, a living room, small kitchen and shower bathroom. A student wife describes the decor as cheerful. She says the apartments "are furnished with second-hand furniture, books, books, books, record players and some of the handsome reproductions of modern art which one can purchase for a modest sum at museums."

Princeton also offers wives of students an opportunity to help put their husbands through by working for the college administration, Princeton University Press and the Educational Testing Service.

The facilities for married students at Princeton are modest indeed compared to those provided by the huge state universities where some 20 percent of the student body is married. On a campus of, say, twelve thousand students there are one thousand married undergraduate students and one thousand graduate students as well as more than one thousand children. Many of these students are women working for their degrees (advanced or otherwise). When married women returned to college in the 1960's to get the degree they abandoned some twenty years earlier, the colleges began to appreciate the urgency of preparing undergraduate married women for their ultimate employment. Girls were urged to keep on with their studies in spite of marriage. Rather than force the married student off campus the new spirit is to encourage him (or her) to stay with it, especially if the college stands to keep an able mind. Colleges are harder to get into and any student who has made the grade ought to finish out. He will be the loser if he doesn't and so, of course, will the college which has invested time and teaching in him.

Parents, too, are willing to subsidize an education for either, or both, husband and wife. They are well aware of the advantages open to those with that coveted degree. The "degree" will likely be more advanced than a simple B.A. Graduate schools claim the cream of the liberal arts crop. These boys and girls are not going to delay marriage while they study law, medicine or whatever.

The differences between GI Joe and the married student of the 1960's are even greater than the generational gap would suggest because of the present emphasis on early marriage and longer education. Your generation expects to be able to handle both marriage and an education because you don't believe in waiting for marriage until you finish getting the degrees you want.

Ask a young couple on campus why they were so determined to marry before finishing their education and both look surprised. "You go read your *Georgics*, I'll tell all about it," the husband says, waving his wife aside. Then he explains, "We didn't like the idea of postponing life until we got through studying. After all, we're going to be studying all our lives. We were going crazy trying to lead a college life in the dormitories. We wanted to see each other while we studied. I figured we wasted a good four hours a day going back and forth from her campus to mine."

Ironically, it seems, today's married couple on campus is likely to be the most serious about academic work. This has served to blunt the case against college marriages which was forcefully put by such critics as Margaret Mead, who complained some five years ago, "There is a tendency to substitute easy domesticity for a period of stretching one's intellectual and ethical muscles before one settles down." Now, however, administrators tend to agree with Dr. Mary Bunting, president of Radcliffe, who says quite pragmatically, "If everybody is doing it you have to change your attitudes." When good students insisted upon marrying before they completed their degrees the colleges simply had to go along. The only stipulation seems to be that if the married student does not do well out he goes.

Sputnik and the subsequent insistence upon excellence has changed the character of campus marriages. It is hard to get into the good colleges and hard to stay in. Serious students are the only ones wanted and if you elect marriage in college you will have to put study first. You can't afford to play house, or practice for life in suburbia the way the GI's did. But neither are you beset with the conflicts which disturbed student marriages of the forties and fifties. In those days the college degree was regarded simply as a passport to professional success. You did not involve yourself in the intellectual life of the college. The frustration lay in seeing the goal so clearly—a house in the suburbs where the children could grow up freely—but being thwarted by the realities of campus life. It was a transitional period to be gotten through as soon as possible. Your parents' generation tried very hard to live up to the suburban standards their parents had established for married couples while earning money on the side and at the same time carrying a full academic load. It seems incredible that they were able to pull it off. Today's student marriages are usually not so burdened with real or imagined responsibilities. Significantly, the students who are managing well have simply eliminated the niceties of domesticity from their schedule. They spend their time studying, not making casseroles or shopping the discount houses.

Making a Go of It: Let the Work Come First

Simply put, the secret of making a go of a college marriage is to give college work top priority.

Today's student marriage is an impressive blend of intense study, casual domesticity and great personal involvement with one another. There are no offspring to interfere with what is now the primary goal—to get a quality education. Sam and Ann, married students at Radcliffe-Harvard, are perfect examples of the new breed. Their world is bounded by the academic advantages open to them but also by their very close personal relationship. They seem to have little contact with "campus activities." They live their own life off campus in a modest frame house.

The living room is bare except for a studio couch. This is their guest room, they explain, "for friends who want to sleep over when they come into Cambridge for a date." Their own bedroom is in the back. A small kitchen is neatly partitioned off the living room and, in contrast to the Spartan surroundings, looks like a gift shop display. Shelves are stocked with silver ashtrays, nut dishes, candlesticks, goblets. "Wedding presents," they explain. "We never use them."

Sam and Ann have known each other since their junior year in high school when, converging on Cambridge from Indiana and Texas, they met on a guided tour of Radcliffe-Harvard. They wrote regularly all through senior year and the summer before college Sam went to Texas to work in Ann's hometown. They took the same courses freshman year thus making sure they would end up in the same classes. When Ann didn't get into a choice seminar Sam badgered the authorities until she was admitted. The summer after freshman year Sam again went to Texas to work. Ann giggles when she remembers how "my mother kept after me to go out with other boys but I discouraged that. They were upset when he decided to come to Texas last summer but

I told them I wouldn't come home at all until they found him a job. I kept hinting that I would like to be married sooner than senior year." Sam says that "we kept moving the date back from senior year to junior year and that last summer we told them we wanted to get married before we returned to college."

Ann's parents finally agreed after insisting that Sam get written proof that his scholarships would continue if he returned to Harvard as a married man. Sam gets twenty-three hundred dollars a year between his National Merit Scholarship and Harvard National Scholarship. Ann's family contributes one hundred dollars a month to her plus her tuition at Radcliffe. She says they are saving about eight hundred dollars a year on her.

Sam and Ann agree that two cannot live as cheaply as one but they believe you can save about 20 percent on your joint college expenses if you are married. "Our book bill is exactly half of what it was," they say earnestly.

So far the marriage has worked out admirably largely, they believe, because they have far more time to study together than they used to have during courting days. Their marks are good. They are both in Group Two which means a mixture of half A's and half B's. To them the future offers an opportunity to keep on studying together since Sam will undoubtedly be able to pay his way through graduate school with grants and fellowships. They intend to put off having a family until they are settled and out of graduate school. Meanwhile they are in the enviable position of having the two things they want most at the same time. They have each other and their education.

Observing the pattern of life Sam and Ann have set for themselves, it is difficult to see how they could do any more studying, be any more dedicated to their work. Their graduate work will probably be at the Sorbonne. Says Sam, "We're interested in French existentialism. We're interested in German existentialism too but we know French."

Daily life revolves around cutting domesticity down to manageable size so there will be more time for study. They get up at seven-thirty on Monday, Wednesday and Friday when they have 9 A.M. classes. Sam fixes breakfast in the small kitchen. "I have to wash my hair every morning," Ann explains. She is a frail, pretty girl who wears little makeup but whose long blond hair is truly magnificent. Sam says, "I let her fix breakfast on Tuesday and Thursday. She can wash her hair after I leave for class."

This is a two-bicycle family. It takes them five minutes to get to class from their small apartment. They come home for lunch. "I fix the sandwiches while Sam reads to me," Ann says. "I had never cooked but Sam came from a large family so he knew something about it." Sam tells you proudly, "Her first question was 'How do I light the stove?'"

Sam does all the shopping. He gets the staples at a supermarket near the apartment. Then he rides on his bicycle further out to a supermarket which has "offbeat things." He goes to the big farmers' market every two weeks. He can save 40 percent on meat and vegetables there. He makes all three trips on Saturday mornings, can do them in three hours. Their menus are built around nourishing, if uninspired, stews and hamburgers and pork chops. "Casseroles are too much work," they say, "but stew isn't because we can study while it's cooking."

Study is, clearly, their prime activity. Everything is built around it, even their social life. On weekends they shop, go to the laundromat, clean house, and study on Saturday afternoons. Saturday night they go to an art film or play or sit around the Cambridge coffee shops. Unmarried friends like to visit them because, Ann believes, "they like the homelike feeling." But that feeling comes more from the marriage itself, not from any elaborate nest building.

Sam and Ann are superior students and perhaps that is one reason they are making a go of marriage. Also, they are reasonably solvent. Parental help and lucrative scholarships eliminate the need for part-time work. How do couples manage who have to support themselves and their college career?

Tom and Laurie go to a giant midwestern university where money-making opportunities for married students are available. So is good, cheap housing. They live in a modern apartment building just a mile from campus along with other married students and faculty. Their large one-room apartment came furnished but they have added a few touches, the most visible of which is a grandmother clock designed by Laurie's father. The room is shining clean and most inviting but there is little time for either of them to use it for entertaining. Tom works on the campus patrol some twenty-five hours a week. This is the best job on campus and pays $1.40 an hour. He made ninety cents an hour when he started and fully expects a pay hike before he graduates next year.

Tom and Laurie pay sixty dollars a month for rent and manage to feed and clothe themselves on another one hundred dollars. Tom's job and Laurie's income from a baby-sitting service she offers graduate students on weekends just about pays for the necessities.

Before they were married they talked the financial problem over with both sets of parents and agreed not to ask for help. Their modest savings were earmarked at this time for tuition and books. Neither minds spending the money on college costs, feeling that it is a long-term investment.

"At least we don't have to borrow money so we can finish college," Laurie says with pride. "We have friends who really have to grind. They take out these huge loans that just about rob you with interest. Then they go to the bank for more and are told, 'sorry, no more loan.'" She shudders in horror.

Tom and Laurie see very little of each other because they are not in the same classes. Tom is a senior majoring in agricultural education; Laurie is a sophomore in the school of education. When Tom graduates he will get a teaching job and she plans to pick up the rest of her credits by going to school nights. Their future is so planned that the present hustle to get through college doesn't bother them.

They are together only one or two hours a day and those hours must be devoted to study. Tom often comes back from class, snatches a quick supper and heads for patrol duty which may keep him out until three or four in the morning. No wonder he maintains somewhat sternly, "If you don't have something more than physical love to hold you together, it's not going to work out—not when you are in school."

He's right.

When It Works

We know more than we did twenty years ago about the factors which contribute to a successful college marriage. Students themselves are often able to analyze why their marriages are going well or why they are coming apart at the seams. Of course, the internal pressures on a college marriage are not going to be any different from those on any marriage. However, the very fact that you are married and living in a community where the majority are single will make a difference. It can work for you or against you.

If you continue with your education after marriage you'll notice a subtle change in the way faculty and other students treat you. One music major at a southern college says the change is one of improved status. "Professors I had before now call me *Mister* O'Neill. I must say I like it. I feel as if I'm on an equal footing with them."

As you move into the adult campus world you are likely to lose some friends among your fellow students. This is inevitable. How are you going to find time for fraternity fun, extracurricular activities when your wife/husband expects you to spend leisure time at home? (Besides, that's where you want to be.)

Something has to give and that "something" is probably going to be the extracurricular activities, student government, sports, the paper, choir, drama group. Dr. David D. Henry, president of the University of Illinois, says, "It's my impression that a smaller proportion of married undergraduates participate in the normal activities of student life but against this statement you have to put the fact that a good many nonmarried students do not participate in these same activities. This is a continuing concern—that the percentage of students participating in what we call 'student activities' is as low as it is."

The sense that student activities are "unreal" compared to marital pleasures and responsibilities will probably be compensation enough for whatever you give up. In one study made of married college women the group was almost unanimous in their opinion that combining college and marriage had strengthened their personal relationship. Many a young husband credits his early marriage with giving him the drive to succeed in college. "I had somebody to work for," explains one. And, an Amherst sophomore who married a Mount Holyoke transfer, puts it this way:

"Being married has given me a much broader context in which to place my studies. My motivation is stronger, because I have someone to work for other than myself, and my goals are better defined. People tend to make a trite distinction when they think that being married teaches you how to 'live in the outside world.' And yet you are faced with some of the practicalities of living—doing dishes, laundry, fixing things around the house. On campus, the College provides everything for you; here, I'm more responsible for myself.

"In a sense, being a married student has deprived me of one important educational advantage—living in close physical proximity with other students. I've missed the 'bull sessions,' but I have also been spared some of the excesses of college living, such as parties where the primary idea seems to be for some students to make fools of themselves."

When It Doesn't Work

Not all married students are as mature as this one nor are they getting as much out of the marriage. They are hard-pressed to keep up with classes, a part-time job and still pay attention to family life. Some of them are extremely articulate in describing their problems. Mrs. Kate Hevner Mueller of the University of Indiana says that married students complain, " 'We are too isolated.' Not enough time to linger in laboratory or seminar for 'shop talk' and professional discussion. 'There's the second jolt,' they tell me. 'You don't see your old friends anymore.' "

Mrs. Mueller is sympathetic with their problems which largely center on "no time or money for social life. If they have no car, too much time is needed for walking home the groceries, for bus and street car to classes, to the doctor and dentist, the laundromat, the library. If they do have a car, too much money for gas and parking, for the emergencies of upkeep. No time for tennis or chess or sailing. No money for concerts or dances or travel. 'Socializing,' they tell us, has top priority in recreation —getting together for bridge or television or just plain gripes and gossip. Shopping and dishwashing every day and cleaning and ironing on weekends, with cooperative baby-sitting and odd-job earning are inescapable routines. The rich life of the campus lies all about them—the free chamber music, the recitals and lectures, the inexpensive concerts and plays, the art exhibits, the seminars with distinguished visitors, the football and basketball, the golf course, the swimming pool—but their participation is at a minimum." "Not enough time for everything," is the chief complaint of married students.

In a study of married couples at a large state university one researcher discovered the usual frictions of married life affected these couples. But there were added ones arising from the peculiar strains of combining study and domesticity. What did they argue about? The wives complained that their husbands did not worry enough about paying the bills. Or that they didn't study hard enough. One wife was angry because her husband didn't make as good grades as she thought he should. One husband resented his wife's show of independence which he thought had to do with the good marks she was getting. Another was upset because his wife suffered so under the strain of their busy lives.

In a study of married women college students Anne M. Lee concludes that "many of the relationship pressures as well as the relaxation and recreation pressures may have stemmed from a lack of time." Frustrations which the married women students felt were expressed in such statements as:

"Not enough time to spend together. Never able to relax. Meals are prepared 'on the run' hence not always something to look forward to.

"Tired at night. Can't find time to get all the housework and studying done.

"Practically all social life has to be eliminated. I work all of the time.

"Many times I feel that I have not completed anything but go from one to another without being completely prepared.

"Not enough time for regular household duties. Physical fatigue affects my patience with the family. Mental strain of all responsibilities may lessen my effectiveness in all roles I have: homemaker, mother, teacher, student."

In this study married women students spent an average of fifty-two hours a week on homemaking duties and more than this if they had young children. Some thirty-eight hours, by comparison, was spent on college work and college activities. It seems then that academic life is less absorbing for the young woman student who is married than her domestic chores. And, say the critics of this way of life, isn't she missing something of consequence? Interestingly, according to Professor Mueller, "only three out of 20 college husbands kept their wives in school and less than half of these wives, what with planning, shopping, cooking and baby tending took full time work."

Let it be said again, at the risk of becoming a bore, that the point of going to college (married students included) is to devote yourself to study. Anything that gets in the way of that goal must go. Married students who have a rough time are inclined to think of themselves as young marrieds first and students second. To them the period spent on campus may be bitterly frustrating. The young husband wants to get moving on a job and resents marking time in college. He feels that he is neither fish nor fowl. He is a married man with responsibilities, but because he is still a student he can't shoulder many of them. His wife feels that she has taken on the duties of a wife but she is not enjoying the privileges of a home of her own, a family and the security of his job. If they have children the situation worsens. If the wife brings to the marriage preconceived ideas of how a husband should behave, she will discover, to her dismay, that a student husband is a different breed. He cannot be a good provider because they have barely enough to live on. He cannot earn much money because he must study. His pride and his masculinity will surely suffer unless he is a dedicated scholar or realistic enough to take the long view. If he brings to the marriage a conviction that wives must cook, clean, bring up children and be emotionally supportive of their husbands, he will be sorely disappointed in his student wife. She may resent cooking for him, cleaning their tiny quarters. She may wonder why he cannot carry some of the load when she has an exam the next day.

Some couples are better able to handle this than others. Those who are truly dedicated to the life of the mind and who share a genuine desire for research or teaching or "pure" learning are willing to make do in order to be together. But those who married in order to set up a home, who yearn for the satisfactions of domesticity, who want a house and a car and a family—right now —are going to find it unsatisfying. The wife will drop out of college in order to work or take care of the children full time. And unless the husband is strongly motivated to go on with his education he, too, may pull out of the situation. The trouble seems to be that too many couples on campus see themselves as young marrieds rather than students. They measure their housing, their finances, their recreation against what they believe to be the "rights" of married couples. They have grown away from the amusements, the schedule and the modest aspirations of the college student. This is why it often seems best for a young couple to separate while in college. They can live in their respective dormitories where the necessities of life are provided.

An Unusual Campus Marriage

There are as many different kinds of campus marriages as there are colleges. Consider the case of Janet and John. They met at the end of her freshman year. He was in his third year of Medical School. They were married at the end of her sophomore year. Janet is a physics major and very intense about it. She recognized, too, that there was something to be gained by staying in the dormitory rather than setting up any young marrieds establishment. They were together every weekend in his apartment. "My parents felt that I needed the undergraduate experience. There was a certain amount of growing up, things to be had from the dormitory life. One other factor was that he worked so hard. He was up at six and worked every other night."

When John graduated he went to Ohio to do his residency. Janet stayed behind to finish college. "We much prefer to be together, of course," she explains and then goes on to describe how precisely they have worked out their part-time marriage. "We see each other Columbus Day, Thanksgiving, Christmas, spring vacation. During the summer we took an apartment together. I went to graduate school out there to get credits for my Ph.D. I'll teach or do research some day. He may practice in South America and there is a great opportunity there. You see, my field is nuclear physics and this attracts so many brains there's little chance to do anything creative. But in South America I should have lots of opportunity since they are just now building their graduate schools. I have to get my Ph.D. in three years so I'll be finished by the time he goes in the Army. I want to go with him wherever he's stationed."

Janet says she feels getting married made it possible for her to put her entire attention on her work. "At first the hardest part was being able to study when I was away from him. But now I can study twice as hard. We've been married a longer time and it's a much more stable situation. If we hadn't gotten married the chance for our growing apart would have been so much greater. If I hadn't married I would feel it was my duty to look around and I would have spent more time on social life instead of on study. If you don't get married one of you will meet someone else."

Janet participates in extracurricular affairs when she is on campus. Student government, choral work, athletics have claimed her attention because she likes to sample different aspects of college life. She looks like any other fresh-faced ingenuous college girl during her winters on campus. During the summer vacation, however, she turns into the young wife of the doctor she married. She manages their apartment while taking courses at the University. She comes closest then to living out the detailed schedule of the more typical undergraduate wife who is truly combining domesticity and scholarship. However, Janet is more absorbed in her work than she is in housekeeping and perhaps because of this is able to cut the domestic chores down to a minimum.

"We wake up around six," she explains. "I go down and put on the oatmeal and eggs while he showers. I drive him to the hospital at seven and go on to classes and study all day. I'd go home and clean the house if we are having company. I try to have company every two weeks so I'll get the house clean. I pick him up at five. We go home and I start dinner. Very simple meals, vegetables and meat. We shop once a week at the supermarket."

Janet is lucky because her husband encourages her professional drive. "He wants me to study. He's not jealous. As long as I have a Ph.D. my husband has his life insurance policy. If anything happened to him I could always support the family. Also I have a concrete background which allows me to work on my interest all my life. After all, a woman doesn't spend her whole life raising children."

Quite consciously, John and Janet have determined not to have children until they have finished their education. With her Ph.D. Janet believes she will be able to keep up with her field while raising her children. She wants to be with them until they are well along in school. It is important, she believes, to get her academic work over with now and not drop out in order to raise a family. Both she and her husband find the load they carry heavy enough and interesting enough to absorb them. They would be physically unable to care for a family under the present setup. They have the self-discipline necessary to carry out their resolve. And, since they are planning a long-term life together, they are able to put first things first and get the education which means so much to both of them. Admittedly, their solution is pretty far-out but it works for them and might work for others.

Putting Hubby Through

Women who support their husbands while they get their degree are supposed to be entitled to one themselves, coyly called a Ph.T. (Putting Hubby Through). Although this group claims to have no resentment about the fact that they are slaving while their husbands enjoy the privileges and distinction of being scholars and gentlemen, one wonders if there will not be some complaining in years to come even though at the time it may be rather thrilling. Said one girl, "It's a great kick, knowing you've helped your husband become a professional man. It's really sharing a career."

Husbands are not always averse to being helped. They know that it will be only temporary and, as one told his wife, "It's the best investment you ever made."

But what if the investment turns out to be a bust? Will his wife, in retrospect, consider her "sacrifice" meaningless? This may be an unworthy conclusion, but entirely human. Even if her husband does fulfill all their career expectations for him she may expect to be "thanked" for her early sacrifice until his retirement, or feel that having done her part she can now sit back. Isn't this very dangerous?

In the first place she is likely to remind him that she was cheated out of her own education and personal development if she sees him forge ahead. In the second place she fears he will become bored by her. The constant reminders to wives not to let their husbands "outgrow" them will only fan her resentment. Unhappily there is some validity in the prediction that a wife who grubs when young so her husband can improve his earning capacity and himself can be "outgrown."

One college dean (Dr. Theodore B. Person of Illinois) asked a group of students what problems (aside from money) plague the married student. The answers are instructive.

"The major problem was the tension created by having a working wife, the bickering of two people with equal responsibility and equal fatigue, the conflict between a wife wanting relaxation at day's end and a husband needing to study. Most students remarked on another problem which seems as acute as finances —the intellectual gulf between a noncollege wife who supports her husband and the husband with a degree. One spoke of an acquaintance who says he has already "outgrown his wife."

Another dean, this time a dean of women, feels that a wife should not allow herself to be "outgrown" even if it means continuing her own education, at considerable sacrifice. She says, "Where the wife gives up her own education to 'put hubby through' there can be real tragedy. A woman's basic education is her best dowry. The girl who drops out of college to work handicaps her own future and the future of her family, both from the standpoint of earning potential and cultural contribution to her family."

Even though studies have shown that the most successful marriages are the ones where husband and wife are about equal as far as education goes there are conspicuous exceptions to this. In a study of the "Young Executives" *Fortune* writer Walter Guzzardi, Jr., found that his group had only a 1 percent divorce rate which is way below the national average. Relating this good news to another statistic, Guzzardi concluded that it may have something to do with his educational status. "The young executive is very well educated. But his wife is not, at least not to the same degree. Over half of the wives do not have college degrees. That happier home life may result in part at least from the fact that the hard-driving, hard-competing young executive, when he finally gets home, is easily the intellectual superior there."

There is plenty of evidence to show that the wife of the hard-driving young executive often feels put down and inadequate because she lacks a college degree. However, she may conclude that her comfortable life, children, husband's devotion make up for her own lack of intellectual credits. Many women are quite able to be the power behind the throne and love it.

If you are happy working in a menial job now so that the two of you can reach your goal that much sooner—fine. But don't let yourself fall into martyrdom, take on the drudge mentality. The difference between your working life and your husband's preoccupations can create resentment. It doesn't have to if you put it in perspective and make some education and career plans for yourself.

You can't help be somewhat jealous of your husband's education—especially if you must abdicate your own. He gets to read the most fascinating books while you spend eight hours in an office. His preparation is for years of responsibility, prestige, authority. You are simply marking time, taking the handiest kind of job so you won't get committed.

There may be good reasons for nonambition at this point. You'll be moving after graduation. You believe that it is pointless to become too involved in a career when, before too long, you'll be starting a family. But if you take stock you may discover that you are deliberately bypassing something good because you are married and you had hoped for total absorption in home and husband.

Don't let yourself go to seed before you have started to bloom. If you deliberately decide to take the dullest job in the world just so you won't have to think about it when you get home, then you certainly need an intellectual supplement. Take a course or two yourself, become involved in a music, theater group. If you're talented enough for painting or piano or design throw yourself into it. Get busy on that novel you want to write. Your husband is going to be so preoccupied studying evenings that you had better develop another interest or you'll end up watching him study. What can be more demoralizing or stunting? Companionship is great but too much can be stifling, even under the best of circumstances. Consider what happened to a young couple named Joan and George. They had waited to marry until Joan had her B.A. degree and George could begin work on his advanced degree. There was no rush to start a family, no pressure on Joan to get a job. The fellowship was ample for their modest tastes. They thought it would be fine if Joan stayed around the house, at least for the summer.

"Since I read a lot anyway," Joan explains, "I just sat and read some more. It didn't bother him or if it did he wouldn't admit it. He has great powers of concentration."

Before long, however, this idyllic arrangement began to pall. Joan discovered that she had nothing to say to her husband. She felt shut out by his concentration on his work. Also, she was limited in her housekeeping and leisure fun because he had to make every minute count. "I didn't like to do any cooking or cleaning or take a nap or listen to records or do anything that would interfere with the work atmosphere. Pretty soon I got tired of just sitting there watching him work so I went out and got a job. It's a temporary one at the library but it gives me something to do. I've never had a real job before and it's quite different from school."

Isn't it hard to come back to a house which has been lived in all day?

Joan admits, "We had to have a schedule. He works in his study and he can do anything he likes in there, be as messy as he pleases. But for him order is important. When I come home I straighten up the study. The rest of the house isn't touched during the day so I can handle the cleaning once a week. I get to work early, around eight, so I can leave at three. I make a regular breakfast for both of us. He has a sandwich for lunch and I eat in the cafeteria.

"When I get home he'll tell me what he's been working on and I'll report on the people I've seen and what happened on the job. We need to be away from each other for a while."

One big problem for the man who studies at home—there's no sense of a time break at the end of the week. For him the weekend is just a continuation of the week. For his wife the weekend is very important—time to go out, see people, dress up, visit the family.

One young wife sympathizes with her husband's ambition and steady work habits but, she says, "I hoped he would reach the point where he needs a break. He had to get used to the weekend idea but he did. We call it 'real people time' because we're out there doing what everybody else is doing—going to the movies or the beach or skiing."

You can forestall that feeling of self-pity which assails even the mature young wife if you schedule some fun for yourself. Also, look out for your own future and that does not necessarily mean a future linked to your husband's career. According to the latest statistics you will be thirty-five when your last child begins school.

What will you do with yourself then if you have not made some preparations now? Colleges and universities appreciate the problem of the older woman who wants to go back to work and they make room for her on campus. However, they would rather have a candidate who has acquired some academic credits no matter how long ago she went to college.

Business firms may welcome you in retraining programs but they, too, like it better if you've had some experience in the working world. If you plan on a profession you can get enough basic training now to qualify you for a beginner's job related to your career ambition. Suppose you decide to be a nurse, a teacher, a social worker, a lab assistant. You can map out a program which will allow you to take academic work in stages, earn money by finding a job in fields related to your interest. If you can type and take shorthand you can at least qualify for office work in the area which interests you.

Your job future is important. You ought to sit down with your husband and plan a career program which includes both of you. Even if your prime responsibility right now is to him and his continuing education you can insure your marriage against corroding resentment in the years to come if you look out for yourself as well.

Don't shortchange yourself in the name of self-sacrifice. You may be paid fifty dollars more a month for a routine job which bores you than for that fascinating receptionist's spot in the art gallery. Take the gallery job. You'll be more fun to live with, you'll be laying a foundation for a future career, you'll have something alive and interesting in your life. Save on something else but take the job that fascinates you even if it doesn't pay as well.

Says one psychiatrist, "Many women have difficulty in understanding that no one is completely selfish or selfless. Too many women think they must either sacrifice themselves completely to their husbands or be considered selfish wives. It is not a black and white choice. There is nothing wrong with wanting to satisfy your own needs. In fact, it is a healthy and realistic attitude. More of the young women putting their husbands through school should realize that they are not being selfish if they want to take an interesting job—even if it means a little less money for their family. They are not expecting too much if they want their husbands to take part-time work so that they can continue their own education, or have more time for their own interests."

Advantages of a College Marriage

If you survive the pressures of a college marriage your future should be greatly improved. You will earn the respect of your parents, the college and, not incidentally, prospective employers.

One college president paid this tribute to his graduating married students: "Young people who have thoughtfully entered into marriage, who have planned their lives very carefully, and their finances, have a pattern of living which helps them in other ways.

"Employers, in general, like to have students who have had some work experience. The experience, if successful, means that the student has learned to budget his time, has learned how to get things done, and very often it has been a maturing experience.

"I was very much interested in a recent report from our student placement office, which described some of our students who are very enterprising in the way they earn money. They have established their own private businesses in a number of cases—repair services, tutoring, cabinetmaking, are examples. They get franchises for selling all kinds of things from cutlery to travel tours. Student wives may contribute earnings from selling also—cosmetics and greeting cards. They do typing and seamstress work and baby-sitting is a major occupation for student wives—sometimes on a cooperative basis and sometimes for money.

"The report from the placement office declares that the married student has proved to be a somewhat more determined individual often more responsible because of his age, experience and obligations and these characteristics are favorable factors in later employment."

Several colleges, among them Antioch, with twenty years of follow-up study, have surveyed graduates who were married in college. Their results indicate that these marriages hold up remarkably well.

For one thing, students who want to marry feel they are ready for marriage. They are willing to forego undergraduate fun and games for the realities of a mature relationship.

Without quite appreciating it at the time, student couples are given a chance to ease into marriage without some of the problems common to young marrieds. They can finance these early years with less money than it would take to live in a big city or suburb. They are somewhat sheltered by the college community, living under its wing so to speak. They have their freedom but also a structured life. One marriage counselor describes it as "a buffer state where they don't have to deal with the real world at the same time they are dealing with an early marriage."

Since they are usually good students their "job" gives them little trouble. Unlike the young husband who must make good in the competitive business world, the student-husband is generally comfortable with his academic responsibilities. He is simply going on with what he has been doing all his life. Even if he is not a brilliant student marriage may improve his performance. A Princeton observer notes, "He straightens up, becomes more serious; far from a distraction, the young lady proves a stabilizer, a gyroscope setting her man on a steady course."

Inevitably college will change you and so will marriage. The impact of both experiences simultaneously can be immensely rewarding—or shattering. Accept the inevitability of change and let it happen. You don't have to know all the answers now, make all your plans, get your future down in black and white. Relax and enjoy those college years, enriched through marriage. You may never have it so good again.

IX

THE IMPORTANCE OF OTHER PEOPLE

The romantic view of marriage shows only two people in the picture—husband and wife. Parents, in-laws, sisters, brothers, the boss, friends and old lovers are conspicuously absent. Yet these significant others will influence your marriage more than you realize. If it is indeed true that no man is an island, it is even more certain that man and wife cannot isolate themselves.

You bring to the marriage relationships which have influenced you profoundly; you aren't going to stop making new relationships even though you have found the most satisfying one of all.

Of all the many people in your life your parents are the most significant. Your mother is quite right when she says, "But I'm *still* your mother!" Her claim is there even though your wife takes precedence. You will have to deal with that claim, honor it in some fashion throughout your married life. If you succeed in loosening childhood bonds without disturbing that deeper relationship between you and your parents you will be truly adult. Your marriage should profit accordingly.

Perhaps you married to get away from home, to free yourself from a clinging parent. Possibly you can put some distance between yourself and that possessive mother or father but you cannot finally cut the umbilical cord. You are still related and this is historic fact. The only thing that changes with marriage is the number of people you become related to through your partner.

You have acquired a new family along with your bride (or groom). The in-laws, sisters, brothers, aunts and cousins, uncles and grandparents will be around for a good part of your married life. You may not know what to expect of them but they are already expecting a good deal of you, especially your in-laws.

If your father-in-law has no sons he thinks he's found one in you. He may simply want another male to talk to at the family gatherings. Or he will insist that you play golf with him, go fishing, talk shop when you come to dinner. One newly married young man found that he finally had to extricate himself from this male togetherness and tell his father-in-law, "I married your daughter; my responsibility is to her."

A mother-in-law who has never had a daughter is likely to express her pent-up longing for a companion who will go shopping with her, take her advice on housekeeping and whom she can indulge.

When you marry you take on a tribe as well as a husband or wife. An old Irish proverb puts it very well, "Marry an island woman and you marry the whole island." Some families are closer than others, larger, more firmly wedded to tradition and the past. But every family has its cherished memories (you are expected to share), its ways of doing things (you must accept them) and its own view of your new mate (often startlingly different from your own). Unreasonably, but secretly, they hope that you will become a second child, a mirror of your mate. You are expected, too, to compensate for whatever your husband/wife has failed to give his parents. A tall order, to be sure.

A recent survey by sociologist Robert O. Blood, Jr., of the University of Michigan turned up the not-too-surprising fact that in-laws become a problem when they come in large doses.

The most unfavorable in-law climate for a young couple, he says, depends on proximity. If the couple settles down in their old childhood neighborhood, where more than half of the relatives on both sides are still living, they will be at a disadvantage. In many cases the young couple continue to eat with parents every night; they may have a separate apartment or house but they are still part of the old family group.

If you live close to your family they will have no compunction about dropping in. Dr. Blood says that unannounced visiting indicates that the boundary lines between family units are not clearly established or respected.

If large family gatherings take place more than once a month the young couple will simply be absorbed into the tribe and find it hard to establish their own autonomy.

A girl whose mother is almost smothering in her attentions advises young couples, "to move away from your hometown right away. At least spend the first year on your own. It makes it easier to establish your independence."

"I suppose you had to do that because your mother would have cooked dinner for you every night?"

"She still tries to but it's easier to say no because we have been on our own."

Must There Be an In-law Problem?

Your needs and those of the in-laws can be reconciled. You can live harmoniously in peaceful coexistence. It may take some frank talk, hard-won compromises, a good deal of understanding and insight but the effort will pay off. It is far pleasanter to get along with your in-laws than to fight with them. Your own partner will be happier if you like his mother and father. (Even the most rebellious child has a secret loyalty to his parents; he can criticize them but let anybody else try!) Your own children will need their grandparents' interest and goodwill. If they are born into family friction they are bound to feel it and react. If you want to make sure that our own children will not be victims of a tug of war between you and the family elders, win your in-laws over at the outset. You need to establish a fresh relationship with your own parents too, once you are married. It is important to show that you like them as people even though you are no longer dependent on them.

Practically speaking, you can use the help and support (emotional as well as financial) that older people offer. If you have their love and respect, their companionship as well as any contribution they can make to your own security, you will have a head start on a happy marriage.

In-laws can help a marriage, not hinder it, says Professor Blood. In reasonable doses in-laws actually provide support for a couple's marriage if they offer love, companionship and tangible help. But the couple must be able to accept the offering, with whatever strings are attached. Either that, or do without cheerfully.

Some newlyweds resolve not to see their parents at all in the misguided hope that this will help their own marriage. Not so, says Professor Blood who has determined that little or no contact with relatives does not seem to strengthen marriage. Why? "People who can't get along with their relatives may not be able to love their marriage partner either." What better argument can there be for establishing a grown-up, mutually helpful relationship with the older generation?

"When will they take us seriously?"

This plea comes from a young married who says her biggest problem is that "our parents don't really believe we've settled down. We went steady in college, decided to get married the beginning of senior year. It's five years later and nothing much has changed for us. We're still 'the kids' and I can't see that we've really achieved the status we should have as an 'old married couple.'"

If you want your in-laws to recognize your individuality you will have to demonstrate that you are capable of handling the responsibilities of marriage. If you can support yourself, pay your bills on time, run a household, you will earn their respect and they will let you alone.

Remember the stories of how Eleanor Roosevelt valiantly fought to create her own identity as a wife and finally succeeded despite the controlling efforts of her mother-in-law Sarah Delano Roosevelt?

Mrs. Roosevelt always acknowledged that her mother-in-law was able to take over with such ease because her own capabilities as a wife were so negligible. "For the first year of my married life, I was completely taken care of. My mother-in-law did everything for me . . . I drove with my mother-in-law in the afternoon. I walked in the mornings religiously, and we practically always took one meal a day together. . . . I was growing very dependent upon my mother-in-law, requiring her help on almost every subject, and never thought of asking for anything which I felt would not meet with her approval."

With what now seems painful insight the young bride came to appreciate how much she feared making decisions. But, as she overcame the fears which beset her and her own self-reliance improved, a break became inevitable.

When Franklin Roosevelt was elected to the state legislature a physical separation was possible. The young couple moved to Albany. "For the first time I was going to live on my own . . . I wrote my mother-in-law almost every day, as I had for many years when away from her, but I had to stand on my own feet now, and I think I knew that it was good for me. I wanted to be independent. I was beginning to realize that something within me craved to be an individual. What kind of individual was still in the lap of the gods!"

We know how the story came out, what kind of individual Mrs. Roosevelt became. She fought to keep her husband active after his polio attack, and was obliged to confront her mother-in-law once more. Sarah Delano's protective wish to have her son retire to Hyde Park was vetoed by Eleanor and so the course of history was changed.

Later, when Eleanor Roosevelt was herself a mother-in-law she established a determined hands-off policy with her children. "I was almost obsessed with the idea that, once the children were grown, they should not be subjected to the same kind of control that has held such sway over me. I am afraid my daughters-in-law sometimes thought that I was not even interested in them, because I was so very anxious to have them feel that I was not in any way trying to control or interfere with their lives, nor trying to demand attention from my children when they had families of their own. I probably carried this theory too far."

The most understanding of parents must necessarily become an "in-law" (with all that hateful word implies) once their child marries. This is a role forced on them and only complicates the adjustment they must make, the sharing they are now obliged to do. Be sympathetic and resist making "in-law jokes," about as funny and valid as the woman-driver type. The meddlesome mother-in-law is rapidly becoming a creature of fiction. You will revive her only if you expect trouble and behave accordingly.

Getting to Know Both Families

Now that you are married you should be able to see your parents in a more adult light. You are going to get a new perspective on them when your partner makes his assessment. Your view of his family should also be illuminating. Beware of hasty judgments. Before you come to any firm appraisal of your new family you ought to know them better than you do now.

If you made some effort to fit in with your new family before the wedding you're that much ahead in the relationship. In-laws tend to resent the boy who calls for their daughter, waits impatiently while she gets ready and then dashes out without so much as a word to them. Even after he marries her they have trouble conquering this early resentment (justified or not). Remember that you are taking something away from them and that the compensation will come only if you encourage their daughter to be available. Incidentally, a boy's mother appreciates some attention from her daughter-in-law. Most particularly, she likes to be consulted on her son's tastes and habits. After all, she knew him first. She may never be able to overcome a kind of primitive jealousy; mothers usually resent the girl who took their boy away. You can get the relationship on a working basis by deferring to her. So much the better if it can be done before the wedding day.

One young couple deliberately set out to woo their respective parents so they could win consent for an early marriage. The boy always made a point of talking to his girl's parents before taking her off on a date. Often enough, the date took place in her home or his. They watched television with the families, ate dinner with them or just sat around. They believe that this careful courtship prepared both families for the engagement. They claim, too, that their in-law problems are minimal because they knew what to expect of the older generation. During courtship they were exposed to family idiosyncrasies.

You can get to know your in-laws after marriage by spending some time with them. Offer to run an errand now and then for your mother-in-law. Take her shopping and out to lunch. Invite her over for coffee now and then. It is up to you to initiate the social life you will have with your elders. Some daughters-in-law are never forgiven because they waited too long to have the family for dinner. You don't have to wait until the house is perfect or until you can get out your wedding china and silver. Invite them for hamburgers or a drink as soon as you are settled. They want to see you in your new life. The sharing is what counts.

Don't tell them everything but do tell them something. The typical parent is dying to know if you're looking for a new job, planning a baby, anxious to buy a house. If you keep her totally in the dark, she will feel so left out that she may determine to push her way in. Talk things over now and then; let your parents know what you are going to do.

Privacy and How to Preserve It

Some aspects of your married life belong to you and your mate. That includes the loving as well as the fighting. Parents are not anxious to be privy to kissing or to quarreling. When you are around them try to restrain yourselves. Giggling, covert squeezes, soulful looks, private jokes, make your parents (and any other observers) uneasy *voyeurs*. Save it for later. You only fan whatever jealousy may be simmering under the surface. Besides, it's bad taste.

Don't expect your parents or in-laws to referee your fights. They aren't anxious to play diplomat or judge. As a matter of fact, modern in-laws would just as soon not be in the middle. One complains that "young people like to have a gallery. Fighting in public seems just as permissible to them as necking in front of us.

"My son-in-law will go out to buy some cigarettes. When he comes back his wife asks, feeling very sorry for herself, 'Didn't you get me any?' (She hadn't said a word about being out of them.) Instead of pointing this out, he says, 'I thought you had plenty.' This is the trigger.

"'You never notice what I need,' my daughter will shriek, and the fight is on.

"I wouldn't think they would want me to watch these rows. They ought to work things out in private. They want me to take sides but I refuse. I just say, 'I have no intention of settling it for you. You can't come home to Mother.'"

Apparently you are damned if you do and damned if you don't interfere. No wonder the mother-in-law role is so ambiguous. Your children have moved out of your jurisdiction but they are very much in your life.

Not only do the new breed of mothers-in-law resent being asked to interfere, they suspect that their children often try to make them compete with the new mate.

One astute mother caught on to what was happening long before wedding bells rang. "In the dating period they tell each other

everything and that includes 'what my mother thinks of you.'
When they get married everybody knows where he stands. After
all, you have heard all the not-so-nice things about your son-in-
law, including what he thinks of you. I can't accept some of the
things my daughter's husband did to her, but I don't think she
should have told me. She says she thought they were 'cute.' I
think she told me so I would be on her side. I said to her, 'Now
that you're married don't do what you did in the previous administration. Don't tell me what Joe does if you think it will upset
me. You think these things are cute but I don't. If you want us
to get along, just tell me the nice things. Stop and think if the
cute thing is endearing or not."

How Much Should You Accept from Parents?

According to the survey of one family agency the in-laws
problem has more than doubled as a cause of marital friction in
the last sixteen years. Couples are likely to have all four parents
still living, thanks to longevity, and quite capable of making themselves heard. The younger the couple, the more likely it is that
they are going to be dependent, economically and emotionally,
on their parents.

Counselors note that some young people actually marry to
escape the dependency on parents which they hate in themselves.
They may try to make their partner into a mother or father and
continue the dependency role, or they will lean on their real
parents much as they did when they were unmarried. They still
feel entitled to help because now they are supporting a family.

If the young couple cannot come right out and ask for help,
they must devise all kinds of circuitous means to get it. Some
insist that they are doing their parents a favor by letting them
provide luxuries as well as necessities. "After all, we can't cut them
out entirely." Others maintain that it is all right to accept help
but not if there are any strings attached. In-laws, according to
this double standard, are allowed to do quite a lot but not make
their opinions known.

An in-law is permitted to baby-sit, co-sign bank loans, put down
payments on cars and houses, ask his lawyer, accountant, doctor,
veterinarian, architect, caterer, seamstress, mechanic, plumber,

banker to "have a look at the kids' problem"—and subsequently foot the bill.

An in-law is not entitled to ask, "Why do you need a new car?", "Don't you think you ought to see the doctor about that?", "Can't you serve beer instead of Scotch once in a while?" Who can blame this mother for complaining, "Young people deeply resent any suggestion that they aren't on the right track, any possibility that through no fault of their own they might fail. My son is convinced, for example, that he is going to get a new job he has applied for simply because 'I got such a strong recommendation.' I try to be a good mother and prepare him for the worst, but he acts as if I am a wet blanket. You are either for them or against them, but you don't have the right to express your own opinion, doubts or fears. You have to have total faith in what they do."

If a parent rebels and refuses to honor the code, he may lose his child's confidence altogether. One father thought he was within his rights to ask for an accounting when his son came to him for a loan. He wanted a month's breakdown of income and expenses, not to check up on the young couple but simply as good business practice. Not incidentally, he probably wanted to show them that credit was not easily come by. The plan backfired. Insulted, the couple went to a loan shark and signed on for an exorbitant credit charge just to prove their independence.

Independence is great. Everybody is pulling for you and your right to do things your own way. Even an in-law can appreciate the obvious fact that her child belongs to somebody else. That somebody may not care whether he eats breakfast, wears his raincoat, gets eight hours' sleep a night, pays bills on time.

All the in-law asks is the same freedom. Why should parents be expected to be orderly, responsible, generous, tolerant and totally adaptable? Why must their door always be open to children who have presumably left the nest? Must they always feed the brood on ceremonial days?

It is easy to sympathize with a mother-in-law who complains, "Why doesn't it occur to the children that their very presence at the groaning board (which represents a great deal of work on the part of the parents) is more than an act of love. It means more mouths to feed, for one thing. They want things to be the way they always were without realizing that tradition takes effort.

They love the Christmas tree but they don't want to decorate it, let alone take it down."

An even more objectionable custom than simple free-loading is, according to one in-law, maneuvering it so that you cancel out both sets of in-laws in one dinner. "We didn't marry our daughter's in-laws," said one mother. "Yet when the holidays come around the children think it is so convenient for all of us to have the big meal together. I suppose they are afraid of hurting one or the other if they don't see that we're all taken care of. (If they only knew how much we'd like to be taken out!) I'm usually the one who does the cooking. The other in-laws try to help while the kids go off by themselves."

In-laws and parents are dying to be asked out to dinner but their married children insist otherwise. One parent complains, "My son keeps telling me, 'We'd have you over but you wouldn't like the way we do things.' They are happy enough to come to us. In fact, I think they would be there every night if we didn't insist on our right to be alone."

One wonders if the real problem for some young marrieds is not how to keep their parents from interfering with them but how to slip back into the family on their own terms.

No doubt your parents expect great things of you—attention and respect—but they are also intent upon living their own lives. Unless you realize this you won't see them for the individuals they really are, and your relationship will falter. You can ask for help but if you want them to take you seriously as a married couple you will have to be businesslike when you ask. You can't have it both ways, cut the strings and still expect support. But it is possible to accept financial help, shelter and advice without losing face or status.

The Subsidized Marriage

There's nothing wrong in letting your parents help you get started if they can afford it, want to do it, and if you feel you need the help.

Money transactions always trigger an emotional response, as anyone knows who has loaned or borrowed cash. It's one thing for a daughter to be given money by her parents while she is dependent on them. It's quite another for her to ask for cash when her husband is supposed to be supporting her. Not that it can't be done, and that it isn't being done but there are certain ground rules that will make it easier, more comfortable for all concerned.

Sit down with a paper and pencil and decide just how much extra cash you need. If you have decided to go back to school, if you want to start a family, if you think it's better for your wife not to work, if you would like to buy a house or a car, you have reason to ask for help.

Don't cut corners. You may want to borrow just as little as you can, but you will defeat the point of the loan if you shave it too close. Listen when your parents give you advice on how much you'll need. If they are willing and able to provide a subsidy, let the loan be adequate. Otherwise you'll be back for more.

Tell them how you would like to have the money paid. Whatever arrangements you make, be sure you are both fully aware of the obligation on both parties. For example, you may need a check on the first of every month to cover the rent. You want it to be paid promptly. If, however, you feel that your father is likely to forget, you might be better off asking that the money be deposited quarterly in your account. The converse is true. If you are not absolutely sure that you will be able to keep from spending your loan on nonessentials you may be better off getting the check the day you owe the payment.

You should make the payments, not count on Dad to do it. Otherwise you will feel like a child.

Put it in writing. You may not be asked to pay back the advance, but you will win your parents' respect and increase your own self-esteem if you contract to return the advance (not necessarily with interest) at some future date.

Don't discuss the transaction after it has been consummated. A genuine thank-you is all that is needed. The helpful parent will not remind you of the loan unless it becomes too much of a burden. At that time it may be wise to renegotiate the whole project.

It is usually best for the boy's parents to provide the subsidy. However, a girl may accept certain tangible gifts from her parents if her husband agrees. She might, for example, accept a car from them, clothes, baby-sitter or nursery-school money, furniture for the house, a washing machine or dishwasher, a ticket home when they feel they haven't seen her often enough. These luxuries or extras can be provided without threatening the natural ambition any young couple has to go it alone.

The big items—house, education, food, insurance, doctor bills —are customarily provided for by the husband. If he needs help and his parents can afford to give it, they are the logical ones to lend a hand.

Once you and your parents have agreed on how much, how it is to be paid out and accounted for later on, let that be it. Don't ask for more, for advances, for extras.

There is no reason to feel inadequate if you do turn to your parents for a loan. Counselors seem agreed that it is the intelligent thing to do providing both parties are willing. In fact, one counselor makes this a condition for the success of early marriage, "that the parents on both sides are very willing to come to the rescue and assist the young couple in emotional and financial crisis. I am not positive, but it seems to me that young marriages work if parents assist them in making it work."

"I believe a subsidy can cement the relationship between parents and children," says a rabbi who has seen many such arrangements work out happily. Basically marriage is a social institution, and while the young people may feel at the outset of their marriage they need no one in this world but each other, they very quickly come to the realization that while having each other is the most wonderful thing in the world, it is even more wonderful to have each other along with family and along with friends who accept and respect them. When a subsidy in marriage is undertaken it should be done with dignity and complete understanding on the part of the parents. They must not consider it a handout. Rather, they are helping to achieve for the child's happiness, just as a parent wants to send his child to the best possible school or give his child the best possible clothes or food. It should be approached from that point of view. And the children should realize the love and devotion of the parent who is willing to subsidize their education while married."

Supplying a case in point out of his own family history, the rabbi continued, "I firmly think subsidizing is good, if you have a healthy situation to begin with. My own brother was going steady his second year in high school. He was married while in college and his wife had just completed high school. Three years of law school were ahead of him. Her parents had their heart set on her going to Sarah Lawrence. Both sets of parents were in a position to help these young people. There had been time for two generations to get to know each other well, so that when the young people decided to get married, their parents wisely gave them their support. They were able to combine college and marriage because they faced the problems they would have and were practical about solving them. They took an apartment near Sarah Lawrence because it was easier for my brother to commute to law school than for her to make the trip from New York to her campus. It has been a successful marriage but it could not have been undertaken without the subsidy of the parents."

Living with Parents or In-laws

Living with in-laws can be an immensely workable arrangement if both parties stand together. However, housekeeping details should be thrashed over before any move is made.

How much housekeeping help is the new bride (and groom) expected to contribute? In other words, is she supposed to pitch in on general chores or, simply, keep her own quarters neat and clean? How much a part of the family will the newlyweds be? Can they live their own life—entertaining, coming and going, shopping, cooking—separately? They can if they are allotted a separate household unit—garage or basement apartment, wing or floor, complete with bathroom and kitchen. This is usually the ideal setup but it is not always possible to achieve.

The T.'s think they have a perfect arrangement. Walter and June moved in with Walter's mother for practical, money-saving reasons, but they were doing her a favor as well. Recently widowed, she had not decided what to do with her good-sized Colonial house. She was lonely living there by herself and welcomed the young couple. Fortunately, two upstairs bedrooms complete with bath could be partitioned off from the rest of the house. They were connected to the main floor by a back staircase. Walter and June could come and go as they pleased without disturbing Mrs. T. She used a downstairs bedroom for herself and the living room for her social life. Both young and old could entertain at the same time without getting in one another's way.

The T.'s, senior and junior, did have to share a common kitchen but they agreed on a schedule satisfactory to both. June got up at six, made their breakfast and cleaned up the kitchen. Both young people were out of the house by eight, on the way to class. Walter is in graduate school (business administration); his wife is finishing her B.A. They met at noon on campus to share a sandwich made by June the night before. Once a week they splurged on a pizza or hamburger.

Mrs. T. had her house to herself during the day. She does the shopping and cooking. June tries to help out on weekends when the house gets a thorough cleaning. "We always have Sunday dinners together and usually Saturday night supper. The rest of the week is sort of haphazard. We may decide to stay at the college working in the library until eight or so. When we get home I'll fix us a hamburger or we might finish up leftovers. My mother-in-law has a lot of friends and she often goes out with them for dinner. We buy our own groceries, pay her a nominal amount for rent. It's a bargain for us but we will get our own place as soon as we're through school."

Clearly this is only a temporary arrangement, mutually satisfactory for the moment. It works because both parties know it isn't forever. Also both are getting a lot out of the present arrangement. The advantages outweigh the liabilities.

Walter says, "When we had our own place we spent a lot of time housekeeping. Now, we don't feel that we have to rush through our studies. I have an altogether different attitude toward my work. I have time to do it and enjoy it more."

They admit that parental subsidy gives them "a little feeling of guilt." And they look back on the year when they had their own apartment with great pleasure. "That year by ourselves. We really had a marriage. We weren't just a couple of kids playing house." On balance, however, they think the present arrangement is very workable.

Accepting Help

For many young marrieds the problem is not that of getting help but of accepting it. They think it is "weak" to take anything from a parent, most particularly advice. Without realizing how they are hurting a mother or father, they go out of their way to prove marital independence.

One mother confessed that the change in her daughter's attitude toward her within twenty-four hours after becoming a bride was nothing less than startling. "Before the wedding it was, 'Can we really have champagne? What kind of linen shall I buy? Do you think this monogram is the right one?' I was privy to every decision, every plan. It was mother and daughter against father, groom, bridesmaids, china buyers, florists, caterers. Now she greets me with, 'I know what kind of house you'd like us to buy, but John and I think . . .' John's taste couldn't have mattered less in June. Of course, he should help her make the decisions now but she acts as if I am trying to interfere. I don't intend to volunteer any advice. After all, what can a woman of forty-five tell a girl of twenty that would be useful?"

It isn't hard to think of a dozen bits of information that mothers could share with their married daughters. Curiously, however, the new brides hardly ever solicit real help. They may ask questions but, as one mother-in-law points out, "They are questions you could find the answers to in the *World Almanac!*" She elaborated, with a touch of humor and more than a little impatience. "If I wanted to know who my senator was I wouldn't ask my mother."

It seems that this is a common complaint among the parents of newlyweds. They are bombarded with pedestrian questions about simple etiquette ("Can you type a condolence note?"), the routine business of living ("Should I switch my registration now that we've moved?"), or even on matters only their children understand ("Do you think I have enough credits for graduate school?").

"They really don't want you to share anything you have personally struggled with and solved—like how to make pot roast or how many drinks you can get out of a bottle of Scotch," complained one mother. "During the last election my daughters called to find out who they should vote for. Not only would I not dream of telling them but I think it's a waste of everybody's time to come to your mother for that kind of advice."

It is possible, as more than one mother-in-law suspects, that the questions are put not to get answers but to involve parents in their children's married life. "They will ask your advice so you won't feel totally excluded but about something completely silly," explains one mother. "I got a call the other night from my daughter who wanted me to settle an argument she and her husband were having. Do you know what the argument was about?" she asked, clearly appalled. "Whether or not you can teach a dog not to sleep on the foot of the bed."

This mother-in-law believes that "the questions are a way of relating to someone, I suppose, but I wish they would find another method."

Parents are wary of trying to dictate to their children but they do hate to see them flounder when a little help could mean a lot. One sympathetic mother reported, after a visit to her daughter, "Sally works and she complains that she has no time to make the money-saving things, like casseroles and stews. So she spends more than she should on convenience foods. As a result the profits from her job are almost nonexistent. I could give her some recipes that take only a minute to prepare but I don't dare interfere.

"They are beginning to use some foresight but it seems to me that it takes them so long to catch onto the simplest things. To take just one example. Bob was always running out of clean shirts because one or the other of them forgot to take the laundry. Now they have discovered, and believe me it's a big discovery, that the best way is to ask the laundry to pick up every Thursday.

"Older people know the shortcuts because they have been coping longer. Why don't they ask us?"

Why? The answer is simple, according to young brides, who don't mind admitting that they are afraid of getting snowed.

"I don't ask for advice because I might have to take it. If I could just say to my mother-in-law, 'You're such a wonderful manager; I wish you could tell me how to get all my shopping done in one or two trips a week.' I really do think she's terrific but if I open the door just a little bit she'll be all over us. First thing you know she'll be picking me up to take me to the store, telling me what to buy, and if I don't want to do it her way she'll never get over it."

You can ask for advice without losing status as a grown-up married person. What harm will it do to get your mother's recipe for pot roast, to ask your father a question or two about real estate taxes, to consult them when you get ready to buy a car? The danger, of course, lies in deciding to follow the advice or not. Perhaps it is better to hedge a little when you ask for it—" Dave and I haven't decided what kind of car we want or whether we'll even get one, but I wondered what mileage you get on the station wagon?" Give them a graceful exit so they won't resort to, "You asked me what I thought and then you go ahead and do just the opposite." You can forestall this kind of problem by telling them in the beginning, "We'll have to make up our own mind but we really would appreciate knowing what you think about it."

In this, the Age of Freud, it is considered downright square, not to say unhealthy, to stay close to your parents once you are married. The parent is off-limits to those who consider themselves mature.

Hasn't the pendulum swung a bit far and wide of the mark? At a time when the generations are closer in age (most mothers are a respectably vigorous forty-odd when their children marry) and tastes (after all, Mother wears Bermudas too), it seems a pity that there should be such self-conscious estrangement.

Of course your first loyalty is to your partner. Let your parents know that this loyalty comes first. There are times when you may have to test their love in order to prove the point.

One young bride was forced to make her loyalties known the first week of marriage. An attack of appendicitis put her in the hospital and of course her mother rushed to be there. "My husband liked the doctor we had but it wasn't our 'family doctor,'" explains the bride. "She kept hounding me to leave the hospital and come back home 'where we could give you the best of care.' I told her 'no,' that Dick and I had decided we would stay with what we had. She wouldn't give up and finally Dick caught her trying to argue me out of it. He just blew up, admitted he was furious with her for sneaking around behind his back. I was amazed how well she took it. I think he's the first man who ever stood up to her."

Clearly, this is one marriage that isn't going to suffer from the so-called "in-law problem" and simply because everybody now knows where they stand. A word of caution, however. While you are gently separating yourself from your parents you might also reassure them that you are still their child. Your relationship can endure even though it is now on a wholly new footing.

The Boss and the Company

Next to your parents and in-laws, the boss and people on the job are going to have the biggest impact on your marriage. You don't have to marry the company but you are going to have to put it first often enough to irritate your wife. She, too, may have loyalties to her own job.

The young man who wants to get ahead is going to make certain sacrifices. His wife may not always agree that they are in the best interests of the marriage. When the boss asks him to work late, to come in on weekends, to travel for the company, his marriage could suffer. His wife feels ignored, unessential, no more than a housekeeper. Her "rights" to his attention and companionship have been usurped by an outsider.

This is how she *could* feel and if she gives in to self-pity she will make her husband feel even worse. Not only will he not be able to keep his mind on the matters at hand (his job) but he will feel abused, guilty and even take on her indignation at being told to give up leisure for company profit.

If the wife has had a taste of the company, been summoned to organization parties, interviewed by personnel, she may feel additionally that she is expected to submerge her own self in the interests of her husband's future.

Company conformity can be a threat, as well as an irritant. "You are supposed to play a secondary role but act like you have some intelligence," comments one young wife. "When we go to the parties I can watch George watching me. The things I do that he thinks are cute at home are forbidden. I'm supposed to be on my best behavior with the Brass. I would be, of course, because that's the mannerly thing to do. But I hate being scrutinized like a five-year-old. It isn't easy to make friends with people who have such a stake in your future. It seems opportunistic and dishonest to me. You try to be pleasant to the boss's wife but she's older. You don't have anything in common. Her children are grown up."

You are going to have to decide early on just how much this ready-made social life bothers you. Some women take to it quite happily. Others detest the idea of making friends with other women simply because their husbands work for The Company. One thing is certain. Your husband spends at least eight hours a day with his company and the people in it. There's no point in being jealous of them, resenting their claim on him. Not if you want to buy the groceries, that is.

You can, however, preserve your personal oasis of time, quite free from company demands. You don't have to make friends exclusively with business contacts. In fact, a number of successful executives have made a point of not seeing their associates on weekends. The Organization Man and his docile wife have been immortalized in literature, but their opposite numbers compose quite a segment of the population. These couples happily pursue their private lives and family ambitions outside the company. They say, quite honestly, "We'd like to come but we promised ourselves that nothing would interfere with our times together." People, even bosses, will respect you more if you are firm about what you owe your marriage and yourself.

Old Friends

At no other period of your life will you have friends who are engaged in so many different activities. Not all of your friends will be married. Those are not all going to live the same way you do. Some are in college, others in the service. Many wives will be working, while a sizable number will stay home to bring up the first baby. A number may be doing both. From age eighteen to twenty-eight young adults are more likely to be in more varied life situations than at any other period.

This variety makes for stimulating friendships but it can also create problems. How can you talk to your best friend when you no longer share the same daily problems and pressures? Aren't you likely to feel out of it if the crowd you used to go around with remains unmarried? Can you be sure you and your husband are making the right decisions, doing the right thing when all your friends are leading a different kind of life?

When you marry you instantly set yourself off from old friends. Someone else has a claim on your loyalties, emotions, time. You change because you belong to another person.

It is, of course, more of a significant change than took place when you went away to college but many of the effects are the same. Remember when you came back that first Christmas vacation. Everyone looked different, less important maybe. You had a hard time remembering just what you used to have in common. The reason was plain—they had made new friends who were sharing their new life and so had you. The landscape was transformed by your recently acquired perspective on it.

When you marry much the same thing happens. You see things in a different light. Let's hope the light won't be too dismal. You can afford to be generous. But things have changed.

You are going to find to your dismay that old friends don't share your opinion of your new mate. Should you cut them ruthlessly out of your life because they don't hit it off with him (her)? Or can you make room for them too?

The chemistry may be all wrong. Or they don't agree on politics. Or, let's face it, a certain amount of jealousy is involved. Worse, your husband can't tolerate your old pals. You had hoped at least for tolerance. "Love me, love my friends." But he wants you all to himself.

One gregarious new bride discovered that she had married a hermit. "Before we were married I was always happy to get away from my friends and be alone with him. I always assumed, though, our married life would include all the people I knew and that I would meet all the ones he grew up with and worked with and liked.

"Now that I look back I realize that I never did meet any of his friends but I suppose I assumed that he was like me, he wanted it to be just us two until we settled down.

"As soon as we got our apartment fixed up I wanted to have a house warming. Bill kept putting it off and putting it off but finally I insisted. I was amazed at the way he reacted to the people streaming into the apartment. He acted as if they were invading his absolute privacy. He didn't make an effort to talk to any of them. After they left he wouldn't gossip with me about them and he didn't seem to care about knowing who they were and how I had gotten to know them.

"I suppose I should have gotten the idea but I was so obtuse. I kept throwing him into my 'other life,' I accepted invitations and then, of course, I had a perfect excuse for having people in— we owe them. But I got mad at having to beg my husband to let me see people I was very close to once and am still fond of.

"I tried to get him to talk about it. I accused him of being jealous. He was very good-humored actually. All he said was, 'You're enough for me. Aren't I enough for you?'

"I really couldn't admit that I missed the shop talk from the office, that I still had bonds with old school friends. I cared about their opinion. I liked to giggle with them, over the good times we had shared. It didn't seem to me I should have to exchange one kind of relationship for another. Why couldn't I have both?

"I did manage to work it out but not without a lot of maneuvering. First, I realized that 'love me, love my school chum' just wouldn't work. There was no reason for Bill to adopt my friends. So I made an effort to see them for lunch or for dinner if Bill had to work. I no longer struggled to drag them into our lives.

"I stopped talking about them too. I could see the way Bill would freeze up when I went on about the opinions of an ex-boss, or old boyfriend. I like to analyze people but you need a receptive audience for that. The other person has to know the subject and appreciate what you're talking about. Since Bill had carefully disengaged himself from my friends the audience wasn't there. I still get some fun out of talking things over with my old pals when Bill is out of earshot.

"The funny thing is that when I quit trying to ram them down his throat he began to expand our social life voluntarily. He would wonder out loud why we didn't see the Randolphs any more. He was quite happy when I suggested that we have them over some night. I guess the whole thing hinged on letting him take the initiative."

Women, too, must struggle with the old pal. Often it is harder for them to take the army buddy who assumes that he can always bunk in with them when he's in town. If your wife seems to spend an inordinate amount of time picking at your friends, you are going to have to straighten her out. Either that or take a hard, cool look at Old Buddy and your feeling for him.

The question to be considered is—Does she not like your friend because he is your friend or because he is himself? Your instinct is to defend him on principle but you might profit from her observations. If she points out (with some justice) that "he does talk an awful lot about himself," don't fly off the handle and pointedly remind her that "so do any number of other people." Hold your temper and consider the charge. Is it justified? Even if she's right do you care? You don't have to fight for his honor. He doesn't have to be the perfect, all-purpose friend. Why not agree she's right (if she is) but make it clear that you still like him.

It will be fruitless to point out that she still likes "silly Jane," even though her friend has on more than one occasion failed to show up when they had a date. "You put up with her," is the obvious rejoinder but don't get into a friend-swapping battle. Keep quiet about Jane and be firm on your own loyalties.

Of course, you may discover that your wife's intuition is right and, despite an uneasy feeling of guilt, you will decide to shed the old friend. Possibly you have outgrown him. Be grateful then to your wife for providing you with a graceful out. Your friend will think it's "her fault" that you never get together. You can have it both ways—retain his approval and prove to your wife that she was right about Joe.

The old friend may or may not survive your marriage but certainly the old flame has got to go. Don't let yourself have lunch with him (or her) even though it may now be the most platonic of relationships. Don't dance too often with an old love at parties, linger over cocktails, reminisce about the good old days.

If you are a wife the easiest way to quench that old flame (if she is still around and single) is to invite her for dinner. Demonstrate how domestic your husband is now, how immune to advances. Chances are, one invitation will be enough. She may not even accept it.

If you are the husband keep your wife's old love at a distance but don't ignore him. Be cordial, helpful and just a little smug.

Neither of you should hide the past but you don't have to keep it alive. Comparisons are odious and unnecessary. The unkindest cut is to remind your husband that "Tom always knew how to treat me like a lady" or tell your wife "how terrific Sally looked last night." This is touchy territory; better stay away from it.

As soon as the old loves are safely married off you may want to regroup. There's no point in turning them out of your life completely. In a small town that would be impossible and uncivilized. Just make sure everyone knows where you stand now—together as man and wife.

X

COPING WITH CRISIS

Ideally you should be better able to cope with crisis now that you are married. You have a partner to depend on, someone whose resources are available in time of trouble. But you also have one more person to consider, one more voice, one more decision-maker. Your partner's mistakes and deficiencies are going to influence your life and future as much as his successes and strengths.

The first year or two of marriage will test your ability to survive the crises any partnership faces. You are going to discover unpleasant things about your mate and either make the best of them or allow them to corrode your marriage. Crisis and change are inevitable; what matters is the grace and strength you develop when confronted with the unpleasant and the unpredictable.

The crises discussed in this chapter are common ones. They can be handled in a variety of ways and no attempt is made here to suggest that the method used by any particular couple is ideal. We are simply describing what can happen and how a couple can survive a crisis. Often enough, the bare description of the crisis only serves to expose a deeper marital problem. It goes without saying that the chronic alcoholic, adulterer, compulsive gambler and big spender needs more than simple, practical help. He probably needs psychotherapy. In this chapter we will review the crises common to early marriage and comment on practical and workable solutions. In Chapter XI the opportunities for counseling and therapy will be explored.

The First Child

According to unromantic social workers, the advent of your first child will be the biggest single crisis you will encounter during these first years.

You may want the baby (both of you), have planned for it and be well equipped to take on parental responsibility. Yet the conditions for crisis still exist. A family counselor explains why the first child can cause problems for even the happiest, best adjusted couple.

"The birth of the first child can be termed a crisis because at this point the couple finds out that this marriage is for real and living together means business.

"The first few months of marriage are usually a continuation of courtship and dating. Housework isn't quite that burdensome yet. In a sense they are playing house. Their sex life is satisfying and they can sleep together whenever they like. They share some property and that is new and exciting. They come and go when they please. Then the baby arrives. When the baby comes, their recreational activities are cut down. For several months before the delivery and for a time afterward their sexual relations must be limited. There will be money problems because the doctor and hospital bills have to be paid. There are practical, mechanical problems such as learning to feed and dress and bathe the baby, getting up in the middle of the night with him. But there are problems on quite another level, on the relationship level. The baby is, after all, a third person and he can stir up all the stuff that's been there under the surface. The rivalry, the jealousy, an older brother felt for his younger brother, can erupt if that brother who is now a father feels once more usurped. Or it can remind the young mother of the period she spent as baby-sitter and substitute mother for her younger sisters. Her resentments may surface. Before they know it they are fighting with one another without quite realizing why. They just know that some of their freedom has disappeared."

He tells of a couple whose great bond had been a love of the outdoor, active life. "They played golf every weekend and really got a lot out of it. When she became pregnant she had to give up golf. Now that she's had the baby she can't take it up again because they can't afford the baby-sitter fees and the course fees. This would be all right if her husband would give it up too but he got in the habit of playing while she was pregnant and he's made new friends and doesn't want to stay home on Saturdays. She's annoyed and feels that he has gotten away from the family. 'He's forgotten all about togetherness' she says."

Despite the prevailing view (heavily discounted by psychiatrists and marriage counselors) that a "baby will bring you together," it seems clear that a baby can drive you apart. If you let it, that is.

In the case of the golfing couple, it turned out that the husband was simply repeating the pattern he had observed in his parents. His mother stayed home with the children while his father kept up his business contacts and got some needed relaxation and exercise on the course. He couldn't understand why this arrangement wouldn't work for him. He loved his wife. He wanted to be with her and indeed he did take her out every Saturday night. Why couldn't she behave like a proper mother and attend to her duties at home?

When young husbands become young fathers they can begin playing an independent role which will infuriate their wives. "I'm not going to be buried in housework just because I am a mother," said the golfer's wife. "My freedom means as much to me as his does to him."

Clearly, the new baby is going to throw a lot of attitudes into bold relief. The husband who has nodded agreeably when his wife described the career she intended to pursue "as soon as the baby is a year old" may turn into a fierce advocate of total mothering and forbid his wife to work.

The young woman who has always championed the differences between the sexes may insist that her husband wheel the baby carriage, change diapers, give the formula so "you can see what it's like."

First-time parents tend to overdo the "baby bit." They center their life on parenthood and then wonder why they are exhausted, snappish and vaguely discontented. "I thought motherhood was supposed to be fulfilling!" one nineteen-year-old complained, "it's just plain drudgery." It doesn't have to be. You can relax and enjoy the baby and probably will in time. Parenthood takes getting used to. You have to try on all the attitudes toward the young you brought with you from your own family and discover the ones your partner possesses. You have to accept the notion that you aren't the youngest ones around; your baby has first claim on youth. Most important, you have to get the hang of handling an infant. He's an unknown quantity and completely dependent on you.

New parents have a natural anxiety about the tiny life they must now nurture. They aren't sure they are caring for it properly and tend to take out their anxieties on one another. One young mother recalls that first year "was all baby care for us. I was exhausted and resented the pressures. My husband felt left out because I was so completely wrapped up in the baby. He kept telling me to relax but I was really scared I would do something wrong. It all seems so absurd now that I have two more. My 'high standards of parenthood' have come down all right and the younger children are much happier than the first one who got much too much attention and probably felt our concern."

If you can talk freely with your pediatrician he will be able to reassure you that most babies are pretty tough. If you give them good basic care and lots of love, they will survive. They will react to the tensions around them and this is something you can control.

The new mother, more than the new father, must take care of the emotional well-being of her family. Admittedly, she feels like being babied herself right after pregnancy. Indeed she may suffer the depression which is not uncommon to mothers right after childbirth. But if she can express her feelings to her husband and doctor she ought to move through this trying period in short order. Then it will be up to her to make sure her husband doesn't feel excluded. Inevitably she will be spending most of her time with the infant. She can schedule that time so that baby's crying, feeding, bath don't always interfere with that companionable drink and dinner hour, sleeping late on weekends and a normal sex life. Babies need scheduling but it can be worked out so that their parents can carry on as usual.

The baby is the mother's responsibility but she is not obliged to carry the full load. In fact, many family counselors advocate some sharing of the physical care of the baby so that the father feels included. This is often hard for the young mother to do because she doesn't think it's fair and she hates to create any more resentment than necessary in her husband. Secretly, she may be a bit possessive of the baby and reluctant to share his dependency. If, however, she encourages her husband to give the evening bottle, to hold the baby while he drops off to sleep, to cuddle it, everyone will be better off. She gets a respite; the husband enjoys the sharing and the baby has a chance at both parents.

No doubt some young fathers are simply not inclined to take care of babies. Don't force it if your husband is frank to tell you he doesn't enjoy changing diapers or burping a baby. Let him handle some of the other chores connected with child-rearing. He might change the bedding on the crib; make the formula with scientific accuracy. Your life does not have to be baby-centered. The crisis will pass as soon as the spotlight fades from the new arrival and he begins to fit easily and naturally into your life.

What if the baby is an unexpected, even unwanted one? There's only one thing to do. Love him. You've got him now so forget the mistakes, the lack of planning and make the most of what you now possess. There's no point in taking your resentment out on him. First of all, he doesn't deserve it. And, in the second place, you'll only cheat yourself. Parenthood, even when forced upon us, can be great.

Premarital Pregnancy

Any bride who is pregnant at the time of her wedding enters marriage in a crisis state. So does her groom. This may not be a "shotgun wedding" by any means if they have planned to marry. However, their decision to do so was certainly made for them when they discovered they were about to be parents.

Peg and Mike are a case in point. They had gone steady through high school and wanted to marry when Mike finished college. They were very much in love and also very aware that they must not let anything stand in the way of Mike's education. Then Peg discovered she was pregnant. Neither of them can recall much about the circumstances that threw their long-range plans off. But, singly, they are quite willing to talk about how difficult the first years of marriage were because they entered it out of desperation.

"I felt really sore," Mike admits. "We went to college—all three of us, Peg and the baby and I—but I was conscious all the time that I was being cheated out of something that should really have belonged to me as a single man. I blamed Peg for what happened and it must have been tough on her, living with so much resentment."

"It was tough," Peg agrees, "but what really bothered me the most was the feeling that I had let my parents down. Not Mike. I figured he was just as responsible as I was for what had happened. I was determined to prove to everybody that we could take care of ourselves and the baby. I wanted that baby to be just about perfect."

The baby seems perfect to Peg, and Mike is pretty proud of her too. In fact, he appears quite content with his family and marriage and so the crisis was weathered. Clearly this couple had something important going for them. They had known each other well and wanted to be married. Even though the crisis they faced created self-doubt and resentment, they were able to keep functioning. In fact, they redoubled their ambition and drive. A desire to "show them" probably created the necessary energy to get them through a bad period.

Not every couple is so blessed. Some young parents do not know each other well, if at all. The pregnancy is obviously an unhappy accident. Should they stick together for the sake of the child? Not unless they really feel they can have a happy life together.

By the time the baby is born they should certainly have some idea of whether they are mismatched or whether they can make a go of marriage. Certainly, they should not have any more children until they have made a well-considered decision about their life together. Why should they, not to mention their child, go through life in misery and guilt?

Your marriage is neither doomed nor damned if you enter it in a state of pregnancy. Your view of marriage is going to be clouded by the crisis of the moment, and you won't really know what you want to do until the baby is born and you can envision life as a parent. If you feel you will spend your life resenting the fact that you were railroaded into a marriage you didn't want (by your partner or in-laws or parents), then you ought to think seriously about dissolving it. A marriage built on recrimination, accusation, resentment can't possibly hold up unless there is a strong counterforce of love and loyalty. You are the only one who can judge whether you have enough on balance to weigh against the inevitable pressures of premarital pregnancy.

Some guidance from a neutral party, such as a family agency counselor or psychiatrist, can help you sort out your feelings. Clergymen can be of help too. The churches are reluctant to endorse marriages which have been forced. They are more inclined to advise the young couple not to marry but, instead, to put the baby up for adoption. If, however, you want to give your child a name and acknowledge parenthood, then marry before you bring it into the world. You may eventually decide to divorce and let someone adopt your child. These are momentous decisions which can only be arrived at intelligently through much discussion. You will need to gain insight into your true feelings. You ought to be frank with one another. It is far better to acknowledge your emotions now (even though you aren't exactly proud of them) than it is to let them eventually destroy your chance for a happy marriage.

Heavy Drinking

"I always knew he liked to take a drink but I never thought he would change as much as he has under the influence of liquor." This statement from a young wife could be repeated by thousands of men and women married to alcoholics. The occasional drink, even the Saturday night bender, are observed and condoned before marriage. After marriage it's different. Living with an alcoholic is no fun. It isn't the drinking *per se* but the personality change that makes for problems.

One young wife was appalled at the brutality her husband showed when he had had more than a few drinks. "Not that he literally beat me up but he said things to me that really hurt. The next day he would apologize and tell me not to pay attention to 'anything I say when I'm not myself.' I claim he is 'himself' when he has been at the bottle; in fact I think he has to get drunk to tell people off—including me."

The alcoholic can be helped to function without liquor through the aid of Alcoholics Anonymous and given other therapeutic assists. His wife can join the AA auxiliary for partners and his children can find solace in the junior chapter of AA. However, it might be worth considering early in a marriage whether you can take the exhaustion of being married to an alcoholic. Some partners are strong enough to manage; some even like the dependency of a drinking man. Others are bound to go under, succumb to liquor or fight for survival by taking up an equally destructive pattern of behavior. Such a pattern might well be martyrdom.

It took Tom and Julia eight years of marriage before they admitted that alcoholism had been their problem since the beginning. Tom had been successful in business and his heavy drinking had no effect on the role of good provider. This was a role he cherished and by which he measured his effectiveness. His criterion for a husband was the ability to earn good money and give his wife clothes, jewelry and a handsome house. He had gotten his drinking under control every time it threatened his work pattern and that, he told himself, was the only time the marriage had been in danger.

Julia had gone along with her husband in maintaining an illusion that their life together was perfect. Underneath her composure, however, she struggled against the resentment she felt almost continually. Although her husband's drinking upset her, his clowning at parties, his habit of scattering his clothes all over the house, his bragging, she never criticized him. She felt very strongly that to preserve the marriage she should avoid arguments and simply swallow her resentments. She was able to keep herself under control because her husband traveled so much on business. When, however, Tom decided to go into a business for himself their problems erupted. Not only did he not succeed in making a go of it but he was around the house more than he had ever been. His drinking problem worsened and she was no longer able to ignore it. She tried working outside the house but this only deepened their conflict. Tom felt he must indeed be a failure if his wife had to go to work to support them. Eventually they landed at a counselor because Julia had decided she simply could not live with the drinking any longer.

If the drinking problem can be recognized in time—by both partners—something can be done to arrest it. Some of the most gifted, engaging people in the world (including women as well as men) have a problem with liquor. Many of them have been able to control it. They were only able to do this, however, when they could admit "I am an alcoholic" and take proper steps to keep their compulsion in hand.

The compulsive gambler faces the same problem as the drinker. He must give up his "vice" completely or go under. There are self-help groups for gamblers comparable to AA and opportunities for husbands and wives to help their partner lick the habit.

Anyone who is in the grip of a compulsive and destructive need to drink or gamble needs help. His partner can lead him to that help and sustain him while the "cure" takes place. In fact, the partner may have a moral obligation to stand by, just as he would in the case of physical illness. However, he too may be in need of guidance and support and entitled to get it.

Deeply in Debt

Without ever intending to get in over their heads financially, many young people find themselves in bankruptcy before the first five years of marriage are up. Ironically, these are the very couples who make good salaries and have the highest living standards. Bob and Elaine are typical.

Although Bob never finished high school he picked up enough technical training during his army service to qualify for factory jobs paying as much as $8,000. Compared to army pay, this looked like big money. Bob and Elaine felt the sky was the limit. They had no trouble getting credit because of Bob's steady employment. They bought whatever they wanted, using installment buying and charge accounts, never keeping any accounts or records of what was coming in or going out. When the situation got to the point where they were hounded by creditors, their solution was to "run away." They simply moved out of the state and started over again. Eventually, they were caught. Then they turned to a loan company and once more tried to borrow their way out of the problem. They still did not grasp what had gone wrong and how they could cope with the crisis.

Their method of handling the debt problem was to spend more money. Each would buy some longed-for item such as a movie camera or a hunting dog. Then each would accuse the other of extravagance and to quiet resentments go buy something else to catch up. It never occurred to them that Bob's salary would not cover all the expenses they were piling up. Like any other optimistic young couple they felt they had plenty of time to make good and resented any suggestion that they might not be able to meet the bills.

Eventually, though, the bill collectors succeeded in bringing them into court. Bob's salary was attached and their credit cut off. For the last five years they have been struggling to get out of debt and pay back every cent they borrowed. "Never again," they promise each other.

This couple reacted to affluence like a couple of drunks on a binge. Once they were obliged to sober up they took charge of their affairs and now give every indication that the future solvency will take precedence over spending.

For other couples the struggle to solve the problem of indebtedness only reveals other, more basic, problems. Sally and Pete discovered that their financial difficulties were secondary to their unresolved conflict over who should take charge in the marriage.

Both worked until Sally became pregnant. During the early months of marriage they handled their financial affairs in a cooperative manner; both were involved in the bookkeeping and billpaying. When Sally stopped work she offered to handle all the family finances because, as she put it, "I have nothing else to do." Pete was glad to let her take over. His mother had been a solid, resourceful person who managed to hold her household together by washing, ironing, cleaning and making every penny count. Sally's mother, on the other hand, was a dependent frivolous woman who was completely dominated by her rather tyrannical husband.

At first Sally's management worked very well but as the family suffered from the loss of her paycheck the outgo began to exceed the income. The more she spent the more the budget fell by the wayside; Sally began to spend even more than she had in order to keep the family establishment going. It was a self-defeating pattern. She became more and more trapped and finally just threw the bills away when they came in rather than open them and face the situation.

The first inkling Pete had of the crisis was when he got a call from one of his creditors. His salary was threatened with a garnishment. Pete quickly took in the situation and acted immediately. He took Sally's mailbox key and checkbook away from her, contacted his creditors to make arrangements for payment, ordered her to go back to work. In little over a year they were out of debt and a year later had a small savings account. At that time he gave her a gold key for the mailbox, returned the checkbook, and suggested that she quit her job and stay home to be a full-time homemaker.

Sally accepted the mailbox key and the checkbook but not his suggestion that she quit her job. She complained that he didn't make enough money to support them in style. He tried to comply by earning more but then she raised her demands so that it still wasn't enough.

One suspects that Sally really likes earning her own money and is not about to become dependent on her husband again. Clearly, their problem is only superficially related to money. Its solution will call for help over and above any provided by financial counseling.

Financial counseling can help, however, if the problem will yield to planning and debt consolidation. Family Service Agencies will put you in touch with legitimate sources of help and, indeed, sit down with you and figure a way out of the debt dilemma.

Often the debt load can be reduced by stringent budgeting. Or the Agency will intervene with your creditors and ask them to bear with you while you make a schedule of payments. Even if you can afford to pay off the debt at only a dollar a week, you should make a start. Otherwise your credit will be ruined. Some young people make the mistake of thinking that if they cannot pay all the debt at once they are better off not paying anything. They have the best intentions in the world of saving up for a final payment but are not always able to make good. When you are bound by a schedule of repayments you slowly and ultimately whittle away at your problem. Before long it is solved.

There are financial outfits which promise "debt consolidations for a fee." Better check them out with your local Better Business Bureau before compounding your financial problems. The "fee" can be enormous and sometimes these intermediaries do not make peace with your creditors as they have contracted to do.

Credit unions, retail credit bureaus, legal aid societies and your employer's personnel department can all be helpful to you. The real solution to the problem, however, lies in your willingness to mend your ways, make a sacrifice now to get out of debt and then stay out.

Changing Jobs

As soon as two people are dependent upon one job the job itself can become a critical focus in their lives. If the wife thinks her husband can do better, that he isn't appreciated, isn't getting anywhere she may nag him into changing.

For Marg and Ralph the job problem was compounded by the fact that he worked for his parents. Marg complained that her husband was too tied to his family. He worked in their business because he was used to letting them tell him what to do. She didn't think he really cared about her. His parents didn't pay him adequately but he didn't have the courage to stand up to them. With all his faults, she loved him but she could wish he had more courage.

In this case it is clear that poor Ralph is being pulled by both his wife and his parents. To prove his independence he eventually found another job but not the kind his wife approved of. He may have only sacrificed his chances of inheriting "the business" to justify his right to make his own job decisions.

When it becomes necessary to quit a job or face the possibility of being let out, the best thing you can do is to consider the options without panic. A hasty or emotionally motivated move can be disastrous. Figure your finances, take your time about looking for the right job if you can afford to, assume that you are going to find another, better spot, and don't let yourself feel down and out just because you are temporarily unemployed. Wives can help by being encouraging, hopeful and always on the side of their husbands. Remember, you are young and promising. You aren't going to be out of work forever.

The Trapped Housewife

Even very young wives find themselves wondering, "Is this all?" after they've done the dishes and gone through another day cleaning, cooking and shopping. If they have worked before marriage, they feel guilty about not keeping up with their career. If they are college graduates, they wonder why they bothered getting that degree. It takes no great brain power or education to run a house. But if their husband wants them to stay home and, if there are children, be a full-time mother they must obey—or think they must.

The crisis comes when their drive to get out in the world becomes too strong to manage. Then they may express dissatisfaction in picking on home and family, in becoming sick, bad-tempered, depressed. The cure is not always a job outside the home but it may well be as simple as that.

This marriage—to take only one example—almost went on the rocks because neither partner could admit that homemaking was not wholly satisfying for a bright, attractive young woman like Jill. She loved her home and her two little girls but she also had a need for adult friendships and activities that were nonhome and nonchild centered. Her husband was a quiet, introverted man whose job in the electronics field satisfied him completely. He put most of his energies into his job and was glad to lead the peaceful life when he got home. He would occasionally invite friends home from work in response to his wife's "I never see anybody who is an adult," but then would disappear into his workshop and let her carry the socializing.

One evening he brought home an older couple who were trying to get a toy and hobby store going. Jill sparked to their plans and begged her husband to let her help them out, if only part time. The job has changed her life and, not incidentally, her husband's. She loves the work and has blossomed into an expert on the merchandise. She has something to talk about besides what the children had, or had not, done during the day. Some evenings she is obliged to help out at the store and her husband willingly baby-sits for her. He gets to know the little girls much better on these evenings when he is responsible for them. Their affection and playfulness delight him. He finds himself eager to discuss their doings with his wife, and this common interest has strengthened the marriage. He has even gotten involved in the toy store, helping his wife with the inventory during busy seasons.

The return on Jill's job has been an increased emotional satisfaction but the financial extras have been welcome. When Jill bought her husband a fishing rig he had wanted, but felt he could not afford, any remaining resistance to the idea of her working dissolved completely.

One marriage counselor points out that "working or not working is not the problem. It is the way working is handled in the marriage that counts. It seems to me that if the wife is working for something other than money, if she sees her employment as secondary to the marriage and keeps in mind that her role as wife and mother is primary, then the job can be a constructive force for good marital relations. If the husband's masculine role is not threatened by his wife's income, this additional income can help solidify the marriage. Essentially, it boils down to the security the man has within himself as a person. If he can see himself as a person of worth who has very necessary functions within the family, and does not have to see himself in terms of his earning power, he will not be very threatened by his wife's outside income. I am stating this clumsily, but the point I am trying to make is that men and masculinity are not rated by pay checks, nor is a woman's femininity necessarily rated by her housekeeping arts. When both husband and wife are mature and secure they are able to tolerate and handle many potential threats to their relationships, including wage earning by the wife. The insecure and immature are more vulnerable to these threats."

You don't have to seek a paying job as a way out of the trap. Volunteer work can provide the outlet you need. Or you might try writing a novel, painting a picture, pursuing that education you never finished. If you find yourself asking, "Is this all?" it is up to you to answer it. If you feel trapped you are going to have to be the one to spring yourself out and into action.

Of course some women feel the real trap lies in the expectation that there ought to be more in life than domesticity. Isn't it enough simply to be a wife, homemaker, mother? Or must you prove yourself by doing things? This is a question every woman must ask herself. She doesn't have to resolve it right away, indeed she cannot. But if she brings the question out in the open, turns it around to see the dimensions of the problem, she will at least know what she's up against.

You owe it to yourself to express your best self. If you are happiest being domestic, feel most fulfilled and productive, then for Heaven's sake go to it. Bake the best bread in the neighborhood, keep your house shining and fragrant, revel in your talents to create a happy home. Don't worry about the college degree you aren't acquiring, the presidencies you don't want, the meetings you don't care to attend.

If, however, you admit that you miss the stimulation of the outside world, then you should plan your life so you can have the best of both worlds. You can attend to your responsibilities as a wife and homemaker and at the same time go after that college degree, hold a job, carry on good works.

The point is, of course, to know your own limits. Some people are blessed with more energy than others. Some are greater perfectionists. They cover less ground but are thorough about what they do.

If you can begin to know your own limits then you won't drive yourself and your family too hard. One young mother finally had to put the brakes on herself. "I was trying to do too much and I knew it. I was president of the voters' league, big in PTA. The house and garden took up a lot of time. We entertained. I even drove fifty miles every week to see my family and old friends. Once I decided to shuck some of the things I was trying to do everything improved. I don't feel as if I'm going to cave in at the end of the day."

Don't assume that your husband doesn't want you to express yourself. A study made by Anne Steinmann reveals that women expect that men want them to be traditional wives—that is, to be more mothering than achieving. Actually the men seem to hope for a balance between nurturer and achiever.

The balance is not easy to maintain. If you become absorbed in your job you are likely not to care whether the beds are made, the laundry picked up. But at least you won't feel trapped.

The Trapped Husband

Increasingly, men are beginning to wonder why their wives should have a corner on frustration and hopelessness. There comes a time in every husband's life when he, too, wonders, "Is this all?" Life can pall when it looks like a series of chores— paying bills, mowing the lawn, washing the car, helping his wife shop for supermarket bargains. Quite understandably, a man begins to get a picture of himself as valued only for the practical functions he performs. He is primarily a breadwinner, handyman and chauffeur but not a man. As a matter of fact, his wife may see him in just that way.

When a group of midwestern researchers asked married women, "What are the roles (in order of importance) of the man of the family?" the women put "breadwinner" first. "Father" ranked second, and "husband" a poor third. These women are living dangerously indeed.

No matter how much a man likes his job it can't meet all his emotional needs. No matter how satisfied he is to be head of a family, supporting it and protecting it, he also wants to be valued for himself. The steady, patient provider is often enough the man who chafes most under the breadwinner label. As he stoically rides the commuter train, predictably rises to the top in his job, conscientiously performs the jobs common to all homeowners, he may secretly feel quite bitter about his marriage. Too often nobody suspects who is wrong until the marriage goes sour. Suddenly, the good husband and father escapes into infidelity or apathy. He loses interest in his job, his appearance, his home life. Or he develops a chronic health problem—ulcer, headaches, fatigue. If he is truly desperate he runs away. The "Disappearing Husband" is familiar to social workers, who frequently comment, "Desertion is the poor man's divorce." This kind of escapist husband may not be basically irresponsible, just snowed by his obligations. He has been pushed too far, too fast, too soon. If he is a natural achiever, he is not reluctant to take on responsibility. But before he knows what has happened he is "saddled" (as he puts it) with house, kids, insurance, bills, car, club dues, etc. He can see precisely what the next twenty years will bring, only more of the same. He hates the treadmill and wonders how he ever got onto it.

Hank was typical of the ambitious young husband who found himself "locked into" a way of life. When he married Helen they agreed to stay in a city apartment until they had accumulated a sizable down payment for a house in the suburbs. Then, one bright spring day, Helen went up to Connecticut to visit an old college friend. She came back brimming over with the possibilities of life in the country. "We wouldn't have to worry about vacations. The beach is right there; tennis, golf and skiing are nearby. When we start our family we'll be all set. Good schools, neighbors, shopping." Before Hank could wonder aloud, "What about my job?" Helen had the answer. "The area is booming with small engineering plants. You won't have any trouble." He didn't. In fact, he got a better job than the one he had in the city. But he never confessed to Helen that he felt out of things working in a country plant. He had not had the chance to live big city life. "I guess I wanted to kick up my heels a bit," Hank says now, "not be tied down right away to middle-aged life."

They bought a small house, put in a garden, took up sailing and within a year were parents. "Then the problems really started to pile up," Hank groans. "I feel we would have waited to have children if we had stayed in the city. We wouldn't have felt rushed. As it was it seemed silly to rattle around in a house in the country without any children. Besides, the country is child-oriented. You have to have kids or you don't belong."

Four years later Hank was the very picture of the unhappy "Trapped Male." He dragged himself to work, reluctantly took care of his property. "It seemed to me that we were always putting up storm windows and taking them down. It was a drag."

Hank's problems did not lead him to any spectacular solution. He didn't crack up or light out or fall into a depression. He did have one piece of good luck, ironic as it seems. He got fired. "I knew I wasn't doing a job for them. I suppose I was kind of hoping that I would be fired. It forced me to face up to what was bugging me. I knew I didn't want to spend the rest of my life driving up the Post Road to work. I wanted to live a little, move around, travel, go in business for myself. I talked it over with Helen and to my surprise she was game. I think she was fed up too but, having pushed us into this way of life, she thought she had to grin and bear it."

Hank and Helen sold their house, moved back to New York. They say quite frankly that they don't think this is the final answer for them. ("The suburbs did rub off a bit.") But for the moment the excitement of urban living has given them a shot in the arm. Hank is full of plans, hoping that his new job will lead to travel and eventually a consultant's spot. Helen is thinking about going back to work now that she has found a good school for their child. Not only have they broken out of a rut but both are convinced they could change their life anytime they feel trapped.

It has been said that the trouble with young marriage is not that the girl is so young but that the boy is. He is obliged to settle into a job, make compromises, avoid risk so that he can support his family. Often enough this means he must give up dreams and ambitions. No wonder he feels trapped, condemned to a life of second best. It is up to his wife to convince him that he can venture as far as he likes and that she will be behind him all the way. She may have to hold back on her own dreams of security, not push too early for a settled, buttoned-down life.

Most important of all, a wife can show her husband how much she values him for himself. She can look at him with pleasure, enjoying his small vanities and his maleness. She can respond to him as husband and lover, not as the family breadwinner.

Separation and Loneliness

Inevitably, you will be separated from one another during the first years of marriage. The army, reserve training obligations, job commitments, illness in the family will oblige you to leave your new home for a period of days, perhaps weeks. How will you take these enforced periods of being apart? Will you feel abandoned, lost, rejected, jealous? Are you going to take it out on your partner (who probably feels miserable away from you) or on yourself?

The lonely wife may not always be able to confront her husband with her anxieties and resentments. Instead, she takes her fury out on herself. She goes on eating binges while he is away, abandons all attempts to keep house, lets her skin and grooming go to pot. When he gets home he is simply irritated by the general disintegration and hard put to hear her side of the story. She does have a grievance even though she isn't solving her problems in a very mature fashion.

When a man is entitled by virtue of his job title to certain luxuries—expense account meals, attentive secretaries, first-class business travel—his junkets away from home inevitably look more like fun than work. His wife resents the gravy train as much as his absenteeism.

One young mother, exhausted from coping with four children under eight, remembers the night she finally blew up. Her husband had just come back from a trip to the West Coast for the company. "He had been wined and dined and he was telling me all about it. In fact, he even said that he couldn't wait to get back there on another trip. He didn't bother to ask me how it had been at home where I was holding on. While he was gone the washing machine broke down and flooded the kitchen floor, all the kids had vile colds and, of course, I caught them too. We had been living on canned soup and crackers. Well, that was the end, when he said he couldn't wait to get back to "the good life." I had had it. I let him have it too. I said, "I thought when we married it was going to be hand-in-hand walking into the sunset. I didn't know it would be Indian file with me at the end carrying the burden." Fortunately, this woman retained some humor about her plight. And some dignity. Her husband, after the light dawned, had to concede that he was getting much the best of married life. He couldn't take her with him on his junkets, but he did manage to cool it when it came to describing them. He began paying her small attentions, took on more of the household chores and, in fact, began behaving like a husband and not like a young tycoon.

The left-behind wife may make her problems worse by imagining the fun and games her husband has at work. She develops a bitterness, martyrdom and jealousy way out of proportion to the situation. One young wife whose husband's job carried over into the weekend became so incensed at being a "Saturday widow" that she barged into his office one weekend. "If you won't come to my house, I'll come to yours," she announced. He was irritated, of course, but secretly rather pleased that she cared so much. She saw for herself just how workaday his world was. He took her out to lunch that fateful Saturday and ever since they have made a monthly ritual of it. He won't be working weekends forever and now they have, at least, reached an understanding on the need for putting up with this particular job demand. She knows that he misses her too, wishes he could be home. Showing concern for the other partner is the best way to make the heart grow fonder.

Sometimes the young wife is obliged to be away from her husband for a period of time. She, too, travels on business. Or she may want to visit her parents. The temptation to go home again for summer vacations is particularly strong if home includes a beach or lake. She reasons, quite sensibly it seems, that it will save money. Her husband can spend his vacation with the family too. Sometimes the plan works. It works best when the young couple can have the place to themselves. It works a hardship on the husband if he is left to fend for himself while his wife is enjoying the leisure life. Weigh the advantages carefully. If you decide the separation is worth it don't let your husband feel he is being shortchanged. Make sure his comforts are provided. Write him every day and telephone when you can. He might be jealous of your other life. ("When you're with your family you're different.") If he feels too frustrated he could even seek the companionship you are witholding elsewhere.

Separation can bring couples closer together if they continue to think of themselves as firmly married. It is a kind of trial you will suffer through and be awfully happy when the trial is over. You ought to be able to go on living even though your partner is away. You shouldn't fall to pieces when he (she) is gone. Let the other know how much you miss him and then prove your love by being your best self during the enforced absence.

When the Roof Caves In

As the old saying has it, "sometimes your troubles come all at once."

For some couples this is only too true. One problem leads to another. Circumstances beyond control accelerate the decline of family fortunes and before long the possibility of extricating yourself seems hopeless. This case from the records of the Family Service Agency shows how a series of disasters can threaten the most stable marriage.

The first five years of their married life were serene and happy for Tom and Jane. During those years there were only the normal ups and downs of married life. Then, about a month before the birth of the second baby, disasters came! They came, not single spies, but in battalions! Even a partial list of those disasters sounds fantastic, but it is true.

Shortly before the baby was due, Tom had a back injury which kept him in the hospital for a month. A few weeks after the baby's birth, the older child had the measles and reacted very badly to the antibiotic. She had to be hospitalized for several weeks. Then while she was still in the hospital, their automobile, a real necessity since they lived seventeen blocks from a bus line, was run into and seriously damaged by a hit-and-run driver. Shortly after that was repaired, Jane herself was in an automobile accident which practically destroyed the car and caused her some physical injuries. Then the baby developed an intestinal condition requiring an operation. The debts piled up and up. It seemed that there would be no end to their troubles.

To all of this accumulation of anxiety, Tom responded by becoming depressed and withdrawn. He was silent and moody. For Jane home became a dreary place, full of worry and fear of what might happen next. She was anxious, too, but her anxiety needed diversion and amusement to take her mind off her worries and fears.

Diversion and amusement were at hand in the person of Joe, a young man, the son of friends from another city. Jane's parents had taken him under their wing so that Joe was usually at their home when Jane and Tom visited.

With Tom silent and depressed on these visits and not entering much into the conversation, Jane and Joe began, as she put it, "to kid around together." They amused themselves talking and laughing about the "dream castle" which Joe was going to build for her, where there would be no money problems and no sick children to worry about. Neither of them realized how all of this must sound to Tom trying to carry on a conversation with her parents while the other two laughed and joked together.

Then, one night, Tom "blew up." He said that he would leave home and Jane could go on off with Joe if she wanted to. Jane was horrified and hurt that Tom could have so misunderstood all of this. For a while they were unable even to discuss it together and it seemed that their marriage was on the brink of failure.

But underneath all of this and through all of this, Tom and Jane were sure they really loved each other. They were able to see this even though their problems seemed insurmountable. "Infidelity wasn't on my mind," Jane says. "I just wanted a little laughter but with Tom of course."

Infidelity

It is always hard to know whether unfaithfulness is cause or effect in a crisis. Certainly, many men and women turn to another person when they have been deeply hurt by their partner. But there is another kind of infidelity which is explained away as "my right to freedom."

Dorothy is twenty-three and, admittedly, unhappy in her marriage. When she discovered she no longer loved her husband she decided that she did not necessarily need to divorce him; that she could simply find sexual satisfaction with another partner.

Dorothy does not complain about her husband's productiveness. He supports them in comfortable style. But she does resent his "indifference, coldness, overattention to this job," and says he never helps her with the children or the house. Her resentment never flared up into a major battle. She just snapped at her husband continually; he responded by withdrawing more and more.

In spite of the cold war carried on at home (or more accurately, because of it) the Browns have a very active social life. They are particularly fond of the couple next door and, in fact, Dorothy and her neighbor Randy are involved in an affair. Dorothy's husband suspects what is happening, never questions it, and goes out of his way to remain friendly with Randy. Dorothy thinks her sexual adventure is completely justified because her husband is so cold. She claims that she would accord him the same privilege. However, she does not want to break with him and lose her status as a married woman, her house and possessions.

This kind of situation is not so rare as it may sound. And this does not make it any more permissible. Infidelity in the early months of marriage is not common because the partners are able to satisfy one another. When, however, a crisis erupts they may show their dissatisfaction by taking on another partner. This, of course, will never resolve the issue at hand.

Infidelity is symptomatic that something is wrong with the marriage. When counselors describe the spiraling effects of conflict during the early years they point out that infidelity represents a definite danger stage.

Escaping from Crisis

Conflict is latent in any marriage. If problems are not brought out, discussed and resolved, then they will accumulate and smolder. Sooner or later a crisis will trigger the stored-up gunpowder and there will be an explosion. The birth of a baby, job problems, debts will precipitate a blowup. Now there is a choice. The partners can try to cope with the immediate crisis and look at what has been festering under the surface or they can escape into another relationship. Some seek allies among their in-laws and family. Others escape into work, hard drinking, socializing. Some find another close relationship. This is the most dangerous solution of all.

"Such a lover presents the most serious and direct threat possible to the existing marriage, for the new love relationship may well supplant the old, at least for a time." This is the considered opinion of hundreds of marriage counselors who have studied marital stress. "Once infidelity has become chronic or a major source of satisfaction to either partner the situation is difficult to reverse."

The only workable escape from crisis is to "work it through." This may well involve seeking professional help. How do you know when you need it? Can you afford it? How long will it take? Can you get your partner's cooperation? The answers to these questions and others will be found in the next chapter.

XI

GETTING HELP

"How do I know if I really need help?" This question put to a family counselor by the young bride seems, on the face of it, a bit ridiculous. But the bride's concern was genuine. She had problems. There was no denying them. But she and her husband were young, just starting out and "won't we outgrow them?" she asked. Besides, wasn't counseling something "old married people who didn't love each other any longer went in for?"

The counselor smiled. "After all, you did seek us out. Something must be troubling you."

"Yes. I am worried but I guess I wonder if I shouldn't be sicker, feel worse before I have a right to get help."

The counselor suggested that she look at emotional disturbance in the same way she had been taught to measure physical pain.

"You are told to see a doctor if the pain persists . . .

"If the sore doesn't heal . . .

"If it interferes with your functioning . . .

"Now then, why not try applying these standards to emotional pain. The sooner you find out why you feel the way you do the better your chances for recovery will be."

"Too little and too late" may be just as disastrous to saving a marriage as in any other kind of rescue work. The chances for a favorable outcome to counseling worsen as the years pass. When the couple still believes in the marriage and is still getting satisfaction from it and when each is willing to accept some responsibility for the marital conflict, they are in the best possible position to use help. Both partners must view the marriage as worth saving and capable of being saved. They must be willing to work with a counselor to find out what has gone wrong.

There does seem to be a "counseling gap" as far as young marriages go. There is plenty of premarital counseling available —from doctors, the clergy, lawyers, social workers, educators. Later in the marriage, if it survives the first decade, there will be professional help for the children and their problems, help to avert divorce, strengthen a faltering sexual relationship. But counselors do not always reach out to young couples during that crucial first five years when they need guidance. The counselors insist that "young people think they know all the answers. They want advice on a fairly practical, quick-and-easy basis." Presumably then they must discover for themselves that they do not know all the answers and return in a humble frame of mind but, unfortunately, when their problems are well along.

Young couples themselves can get the help they may need right at the beginning of their marriage but they will have to indicate that they are serious about taking care of the little problems before they erupt into big ones.

What Kind of Help?

Your options are considerable and as a matter of fact the choices open to you may be confusing. You will probably be most comfortable seeking advice from someone who has guided you in the past—your doctor, minister, school guidance counselor. This individual may not feel qualified to treat you as a client now that you are married, but certainly he will be able to refer you to someone who can be useful.

Most religious groups now train their clergy for pastoral counseling. If you are a Catholic you can attend "Cana conferences" —meetings held for married couples and led by a priest skilled in marriage counseling. Reverend George A. Kelly, who is director of the Family Life Bureau of the Archdiocese of New York, explains the purposes of Cana.

"These conferences are named, of course, for the wedding feast at which Our Lord performed his first miracle. They are now regularly conducted in about one hundred dioceses throughout the United States. They have helped hundreds of thousands of

couples to gain new insights into the harmony and sanctity it is
possible for them to achieve together . . .

"Conferences usually are organized by a few couples in the
parish, working with a parish priest. They are made as informal as
possible and are usually held in a small hall where smoking is
permitted and light refreshments are served.

"At a typical conference, there are two talks by the priest-leader.
He discusses common problems in marriage—perhaps difficulties
that arise over in-laws, money matters, physical relations, and the
bearing and caring for children. Your down-to-earth problems,
with which you may have grappled for months, are considered in
a realistic way. When they are analyzed and discussed against the
background of the true, spiritual meaning of your marriage, their
solutions often become clear.

"After the second talk, there is a half-hour break for simple
refreshments. During this time you have a chance to talk to couples like yourself. The third session usually consists of a question-
and-answer period; without identifying yourself, you can submit
written questions about problems or questions which you want
clarified. These are discussed by the priest in a friendly, relaxed
way. Discussion by other members of the conference is always
invited. The typical conference ends with a renewal of the marriage vows and benediction."

Catholics are urged to keep in touch with the priest who married them. Father William F. McManus, who has worked with
Cana, reminds young Catholics: "His interest is not confined to
the smooth operation of the marriage ceremony alone but in your
happy adjustment as husband and wife, father and mother,
throughout your lifetime. Nor should you fail to review the goals
of your vocation often. Just as priests make retreats to keep the
ideals of their vocation fresh in their minds, so too should you
frequently remind yourself that your marriage is the means designed by God to enable you and your spouse to achieve your
eternal salvation. You can attend marital check-ups and look into
the state of your marriage each year by attending Cana conferences for married persons. You can also strengthen your marriage
by participating in the Christian Family Life Movement, by joining hands in family communion, and by attending family
retreats."

The Catholic Church provides other counseling resources for couples who need private consultation.

Protestant churches also offer their members a chance to air marital problems either in discussion groups or in a private session with clergymen who have had training in counseling.

Jewish couples will discover that their religion offers a wide variety of counseling help—ranging from the supportive advice of their rabbi to psychiatric therapy.

Increasingly, clergymen are becoming conversant with psychiatric techniques, aware of legal issues involved in marriage and divorce, and they are also quite capable of giving young couples help in resolving emotional and sexual problems. They are also quite conscious of their limitations and will not hesitate to refer the young couple to professionals who specialize in marriage counseling. The churches themselves sponsor and subsidize family agencies where counseling is available for a modest fee.

Your family doctor, who in the past was inclined to pat the young couple on the back, urge them to "start a family" and predict that "everything is going to work out," today encourages any couple in trouble to seek professional aid.

Family Service Agencies

This teen-age marriage is considered a success by the Family Service Agency which worked on it. But had the young couple not been able to call on both the agency and the church it is doubtful if their adjustment would have been so effective.

Francisco and Patty were married during Patty's eighth month of pregnancy. She had been brought to the Family Service Agency by her mother, who admitted she did not know how to handle this crisis. Patty's father was a strict, rigid, cold man whose children did not respect him. He either ignored them or blew up impulsively when they annoyed him. He spent much of his time away from home. Patty was fifteen when she came to the agency. A petite, dark-haired, attractive girl, she seemed reserved at first but around her young husband she was quite gay and girlish.

Francisco's father had died when he was just a baby. He never did well in school and had dropped out of the ninth grade when he was sixteen. However, he is a good worker and quickly got a job as a roofer's helper.

When the two decided to marry they had several strikes against them, not the least of which was a difference in religion. Francisco's family was Catholic. Patty was Protestant but she had no religious training and planned to take instruction in the Catholic faith. In addition to the religious issue, the matriarchal structure of Francisco's family had led him to expect a strong wife and mother, a role Patty was unprepared to play.

The couple, and their families, needed the support and guidance from an understanding caseworker in clarifying and resolving the religious question. The young couple needed to understand the decision of the church that Patty was too young for a Catholic ceremony. They then were able to get needed information about the procedures for forced marriages of minors. The agency worker helped them follow through with these plans. Most important, she obtained medical care for Patty at a public clinic. With this support and guidance the family was able to make decisions and take effective action on those decisions.

After the marriage the couple lived with Francisco's mother but the home was crowded and the couple, with the help of the caseworker, moved to a small apartment and made more adequate living plans. Francisco especially needed encouragement, support, understanding and guidance in his decision to move away from his maternal home and to establish one of his own.

The community offered many services that neither Francisco nor Patty were aware of such as: expectant parent classes and visiting nurse service for Patty for a time after the birth of the baby.

The caseworker and the young couple continued to be concerned about family relationships, child care, future educational and/or vocational plans and financial planning.

Teen-age marriages have a high rate of failure. This one was contracted under unfavorable conditions but there also existed some positives such as: the motivation for marriage, the similarity in backgrounds, the attitude toward marriage of the Catholic Church and the acceptance of Patty by Francisco's family.

Although Family Agencies do spend a good part of their time working on cases as full of problems as this one, their services are available to couples who are not in desperate need. You don't have to be poor, physically sick, or emotionally disturbed, on the verge of divorce, referred by "the authorities," before you can qualify for the kind of assistance Family Agencies provide.

However, there is always a long waiting list of clients to be served. The sooner you seek help, the better your chance of receiving it. Workers stress the importance of doing something about your problems as soon as you know the marriage is not going well.

Now, of course, they don't mean that you will run to a counselor every time you have a fight. But, the very first minute you feel any serious dissatisfaction with the marriage, you ought to find out what is wrong. At this point you and your partner have the flexibility and the inner resources to make a new adjustment. If you wait too long your defenses will solidify. You'll have all kinds of reasons why you are right in what you think and do and why he is wrong. You will be looking for an ally and a judge instead of a professional who can help you put your problem in perspective.

What Happens in Counseling?

Many a couple could be helped to cope constructively with their problems if they would just seek that help early in the marriage. Not only are they somewhat ashamed to admit they have any problems but they wonder what it would be like to visit a counselor. "He might tell us what to do." "Who needs a referee?" "He'll take her side."

Every case is different and so is every caseworker. However, the techniques of marriage counseling have evolved over the years to the point where certain standard efforts are generally made by the counselor. This is what you can expect when you consult an expert in this field.

The worker never allows himself to become an active partisan, judge or prosecutor. He must be free to carry on his role of the sympathetic, yet perceptive, observer of the action. It is his job to reveal to both of you what is going on. Ideally, he does this by reminding you of what you have been saying, of how important this or that is to you, of how you have lost sight of what is really going on.

The worker tries to analyze just how the balance of the marriage became upset. How deep is the conflict? In this sense the worker is diagnosing the problem. Then he tries to show (not tell) the participants how they are creating a vicious circle in their relationship. Perhaps the problem is one of communication.

Often, a wife will persist in thinking, "There's no point in talking about it. He just doesn't listen." The worker may encourage her to try again. "Perhaps you aren't getting through to him because you assume he won't listen." One woman, with the worker's help, did manage to tell her husband just how seriously his heavy drinking upset her. She had never revealed this to him in words before. She thought she was letting her disapproval show in the way she treated him and that "he should know how I feel." Once they got it out in the open the wife felt considerable relief. The husband was able to discuss some of his feelings. It turned out that he actually appreciated her frankness and was quite willing to talk about his "problem." He had always felt like a little boy being punished by silence and retaliated by drinking even more. His wife was amazed that he did not "jump all over me for saying what I think." She felt more confident that they could find a solution to the drinking problem.

The worker helped both of them discover what they were doing to one another. With her interpretation and reassurance they could work out a new way of relating. At first it was pretty self-conscious. They were trying out new ways of operating. They had to accept the fact that this was a part of the readjustment process. Gradually what was conscious became more second nature and came to be a pattern of their behavior. In essence they came through the readjustment pretty well.

Intelligent compromise marked the beginning of their readjustment efforts. She did not demand that he cut out his drinking completely but he, on the other hand, agreed to keep his drinking within reasonable limits. He expected her to quit work but it was with the understanding that she would work until they were able to eliminate the enormous debts that they had accumulated.

One of the basic changes was the fact that she learned to express her feelings honestly and frankly. This fostered a growing feeling of self-respect and a development of mutual respect, not to mention a much better understanding, and sympathy.

Basic to the improvement in their relationship was her fuller understanding of her husband's strong needs to feel adequate as

a man, husband, and father. She adjusted her thinking and behavior accordingly. She became less independent and more femi-
nine in her approach to him. Her husband responded by being
more affectionate and considerate. She was beginning to meet his
needs and in having his needs met he was able to begin to meet
hers.

At the time that the couple terminated counseling interviews
they were still having their ups and downs. A measure of the
stability that they had been able to achieve in their marriage,
however, was in the fact that they felt quite competent that they
could weather the stresses in their marriage and come out feeling
the stronger for their experience. They felt that they had gained
enough understanding of themselves and their relationship to
each other that they could continue in their marriage and on
their own. They left the agency with the understanding that they
could return for interviews any time if they felt they needed further help, but so far they have not been back.

The counselor tries very hard to reverse the process of disintegration. If the marriage has been going badly for some years
the chances for reversal are not very hopeful. But if caught early
even the most serious problems will yield to treatment.

The worker never blames either partner. He listens attentively
and sensitively, then interprets what is happening. Joint interviews with husband and wife are considered very useful because
the interaction between the couple becomes apparent to the
worker. And—to each other.

After the couple has talked out the problem, what else happens? Is talk enough? It can help in airing differences, relieving
anger and resentment. And once someone cares enough to listen
to your problem you feel a bit better about yourself. Not so hopeless. Not so wronged. This improved self-esteem can work wonders
in any marriage.

Barbara and Arthur were twenty-one when they came to a Family
Service Agency. They had seen a lawyer about getting a divorce
and he referred them to the agency, feeling that they were too
young to consider divorce. Besides, they were the parents of two
small daughters.

Arthur was out of a job at the time and this only added to his
marital problems. His wife was convinced, and said so, that "he
will never amount to anything." Much of the counseling that

took place was directed at getting Barbara to give her husband the support and confidence he so badly needed. He wanted to be the family breadwinner but the more she tore him down the less capable he thought he was. When his wife began to show some respect for him as a man his prospects brightened.

What made her change so miraculously? She was working with the counselor who helped her see that she was only defeating herself by harping on her husband's inadequacies. "Actually, he has some wonderful traits," Barbara admitted. "Show him you think so," the counselor advised.

Arthur got a job and then, to his surprise, was offered a better one. This involved moving away from his hometown and family but he and his wife thought he could do it. Barbara even looked upon this move as a chance for her husband to demonstrate his abilities and maturity far from home. She encouraged the move and they are now happily settled and on their own.

Of course there are plenty of cases which do not have happy endings. A recent survey of family caseworkers indicated that nearly half of the clients seen leave treatment without resolving their problems.

The worker may feel that the problems presented by a client are too complicated for the treatment he can offer. He may then refer his client to a psychiatrist for intensive therapy. Or he may recommend a private marriage counselor.

In some cases divorce is the only answer. Indeed, many workers have commented that counseling which helps one partner "move out of a destructive marriage with minimum damage should also be considered a success."

Legal Facts About Divorce, Separation and Annulment

Legal and religious laws governing divorce, separation and annulment are complicated and vary widely among the states and major religions. For example, you may have a general idea of the difference between divorce and a separation. But what is a limited divorce? An "Enoch Arden divorce"? A separate-maintenance decree? Virtually all religious denominations encourage premarital and marital counseling to prevent divorce by helping to assure sound and stable marriages. But when a marriage, for whatever reason, fails, these *basic* principles of law and attitudes of religion govern its termination:

An absolute divorce, also called a complete or final divorce, legally dissolves a marriage. The law views marriage as a *contract*. A divorce is a legal contest or lawsuit in which an "innocent" party seeks to prove that a "guilty" party has committed a wrong which is legal basis, or *ground*, for divorce. In most states, only one spouse can be guilty. If both are at fault, or if both are innocent, no divorce will be granted. A complete divorce usually involves settlement of property rights and custody and support of children. It may include *alimony*, support payments for the wife. In some states the divorced person must wait (usually one year) before remarrying.

A *limited divorce*, also called a qualified or partial divorce or a legal separation, requires the spouses to live apart, but does not end the marriage. Like a complete divorce, it usually involves a property settlement, child custody and support, and support for the wife. Neither spouse can remarry.

An "Enoch Arden divorce" is granted in some states when a spouse has been missing for some years (three to seven years, depending on the state).

Grounds for divorce vary widely. The most commonly recognized grounds are adultery, desertion, physical or mental cruelty, conviction for a felony (that is, a serious crime) and habitual drunkenness. Some states are strict in allowing only one or a few grounds for divorce. Others have ten to fifteen grounds, and some, notably Nevada, make divorce relatively easy because of short residence requirements. A *migratory divorce* is one obtained by moving to such a state. The person must intend to reside in the state.

Separation leaves a couple legally married, but limits or severs certain marital rights. The right and duty to live together is suspended for a fixed or indefinite period. The wife is entitled to support from the husband if she is the "innocent" party; the amount is fixed by the court. Provision is made for child custody and support. Neither is free to remarry.

A *legal separation* is the same as a limited divorce. However, a couple may also separate without asking court permission to live apart. This may be formalized by a *separation agreement* which settles property rights, support for wife and children and custody of children. The agreement is no longer binding when and if the couple resumes married life.

A wife whose grounds for divorce or legal separation are not allowable in her home state can sometimes sue for *separate maintenance*. In such a case the wife must be the innocent party and must show good reasons, similar to divorce grounds, for the separation. The couple is free to resume married life without court permission.

Annulment is a finding by the court that a marriage was invalid, or *void*, from the start. Thus, in effect, a marriage never existed. Many different grounds exist for annulment. They generally include *nonage* (being under the legal minimum age for marriage), impotence, bigamy, fraud such as concealed pregnancy or concealed venereal disease, drug addiction, and *duress*, or forcing marriage by threat or physical force.

Religious attitudes toward divorce vary widely among the major faiths, though all are generally opposed to it. *The Roman Catholic Church* holds that a valid, consummated marriage of two baptized persons is dissolved only by death. A Catholic may not obtain a civil divorce unless a court of his church has granted an annulment of the marriage. In this case the parties are free to remarry. In some cases, too, the church allows a civil divorce if a separation would put the innocent party at a serious civil disadvantage. However, in these cases the marriage bond *still exists* in the eyes of the church and the Catholic may not remarry during the lifetime of the spouse. A Catholic who attempts another marriage after obtaining such a divorce is subject to penalties which curtail his rights as a church member.

Judaism contains three major groups: Orthodox, Conservative and Reform. While Judaism discourages divorce, the Orthodox and Conservative groups provide religious courts and laws through which *religious* divorce may be granted. In these cases a couple must obtain a religious divorce before they remarry. In Reform Judaism, only a civil divorce is required.

Protestant denominations differ considerably in their attitudes toward divorce and remarriage. For example, Southern Baptists generally oppose divorce for any reason but adultery. For the most part, they hold that a divorced person who remarries is guilty of adultery himself unless he was the innocent party in a divorce based on adultery. Many American Baptist ministers accept divorce in some circumstances and feel that divorced persons should have the right to remarry. The Episcopal Church maintains that "true Christian marriage is indissoluble," but has a procedure for deciding whether, in specific cases, such a marriage exists or has existed. Methodist and Presbyterian ministers have authority to perform marriages of divorced persons whom they have counseled about remarriage.

Picking a Reputable Counselor

If a Family Agency refers you to a private counselor you can be confident that his professional credentials are sound. If, however, you pick one from the telephone book or rely on a friend's recommendation you may find yourself going to a quack. Here's how you protect yourself.

The legitimate counselor has had training in his profession. He may have a degree in counseling or have come into the field by way of the ministry, psychiatry, social work, medicine, the law. He should be able to prove his qualifications as a member of the so-called "helping professions." Ask to see his credentials.

The legitimate counselor does not promise quickie results. He has no way of knowing just how long treatment may last. There is no such thing as a "course of treatments" as far as he is concerned. The patient comes until the problem has been relieved or until he decides he can make it on his own.

The legitimate counselor does not advertise his services any more than a doctor or lawyer would. He observes professional ethics.

If you have any doubts about the qualifications of a counselor or if you are interested in finding one you can get in touch with these national agencies. They will be happy to direct you to qualified counselors.

American Association of Marriage Counselors
27 Woodcliff Drive
Madison, New Jersey 07940

Family Service Association of America
44 East 23rd Street
New York, New York 10010

National Council on Family Relations
1219 University Avenue, S.E.
Minneapolis, Minnesota 55414

What About Psychotherapy?

Marriage counseling, in or out of a Family Agency, usually involves work on "the marriage." Psychiatric therapy is generally
devoted to work on individual personality problems. You may
come to therapy because your marriage is in trouble but you will
end up analyzing the personal problems which are creating the
difficulty. To be sure, in any kind of counseling this discussion of
personal problems takes place. But in therapy the goal is a highly
individualistic one—to improve self-fulfillment and self-realiza-
tion. Improving the marriage may be only a secondary goal.

Little wonder that partners are often jealous of the analyst,
resentful of the time and expense involved in treatment. The
partner who is not in treatment may feel left out, worried that
the analyst is conspiring to wreck the marriage. "Do you talk
about me?" is the natural question. If the other partner is deeply
troubled he, or she, may encourage the jealousy and anxiety.

If you need psychiatric help you ought to get it, even though
your marriage may not be able to survive the stress. Your partner
may need help too although not necessarily the intensive kind.
Certainly he will need someone to talk to while you are in treatment. The decision to go into analysis, or stay with it if you married during treatment, is an individual one, subject to your
decision and professional advice. The whole point of treatment is
change and that change may have various consequences for your
marriage.

The cost of treatment varies with the frequency of visits and
that, in turn, must be determined by your counselor or therapist.

The most expensive treatment is private analysis which can
cost up to fifty dollars a visit. In intensive analysis patients go
every day. Most private analysts charge fifteen dollars a visit and
usually set up three visits a week. Low-cost treatment is available
through the major psychiatric centers but the waiting list is long.

Group therapy offers one low-cost method of getting help and, indeed, analysts believe that it is remarkably effective for some patients.

Family Service Agencies charge clients on their "ability to pay," fees running as low as five dollars a visit.

You will have to equate the cost of getting help in terms of benefits to you and your marriage. No price is too great if it pays off in years of contented, fruitful relationship. In this sense help is not a luxury. It is a necessity.

Clark W. Blackburn, general director of the Family Service Association of America, says: "It is important for men and women to learn to distinguish what they *must* have and what they would *like* to have because we all have one thing in common. Our emotional needs are what we all must have fulfilled in order to function. Our desires are pleasant but we can get along very well whether they are satisfied or not. In other words, our emotional needs are necessities."

XII

THE HAPPY MARRIAGE

Marriage is the most complex, exasperating, yet wholly satisfying, experience known to man. It is our invention and it reflects our imperfections as well as our dreams. No marriage can be perfect. But any marriage can be happy if both partners are getting enough out of it. What is enough? Why do people get married anyway?

The prime reason for marriage offered by men and women who have been interviewed on the question is that they wanted companionship. Not support, or security, or sex. They wanted someone they could depend on, someone who would be their own, someone they could level with.

Implicit in this companionship are other qualities, all essential to a happy marriage. You have to feel there is a full measure of caring. You must know that to one person in the world your happiness is all-important. Of course, that person is concerned with his own comfort and well-being but yours is just as important.

Is this kind of caring simply a providing of creature comforts —putting the pillow behind his back, fixing her a drink, seeing to it that dinner is on time? Or is it a deeper kind of caring which may seek expression in small gestures but is really fundamental to the marriage. One long-time married man, in seeking to define comfort, says it is what makes him feel at home in the world. "This is what makes you feel adequate and able to cope. Marriage may be a retreat, a cozy place where you are most at home." He puts comfort and adequacy ("A woman just has to make her hus-

band feel adequate.") at the top of the list when trying to assess
the ingredients of a happy marriage.

"What about honesty?" he was asked. "Don't young couples in
particular prize honesty, insist upon being frank and open with
one another?"

His answer is worth considering. "Honesty is great. It is absolutely essential. But not at the expense of comfort and adequacy."

This man is more direct than most. He cheerfully admits that
he married to gain a warm berth, a reliable source of love. He
wants someone to care for him and about him, to minister to his
needs. Another man calls it "convenience." He says, "I wanted a
home, someone to look after me, talk to me, hear me out, raise
my children. If that sounds crass, well I suppose it is. But marriage was created to perform a function. Hopefully, your partner
will have the same goals you have and together you can help each
other reach them."

The Goals Are Important

Anyone who has ever observed a happy marriage is immediately
struck by the fact that both partners are agreed on a common
goal. It may simply be a life style which suits them or a point
of view they share. Or they are resolved to acquire property, raise
a large family, go into business for themselves, travel widely.
Whatever the goal, it is mutually agreed on and their efforts
jointly committed to realizing it. In this kind of marriage neither
is likely to outgrow the other because they have something in
common. They are together.

When you have shared something important—the birth of a
child, the ups and downs of a career, the death of a parent—your
commitment to one another will be reinforced. You will come to
know what kind of person you married as you experience life
alongside him. You will learn to trust the other person, depend
on him, share confidences. What you find out about him will determine the texture of your marriage.

Is it going to be close, warm, sustaining? Or will you settle for
the externals, content to be "that attractive young couple." You
may look successful in the eyes of the world but are you really

happy? If you are to be truly satisfied with marriage you will demand more intimacy, more trust, more sharing.

You can settle for a "congenial marriage," one where the relationship is more brother-and-sister than husband-and-wife. Any number of marriages coast along on this level. They don't end up in the divorce courts primarily because the partners don't know what they are missing. Or you can have the kind of marriage where sparks fly, fights are common and both husband and wife depend on a love-hate relationship. You may survive but will you like it?

The most desirable kind of marriage is one in which vitality is predominant. Neither partner could live happily without the other. Both put into the marriage a lot more than they could reasonably expect to get out of it. They make an effort. They are willing to change. But, of course, they hang onto their own identity, convinced that as individuals they contribute something terrific to the marriage. They are sold on marriage *per se*.

"Every variety of marriage, if it is to be successful and enduring," says Dr. John Levy, "has one requirement; two people shall be ready to sink themselves in the creation of a new unit bigger than either of them. The creation must be important to them. They must accept their relationship as the permanent framework of their lives."

Success Takes Time

Only if you take the long view will you be able to manage your married life so that it gives you maximum satisfaction. Of course you are going to be disappointed, frustrated, occasionally lonely and depressed. It takes a long time for a marriage to ripen. You have to give it a chance and assume from the start that marriage is forever. Don't be impatient if everything doesn't fall into place immediately. The wife may worry that it will be years before she is living the way she hoped she would. The husband may chafe under the "system," anxious to give his family everything right away. Both of them are losing something important, the feelings they are entitled to in the present.

Let yourself open up to the experiences around you. Don't be so concerned with the ultimate goal that you fail to enjoy everyday pleasures. What does it matter if you aren't eating steak every night? Relax and enjoy the hamburgers. You don't have to keep up with the status seekers. In this time of your life you can afford to be experimental. Stay loose.

Suppose you decide to change your style of living. Go ahead and do it. Throw out the antiques and trade them for modern if that is your taste of the moment. Spend your all on a large apartment and forget about saving for the house in the country. Decide to invest in more education instead of a car if that's what you want. You don't have to decide irrevocably to live a certain way. You have freedom of choice. Marriage offers freedom, as well as security. Even though marriage imposes its own restrictions—the obligation to support a family, forego other sexual involvements, keep house—it affords unparalleled freedom. When you are living intimately with someone who cares you have freedom to be yourself. Make the most of it.

Let yourself express tenderness. Write notes, send flowers, bake him a cake, make telephone calls. Don't feel inhibited. If you feel like kissing or making love go ahead and do it. Seize the moment. If you worry about whether you should behave in a certain way— "Is this what married couples do?"—stop and ask yourself, "Do I care, if it's what I want to do?" Trust yourself. If it feels good and solid then you are on the right track.

Your Future and What It May Bring

Whenever people try to dissect a successful marriage they are obliged to take their models from the past. But this is hindsight. What works for one generation will not necessarily succeed for another. Nobody can predict how your particular marriage will turn out but we can see the shape of the world to come. Your marriage will have a better chance to succeed if you are prepared to live in that world—as well as with each other.

You will probably have more leisure. When you were courting you spent your leisure time together because you didn't have a house or apartment to maintain. Once married you may find that leisure time is spent in doing chores or going to bed. Before you fall into the habit of just killing time when you aren't actively occupied with job, housekeeping, each other make an assessment of your other interests. How can you develop them to the fullest? You don't have to spend every waking moment together but certainly you ought to share some outside interests. If you are close only when involved in the traditional marital responsibilities your marriage will suffer. A process known as "disenchantment" usually takes place at some point during the first few years of marriage. Both husband and wife are conscious of losing some of the satisfactions they felt at the beginning. Significant losses are felt in the sharing of leisure-time activities. Don't let this happen to you. Build a full life together and that includes creating a stimulating and restoring leisure life.

Another sign of the times to come concerns privacy. There will be more of us, less space and consequently more pressure to preserve privacy. You need to create your own oasis of privacy, make sure your home provides you with a chance to be yourself. Don't run with the crowd all the time. Instead, from the very beginning put a high value on "aloneness." This is not the same as loneliness. You can reach out to your partner, feel comforted that he is there but accord him a chance to develop his own self. Both of you will need a time and place to get away from it all. Privacy is going to be even more precious than it is now.

In the new world to come your abilities will be tested as never before. Help each other meet the challenges of the future. You may want to go back to school or continue your education. This decision will affect family budgets and other plans. A wife should be supportive (literally in many cases) if her husband wants to get more training, switch jobs, move into a different and more promising field. He, on the other hand, should help her develop a career or outside interest which will provide enduring satisfactions in the years to come.

Change Is the Key

If, in the years to come, your partner says accusingly, "But you've changed," take it as a compliment. Of course you are going to change. If you don't your marriage will be in serious trouble. Marriage is not a static state. Its very excitement springs from the interaction of two people who are alive and thinking. When one of you changes the other will react. The dynamics of married life are not easily analyzed but you can feel them.

You may wonder whether you made the right choice, whether you are really ready for marriage. These are natural questions. Don't feel guilty about thinking them. Instead, take comfort from the fact that you and your partner are going to change. You're going to have to meet the demands of married life. You'll discover your strengths and weaknesses as you go along but if you are together in the search for a happy marriage the discovery will be exhilarating.

One young wife who had entered marriage with qualms, even apprehension, describes how the first year changed her. "I enjoy planning now. I never wanted to look ahead but now I feel that even if I don't get everything I want right away it's fun to talk about it with my husband. I would like a house on a nice piece of land and some children but I don't have to have it right away. That's what's changed for me, being willing to wait. Three years is just nothing to me now. It used to be an eternity. I'm getting used to the idea of keeping fluid. Marriage has helped me get a new sense of time."

No marriage could possibly satisfy the expectations most of us hold for it. But any marriage can work. You may feel let down at first, vaguely disappointed in yourself and your partner. This is only a temporary state. Let yourself become absorbed in marriage, give it all you've got before you decide it is not working.

Marriage is a daily kind of thing. In fact it is the very dailyness that becomes most satisfying. A young wife describes the essence of a happy marriage this way: "I thought it was going to be worse than it is, living with somebody. But it is better than I would have anticipated. The day-to-day part is just so much more enjoyable. A happy marriage isn't what they tell you it is—all rapture. It is a matter of plugging along but that's what it is all about. When I go to sleep at night I am conscious of what has happened to me since marriage. I go to sleep very content. I've had a good day."

READING LIST

Bride in the Kitchen. Betty Wason. Doubleday. The ABC's of cookery for the newlywed with drawings and how-to-do-it techniques.

The I Hate to Cook Book. Peg Bracken. Crest. Useful recipes with amusing comments for the cook who has to but hates to.

The I Never Cooked Before Cookbook. Jo Coudert. Stein & Day. A valuable cookbook which assumes the reader knows nothing about cooking or its vocabulary, with taste-tempting recipes requiring a minimum amount of ingredients and easy-to-understand directions.

The James Beard Cookbook. James Beard. Dell. A basic cookbook for beginners and the gourmet by a gastronomical expert.

The Joy of Cooking. Irma S. Rombauer. Bobbs-Merrill. An all-purpose cookbook, a classic American volume.

Mastering the Art of French Cooking. Simone Beck, Louisette Bertholle, and Julia Child. Knopf. The most widely read cookbook that explains how to create French dishes in American kitchens with American foods.

Amy Vanderbilt's New Complete Book of Etiquette. Amy Vanderbilt. Doubleday. The classic guide to gracious living including dress and manners, home entertainment, correspondence, travel, etc.

The Complete Book of Home Remodeling, Improvement, and Repair. A. M. Watkins. Doubleday Dolphin. A handbook for the owner who wants to do it right—but not do it himself.

A Complete Guide for the Working Mother. Margaret Albrecht. Doubleday. Practical advice to working mothers on the risks and rewards of working while being wife, mother and homemaker.

Consumers All. U. S. Department of Agriculture. Pocket Books. This book tells consumers how to buy, use or make food, clothing, household furnishings and equipment, how to manage money, care for house and garden, use leisure time and stay healthy.

Good Housekeeping Guide for Young Homemakers. Edited by William Laas. Harper. A handbook for successful home management.

The I Hate to Housekeep Book. Peg Bracken. Crest. For "the occasional or random housekeeper," with clues for accomplishing housekeeping with the minimum amount of worry.

Sense with Dollars. Charles Neal. Doubleday. A challenging presentation of spending, saving and investing by a financial counselor.

This U.S.A. Ben J. Wattenberg and Richard M. Scammon. Doubleday. A portrait of the wide range of information supplied by the 194,067,296 Americans in the 1960 census.

The Challenge of Youth. Edited by Erik H. Erikson. Doubleday Anchor. Psychological and sociological aspects of modern youth.

Childhood and Society. Erik H. Erikson. Norton. A classic work on growing up in a variety of cultural and social settings by a professor of human development at Harvard University.

I and Thou. Martin Buber. Scribner's. A distinguished theologian offers his challenging philosophy on human relationships including marriage.

The Interpersonal Theory of Psychiatry. Harry S. Sullivan. Norton. Significant papers by the man who pioneered interpersonal psychiatry discussing human conflicts and potentialities.

The Natural Superiority of Women. Ashley-Montagu. Macmillan. A plea for more mutual love and understanding as well as complete social equality of the sexes, emphasizing woman's superiority, by a physical anthropologist.

The Psychology of Women. Helene Deutsch. Lippincott. Psychoanalytic interpretation of development in girlhood (Volume I) and motherhood (Volume II).

The Art of Loving. Erich Fromm. Harper. Discussion of love in all its aspects.

The Catholic Marriage Manual. The Rev. George A. Kelly. Random House. A complete book of practical guidance and inspiration on every aspect of family life, written by the former director of the Family Life Bureau of the Archdiocese of New York.

The Complete Book of Birth Control. Alan F. Guttmacher, M.D., with Winfield Best and Frederick Jaffe. Balantine Books. The complete how-to including the latest methods by the president of Planned Parenthood Federation of America, Inc., and colleagues.

Engagement and Marriage. Ernest W. Burgess and Paul Wallin. Lippincott. A standard text used in college marriage courses.

The Folklore of Sex. Albert Ellis. Boni. A book by a free-wheeling sexologist.

Human Sexual Response. William H. Masters and Virginia E. Johnson. Little, Brown. This pioneer volume is the product of eleven years' research into the anatomy and physiology of human sexual response. The authors have been able to record the physical reactions that occur when the human male and female respond to sexual stimulation.

Love and Conflict. Gibson Winter. Doubleday. New patterns in family life.

Love Without Fear. Eustace Chesser. Signet.

Male and Female. Margaret Mead. Morrow. Extensive study of sexes in a changing world examining basic human relationships.

A Marriage Manual. Drs. Hannah and Abraham Stone. Simon & Schuster. Practical guidebook to sex and marriage with anatomical, physiological and psychological facts, accurate and clear presentation in the form of questions and answers between an engaged couple and their doctor.

Modern Woman's Medical Encyclopedia. Edited by Anna M. Fishbein. Doubleday. Valuable reference book on special health problems of women by ten noted women doctors covering all stages of female development and concluding with an encyclopedic section of definitions and descriptions.

The Organization Man. William H. Whyte, Jr. Doubleday Anchor. An examination and indictment of the pressures of the organization as experienced on and off the job.

Premarital Intercourse and Interpersonal Relations. Lester A. Kirkendall. Julian Press. A research study of the effects of premarital intercourse on interpersonal relationships, based on case histories of the experiences of college-level males.

The Rights of Infants. Margaretha Ribble. Columbia University Press. The results of a study of the early psychological needs and satisfactions of infants and the nature of the relationship between baby and parents.

Sexual Behavior in the Human Female. Alfred C. Kinsey, et. al. W. B. Saunders. Scientific research study including sex development, premarital and extramarital relations, the sexual factor in marriage, anatomy and physiology of the sexual response.

Sexual Behavior in the Human Male. Alfred C. Kinsey. W. B.

Saunders. Comprehensive scientific study of American male sexual behavior.

The Sexual Responsibility of Woman. Maxine Davis. Permabooks. The process of the sexual relationship, problems and solutions for the ultimate satisfaction from the sexual union and the attainment of marital happiness.

The Social Context of Marriage. J. Richard Udry. Lippincott. A basic text on the sociology of marriage written to be understood by the layman.

Successful Marriage. Edited by Morris Fishbein and Ernest W. Burgess. Doubleday. A modern guide to love, sex and family life by thirty-eight of the most distinguished specialists in their fields.

Your First Year of Marriage. Dr. Tom McGinnis. Doubleday. A helpful book dealing primarily with the psychological adjustments of the first year, written by an experienced family counselor.

INDEX